Miriam Lichtheim

Maat in Egyptian Autobiographies and Related Studies

ORBIS BIBLICUS ET ORIENTALIS

Published by the Biblical Institute of the University
of Fribourg Switzerland
the Seminar für Biblische Zeitgeschichte
of the University of Münster i.W. Federal Republic of Germany
and the Schweizerische Gesellschaft
für orientalische Altertumswissenschaft
Editor: Othmar Keel
Coeditors: Erich Zenger and Albert de Pury

The Author:

Miriam Lichtheim grew up in Berlin. She studied Semitic languages, Egyptology, and Greek at the Hebrew University in Jerusalem, finishing with a M.A. degree in 1939. Continuing at the Oriental Institute of the University of Chicago, she obtained a Ph. D. in Egyptology in 1944. Subsequently she became a professional librarian, working first at Yale University and later at the University of California, Los Angeles. There, until her retirement, she held the dual position of Near Eastern bibliographer and lecturer in ancient Egyptian history. Apart from articles, her publications include: Demotic Ostraca from Medinet Habu, 1957, the three-volume Ancient Egyptian Literature, 1973-1980, Late Egyptian Wisdom Literature in the International Context, OBO 52 (1983) and Ancient Egyptian Autobiographies Chiefly of the Middle Kingdom. A Study and an Anthology, OBO 84 (1988).

Orbis Biblicus et Orientalis 120

Miriam Lichtheim

Maat in Egyptian Autobiographies and Related Studies

Universitätsverlag Freiburg Schweiz
Vandenhoeck & Ruprecht Göttingen

Die Deutsche Bibliothek – CIP-Einheitsaufnahme

Lichtheim, Miriam:
Maat in Egyptian Autobiographies and Related Studies / Miriam Lichtheim. – Freiburg, Schweiz: Univ.-Verl.; Göttingen: Vandenhoeck und Ruprecht, 1992
(Orbis biblicus et orientalis; 120)
ISBN 3-525-53754-9 (Vandenhoeck und Ruprecht)
ISBN 3-7278-0846-2 (Univ.-Verl.)
NE: GT

Die Druckvorlagen wurden von der Verfasserin
als reprofertige Dokumente zur Verfügung gestellt

ISBN 3-7278-0846-2 (Universitätsverlag)
ISBN 3-525-53754-9 (Vandenhoeck & Ruprecht)

CONTENTS

PREFACE

Not formally but in effect, this book is a sequel to my Ancient Egyptian Autobiographies Chiefly of the Middle Kingdom (Fribourg 1988). Its five studies deal with certain aspects of Egyptian Autobiography, and the time span now is predominantly that of the New Kingdom and the Late Period.

1. The essay on Maat was prompted by observing the imbalance between the plethora of broad treatments of the topic "Maat" and the lack of detailed textual studies. My enterprise is an assemblage and paraphrase of texts, mostly autobiographic ones, arranged in chronological sequence, in which the Egyptians declare and define their doing and thinking of Maat. While the word "maat" translates readily into "right/rightness", "truth", and "justice", Egyptian thinking about Maat resulted in formulating the systematized attitudes which in modern languages are called "ethics" and "morality". Studying the ethics of the ancient Egyptians means examining Maat in the context of the Egyptian experience with "knowledge/wisdom" *(rḫ)* and with the Egyptian's sense of the divine, his piety. Thus, in the sources here assembled the triangle ethics-wisdom-piety will be in constant view.

2. The second study traces the connection between autobiographic self-praises and the "Negative Confessions" of chapter 125 of the Book of the Dead. And since the "Negative Confessions" were motivated by the idea of a "Judgment of the Dead", the autobiographic texts are also examined for their bearing on the concept of that "Last Judgment".

3. The brief third study is in the form of an annotated Index, which assembles and translates the moral vocabulary of the texts cited in Studies 1 & 2 and draws some conclusions about the ranking of moral values in Egyptian thought.

4. The fourth study is a grammatical investigation of the portion of Autobiographies known as the "Appeal to the Living". It

reaches certain conclusions about changes in the grammatical structure and meaning of the "Appeal" which have hitherto not been recognized.

5. Lastly, there is a new edition of the text on the verso of the Ptolemaic stela of Padisobek (Cairo JE 44065) which was first published by Daressy in Recueil de Travaux 36, 1914, 73ff. Known as the stela of the "childless man", it has an unusual autobiographic text on its verso which has been discussed by several scholars; but no photographs were published and Daressy's unreliable printed text prevented a clear understanding. The photographs here published now allow an almost complete reading, and some improvements over what I have read and understood could still be made.

The camera-ready copy of my typescript was computer-typed with care and competence by Hanna Jenni of Basel. And once again I thank Prof. Othmar Keel for the hospitality of his OBO series.

Jerusalem, July 1991

Miriam Lichtheim

I

MAAT IN EGYPTIAN AUTOBIOGRAPHIES

1. Basic Recognitions

The earliest statements of "doing Maat" occur near the end of the 5th dynasty.

1) Tomb inscription of the priest *Wr-ḥww* from Giza. (Urk. I, 46.8ff.; Baer, Rank and Title, no. 118; end of 5th dyn.)

pr (.i) m niwt(.i)
h3.n(.i) m sp3t(.i)
ḏd.n(.i) m3ʿt im
ir.n(.i) m3ʿt im
....
n sp ir(.i) šnnt rmṯ nb
n sp di(.i) sḏr s nb špt ir(.i) ḥr ḫt nb
ḏr mswt(.i)

I went from my town
and have descended from my nome,
having spoken Maat there,
having done Maat there.
....
I never did what is hurtful to people,
I never let a man spend the night angry with me about something,
since I was born.

2) Tomb inscription of *Sšm-nfr* from Giza. (Urk. I, 57.11ff.; Baer, Rank and Title, no. 479; end of 5th dyn. or later)

iy.n(.i) m niwt(.i)
pr.n(.i) m sp3t(.i)

qrs(.i) m is pn
ḏd.n(.i) m3ʿt mrrt nṯr rʿ nb
bw nfr pw
wn(.i) ḏd(.i) ḫr nswt 3ḫ n rmṯ
n sp ḏd(.i) ḫt nb ḏw r rmṯ nb
ḫr ḥm n nb(.i)

I have come from my town,
I have gone from my nome,
I am buried in this tomb,
having spoken Maat, the god's wish, daily -
it is the good.
I used to tell the king what serves people,
I never told an evil thing against people
to the majesty of my lord.

In both texts the affirmation of having done and spoken Maat comes after the "I-came-from-my-town" opening, and is followed by specifications of what the doing and speaking of Maat is. Such tripartite declarations became standardized as the non-narrative part of the autobiography, the part that outlined the moral personality. As for the motivation of acting by Maat, the second text states it tersely: the god loves/desires it, and "it is the good".

3) Tomb inscription of the priest and judge *Ḥtp-ḥr-3ḫt(i)* from Saqqara. (Urk. I. 50.1ff.; Baer, Rank and Title, no. 357; 5th dyn.)

ir.n(.i) is pw m išt(.i) m3ʿ
n sp iṯy(.i) ḫt nt rmṯ nb
ir rmṯ nb wnw ir.sn n(.i) ḫt im
ir.n.sn dw3.sn n(.i) nṯr ḥr.s ʿ3 wrt
....
n sp iry(.i) ḫt nb m wsr r rmṯ nb
mr nṯr ḫt m3ʿ
ink im3ḫw ḫr nswt

I have made this tomb from my rightful means,
and never took the property of anyone.
All persons who worked at it for me,
they worked praising god for me greatly for it.
....

I never did anything by force against anyone.
As the god loves a true thing,
I am one honored by the king.

4) Tomb inscription of the nomarch Inti of Deshasha. (Urk. I, 69,16f. & 71.5ff.; Baer, Rank and Title, no. 44; 6th dyn.)

ir.n(.i) is pw m išt(.i) m3^{c}t
n iṯy(.i) ẖt nt rmṯ nb
....
ink im3ẖw ẖr nswt
ink im3ẖw ẖr nṯr ^{c}3
ink mr.f nfrt msḏ.f 3bt
mrrt nṯr pw irt ẖt m3^{c}

I have made this tomb from my rightful means,
and did not take the property of anyone.
....
I am one honored by the king,
I am one honored by the great god;
I am a lover of goodness, a hater of crookedness,
doing the right thing is what the god desires.

So far we have seen Maat in two contexts: in texts 1 and 2 Maat was viewed by looking back at life from the moment of burial. In texts 3 and 4 Maat presides over a man's building his tomb while he is in the midst of life. Thus most of the good deeds claimed in the latter context have to do with honesty and liberality in connection with tomb building. The final quatrain of text 4 adds an effective definition of what doing Maat is and what its rewards are: loving the good, hating wrongdoing, and obtaining a state of honor with the king and with the god. And note the amplified motivation for right-doing: not only does the god love Maat; it is man who loves good and hates evil. Observe also how "the god" and "the king" are set in parallel functions.

5) In the Giza tomb of *Ḥtp.n-Ptḥ* (Urk. I, 187-188; Baer, Rank and Title, no. 356; early 6th dyn.) there are two references to Maat in a broken context which Edel has restored and explained (Hierogl. Inschriften des AR, 1981, p. 93):

iw ir.n.f m3ᶜt nfrt [n nb.s]
[iw] ir.n.f ḥtpt n mrr sy m nfrt rᶜ nb

He has done good justice [for its lord],
he has daily made peace for him who loves it for its goodness.

6) One of the several Ptahhoteps at Saqqara (Urk. I, 188-189) bears the title *ḥm-nṯr m3ᶜt*, "Priest of Maat", a title often found since the 5th dynasty, though a cult and temples of Maat are known only from the New Kingdom onwards.

7) Now we come to the vizier Kagemni in his Saqqara tomb (Urk. I, 194-196; Baer, Rank and Title, no. 548; 6th dyn. Edel, Inschriften des AR, II: Die Biographie des K3j-gmjnj (Kagemni), MIO 1, 1953, 210-226). The autobiography is inscribed on the right and left sides of the entrance. Here are sentences from cols. 2-5 of the right side (Urk. I, 195 augmented by Edel's restorations).

sk nḫt ib n ḥm.f r ḫt nb wḏt.n ḥm.f irt
n mnḫ.n(.i) špss(.i) ḫr ḥm.f
i --- ir bw m3ᶜ n nswt
m3ᶜt mrrt nṯr
ḏd bw m3ᶜ n nswt
mrrt nswt m3ᶜt
i --- im.ṯn ḏd n.f is ḫt r(.i) ḏw n nswt m grg
ḏr wnt ity rḫ qd(.i) sšm(.i)
nḫt ib n ḥm.f r(.i) r sr.f nb ...
ink ḏd m3ᶜ wḥm nfr
m ḫt mrrt nswt
i.mr(.i) nfr n(.i) im
ḫr nswt ḫr nṯr ᶜ3

His majesty relied on all that his majesty ordered done,
because I was worthy and valued by his majesty.
O you --- do what is right for the king,
the right which the god loves!
Speak what is true to the king,
what the king loves is truth!
O you --- do not speak evil against me to the king in falsehood,

for the sovereign knows my character and conduct,
his majesty relies on me more than on all his officials ...
I was one who spoke truly, reported fairly,
in the way the king loves,
for I wished to stand well through it
with the king and with the great god!

As Edel observed, there is here a strong emphasis on Maat doing, the nouns and adjectives of Maat occurring eight times. This emphasis of course reflects the fact that Kagemni was vizier and chief judge. The judicial function, then, is the third context in which we encounter Maat statements in autobiographical inscriptions.

Returning to the first of the three contexts - the declaration of right doing attached to the "I-came-from-my-town" formula - we find that these declarations are gathered into lengthy sequences which appear with minor variants in a number of 6th dynasty tombs. From four such versions, being those of *Nfr-sšm-ptḥ*, *Nfr-sšm-rᶜ*, *Idw*, and *Iẖẖy*, and using that of *Nfr-sšm-ptḥ* as the leading one, Edel reconstructed a standard text in his Hieroglyphische Inschriften des Alten Reiches, pp. 77ff., which supersedes the partial editions of Sethe in Urk. I, 198; I, 200; and I, 204.

8) Tomb of *Nfr-sšm-ptḥ* at Saqqara (Edel, Hierogl. Inschr., 77ff.). On the right side of the façade:

[pr.n(.i) m niwt(.i)]
[h3.n(.i) m sp3t(.i)]
[ir.n(.i)] m3ᶜt n nb.s
sḥtp.n(.i) sw m mrrt.f
ḏd.n(.i) nfr wḥm(.i) nfr
[iṯ.n(.i) tp-nfr]
[mr(.i) nfr im] n rmṯ
wp.n(.i) snnw r ḥtp.sn
nḥm.n(.i) m3r m-ᶜ wsr r.f m sḫmt.n(.i) im
[ḏd.n(.i) m3ᶜ ir.n(.i) m3ᶜ]
[rdi.n(.i) t n ḥqr] ḥbs n ḥ3y
sm3(.i) t3 m iwi
qrs.n(.i) iwty s3.f
ir.n(.i) ẖn [n iwty ẖnt.f]
[sm.n(.i)] nmḥw

n sp ḏd(.i) ẖt nb ḏw r rmṯ nb n sẖm-irf
.... (several more sentences)

[I have gone from my town,]
[I have descended from my nome,]
[having done] justice for its lord,
having contented him with what he loves.
I spoke the good, I repeated the good,
[I grasped the right manner,]
[for I wanted the good] for people.
I judged two parties so as to content them,
I saved the weak from one stronger than he as best I could,
[I spoke truly, I acted justly.]
[I gave bread to the hungry,] clothes to the naked,
I landed one who was stranded,
I buried him who lacked a son,
I made a boat [for the boatless,]
[and supported] the orphan.
I never spoke evil against anyone to a potentate.

9) When the main features of right doing had been established, a man could present his moral self-portrait without mentioning Maat, the underlying moral principle. For example, Pepinakht-Heqaib has the following self-presentation (Aswan tomb 35, Urk. I, 132-133; Lichtheim, Autobiographies, p. 16):

ink ḏd nfr wḥm mrrt
n sp ḏd(.i) ẖt nb ḏw n sẖm-irf r rmṯ nb
mr.n (.i) nfr n(.i) ẖr nṯr ʿ3
iw rdi.n(.i) t n ḥqr ḥbs n ḥ3y
n sp wḏʿ(.i) snwy
m sp sšwy s3 m h̲rt it.f
ink mry n it.f ḥsy n mwt.f
mrrw snw.f

I am one who speaks the good, repeats what is liked,
I never spoke evil against anyone to a potentate,
for I wished to stand well with the great god.
I have given bread to the hungry, clothes to the naked,
and never judged between two parties
in a manner depriving a son of his father's property.

> I am one loved by his father, praised by his mother,
> beloved of his siblings.

In its brevity this is the essence of right doing as then conceived. Its features are: kindness, charity, fair judging, and love of family. Its ultimate goal: "to stand well with the great god".

Kagemni (text 7) had wished "to stand well with the king and the great god". Being vizier, Kagemni was much closer to the king than Pepinakht at Aswan, and his judicial function entailed constant reporting to the king. What we must clarify at this point is the identity of "the god" and "the great god". Kagemni, and Inti (text 4) drew a clear distinction between "king" and "great god" by setting them side by side. The first question then is whether *nṯr* and *nṯr ꜥ3* refer to the same being. In his Untersuchungen (1944, p. 9) Edel assembled variants of the phrase "for I wished to stand well with the god", which showed that "god" and "great god" were used interchangeably. And in discussing the versions of "I have done Maat beloved of the god", Edel wrote (p. 39): "Die Ausdrücke, 'dem Gott', 'ihrem Herrn', 'dem, der sie liebt', dürften sich auf den Sonnengott Re beziehen." Edel returned to the matter in his discussion of Kagemni, where he observed: "Die Bezeichnung des Königs als 'Gott' ist in biographischen Texten des AR nicht gerade häufig; ein gutes Beispiel bot immerhin die Biographie des Izj ('ich tat alles, was dieser Gott liebt' Izj, B 2/3)." Now for the passage in the text of Izy one should know that the sentence "I did what this god loves" comes directly after king Teti has been mentioned by name; and this is the normal usage: the king is called "god" or, quite rarely, "great god" when he has just been named. Otherwise, in autobiographical inscriptions from the 5th dynasty onward, "god" and "great god", the latter often described as "lord of sky", "lord of the west", or "lord of judgment", is the god, be he Re, or Atum, or another. (The reader should consult Junker, Giza II, 52-57; Kees, Götterglaube, 270-278, and Kees, Totenglaube^{2}, 110). Assman's general equation of "great god" with "king" (Ma'at, pp. 106 & 128) is unsubstantiated.

For perspectives on Maat thinking outside of biographical sources we now turn to the Instruction of Ptahhotep, Maxim no. 5 (P.Prisse 88ff.):

10) Great is Maat, lasting in effect,
undisturbed since the time of Osiris.
For one punishes the breaker of laws,
though the greedy one *(ꜥwn-ib)* overlooks this.
While baseness *(nḏyt)* may seize riches,
crime *(ḏ3yt)* never lands its wares.
In the end it is Maat that lasts,
man says, "it is my father's ground".

The verses convey that Maat was viewed as a primordial condition, one firmly founded and lasting, which when activated overcomes all crime. Maxim no. 19 (P.Prisse 312ff.) elaborates:

That man endures whose rule is Maat,
who walks a straight line.
He will make a will by it,
one who is greedy has no tomb.

The emerging picture of Maat has weight but is still incomplete. In particular, the connection between Maat and the gods has not been explained beyond the affirmation that "the god" is lord of Maat, and that he loves/desires that men do Maat.

The Pyramid Texts supply the heavenly dimension of Maat, but just barely. Two passages relate Maat to Re, the first being a broken one:
Pyr. 1774b: --- *m3ꜥt m-b3ḥ rꜥ*, "--- Maat before Re" and
Pyr. 1582a: *psḏ m rꜥ dr ḏ3t / sꜥḥꜥ m3ꜥt r-s3 rꜥ*, "May you shine as Re repressing wrong, and let Maat stand behind Re."

Another passage tells that the Four Sons of Horus "live by Maat"; the king does not, he merely aspires to it: Pyr. 1483a+c:

n P. is pw wꜥ m 4 ipw nṯrw
Imst Ḥp Dw3-mwtf Qbḥ-snwf
ꜥnḫiw m m3ꜥt tw3iw ḥr ḏꜥmw.sn
mnhsiw t3-šmꜥ

For Pepi is one of these four gods
Imsety, Hapy, Duamutef, Kebehsenuf,
who live by Maat, who lean on their staffs,
who watch over Upper Egypt.

As for the king as bringer and doer of Maat, it is said in three passages, one of them broken:

iy.n W. m iw n sisi
dn W. m3ᶜt im.f m st isft (Pyr. 265b-c)

Unas has come from the isle of fire,
Unas has set right in it in place of wrong.

pr W. ir m3ᶜt
int.f s is ḫr.f (Pyr. 319b)

There comes Unas, doer of right,
he will bring it with him.

pt m ḥtpw t3 m 3wt-ib
sḏm.n.sn dd N. m3ᶜt [m st isft] (Pyr. 1775a-b)

Sky is at peace, earth in joy,
when they hear the king has set right [in place of wrong] (restoration by Sethe).

In a number of passages, the king on his journey to the sky, addressing the gods in prayer or by threats, insists that he is just and demands his justification. That means he is not himself the bringer of Maat. Pyr. 1188a-f is among the spells that are least governed by the presumption of magical power, hence closest to an ethical view of the royal claim to Maat:

i ḏ3 iwy m3ᶜ
mẖnty sḫt i3rw
P. pw m3ᶜ ḫr pt ḫr t3
P. pw m3ᶜ ḫr iw pw n t3
nb.n.f spr.n.f ir.f
nty imiwt mnty Nwt

O boatman of the boatless just,
ferryman of the reed field!
Pepi is just before sky and earth,
Pepi is just before this isle of earth,
whereto he has swum and come,
which lies between the thighs of Nut!

Note how the lines are governed by alliteration and internal rhymes.

On the other hand, in Pyr. 361a-c the king declares his vindication by means of a proclamation:

ḏd.tn sw(t) rn nfr n P. pn n Nḥb-k3w
hny n P. pn hny n k3.f
m3^c-ḫrw P. pn m3^c-ḫrw k3 n P. pn ḫr nṯr

Announce the good name of Pepi to Nehebkau!
Hail this Pepi, hail his ka!
Pepi is justified, Pepi's ka is justified before the god!

A summary of what the Old Kingdom texts that speak of Maat yield for the meaning of the term is now called for.

The nouns *m3^{c}t, m3^c*, and *bw m3^c* translate readily into "right", "rightness", and "truth". In the context of judicial action "rightness" acquires the sense of "justice".

To denote the opposite of *m3^{c}t*, the Old Kingdom texts use the terms *isft* and *grg*, "wrong" and "falsehood", they also contrast *m3^{c}t* with *ḏw*, "evil".

The nominal form *m3^c* might be (as Westendorf suggested in his Ursprung und Wesen, 203) the passive participle of the verb *m3^c*, "to guide, direct", hence "that which is regulated", i.e. "right".

Since the 5th dynasty, when the texts begin to speak of Maat, performing Maat is described by the verbs "to do" and "to speak". And given the presence of the opposite pair "wrong" and "falsehood", it is clear that the two meanings "right" and "truth" were present from the beginning.

Old Kingdom spellings of Maat with the standing goddess determinative (Wb. 2, 20) and the title "priest of Maat", where the determinative occurs, convey the mythological aspect of Maat as a forceful divine being.

The Pyramid Texts suggest that Maat came into being together with the gods and is continually upheld by them.

The biographical texts, working out actual experience, declare that Maat is "the good"; and "doing Maat" consists of performing acts of honesty, fairness, and kindness.

In sum: man did Maat because it was "good" and because "the god desires it". It was the principle of right order by which the gods lived, and which men recognized as needful on earth and incumbent upon them.

2. Exploring the Self

In the autobiographical inscriptions of the First Intermediate Period mentions of Maat are rare. The rarity probably has several causes, the first of which might be an external one: the small number of presently known inscribed tombs, and their poor state of preservation. Even so, three occurrences of Maat can be culled from the inscribed fragments of tombs at Dendera.

11) Inscriptions from the tomb of *Mn-ᶜnḫ-ppy* called *Mni* are included in Urk. I, 268f., but they are likely to be of post-Old Kingdom date, as was argued by Fischer, Dendera (pp. 85ff., 131, 170ff.). From some fragments of the frieze Sethe reconstituted the sentence:

[ḏd.n(.i)] m3ᶜ n mrwt siᶜt m3ᶜt n [nb.s]
[I spoke] truly so as to raise up Maat to [its lord].
(Petrie, Dendereh, pl. 2a = Urk. I, 269.9)

12) On the false-door from the tomb of *Sn-nḏsw-i* (Petrie, Dendereh, pl. ix; Schenkel, MHT, no. 128, pp. 141f.) we read:

pr.n(.i) m pr(.i)
h3.n(.i) m is(.i)
ḏd.n(.i) mrrt ᶜ3w ḥsst nḏsw
n mrwt s(i)ᶜt m3ᶜt n nṯr ᶜ3 nb pt

I have gone from my house,
I have descended to my tomb,
having spoken what the great love and the small praise,
so as to raise up Maat to the great god, the lord of sky.

13) On the frieze from the tomb of *Ḥtpi* (Petrie, Dendereh, pl. 11, reconstituted by Fischer, Dendera, pp. 166-168 & fig. 31b at p. 158) we read:

n rdi(.i) s n wsr r.f
n mrwt s(i)ᶜt m3ᶜt n nṯr ᶜ3 nb pt

I did not hand a man over to one mighter than he,
so as to raise up Maat to the great god, the lord of sky.

The dates of the tombs of *Sn-nḏsw-i* and *Ḥtpi* are clearly post-Old Kingdom (see Fischer, Dendera, pp. 128fff.). Thus all three tombs yield the same phrase, one which declares that acting with justice and compassion meant offering to the sungod what was essentially the god's own creation. When in temples of the New Kingdom and Late Period the king is shown performing the act of offering Maat, the scene depicts what had been conceived a thousand years earlier by men who practised self-reliance and initiative undirected by royal command: it was the man of standing who raised up Maat to the deity.

As for the "I-came-from-my-town (or, my-house)" formula, when found at this time it could introduce a declaration of good deeds done without references to Maat, as is the case in Siut tomb no. 4 of Khety, in the façade inscription (lines 61-66, cited after Edel, Inschr. der Grabfronten der Siutgräber, pp. 96ff.):

14) iy.n(.i) m niwt(.i)
h3.n(.i) m sp3t(.i)
ir.n(.i) mrrt rmṯ ḥsst nṯrw
iw rdi.n(.i) t n ḥqr ḥbsw n ḥ3y
sḏm.n(.i) sprt n ḫ3rt
di.n(.i) pr n nmḥw
wḏb.n(.i) s3(.i) n mrr grg
n wḏʿ(.i) iwty sp.f r ṯs.f
wšb.n(.i) bin m nfr
n ḏʿr(.i) bw ḏwy
n mrwt w3ḥ tp t3
sbt r im3ḫ

I have come from my town,
I have descended from my nome,
having done what people love and gods praise.
I have given bread to the hungry, clothes to the naked,
I listened to the plea of the widow,
I gave a home to the orphan.
I turned my back on the lover of lies,
and did not judge the blameless by his (the liar's) word.
I answered evil with good,
and did not seek wickedness,
in order to endure on earth,
and attain reveredness.

Where in the past the I-came-from-my-town opening was rounded off by the statement of having done Maat (text 8), there is now the "doing of what people love and gods praise" (and its variant in text 11). Altogether, the handsome self-laudation of Khety of Siut shows the ongoing innovations in phrasing.

The many small stelae that now constitute the bulk of the source material present their owners as men who acquired possessions, supported their fellowmen, and loved their families; and the common terms with which to describe their virtue were *nfr*, "good" in all its applications, and *mry*, "beloved".

15) Stela of *Iti-ᶜ3* (Dunham, Naga ed-Dêr, no. 73, pp. 85f.: Schenkel, MHT, no. 241, p. 176). After a brief offering formula:

> ink ḏd nfr wḥm nfr
> rdi ẖt n tp-nfr
> ink mry n it.f ḥsy n mwt.f
> mrrw snwt.f im3 n 3bwt.f
>
> I am one who spoke the good, repeated the good,
> and settled matters for the best.
> I am the beloved of his father, the praised of his mother,
> loved by his siblings, kind to his kindred.

Evidently, the average person could lay claim to virtuous behaviour without speaking of Maat - and it is the common man who speaks on these many small stelae. *M3ᶜt*, then, was a weighty and solemn word; and one that had to do with public service and with rank. Here is one man who used it, the Theban *Ṯbw* (CG 20005) who had a substantial stela, unfortunately now broken (TPPI, no. 3; Schenkel, MHT, no. 90). Near its end he declared:

16) iw ir.n(.i) imi-r3 pr n ḥq3 6
> n sp iwt ẖt im
> ink ir m3ᶜt
> sb n im3ẖ
>
> I have served as steward to six chiefs
> without incurring blame;
> I am one who did right,
> and attained reveredness.

The time of the rising 11th dynasty was a time of driving creativity during which the Egyptians discovered the sources of their selfhood: the heart *(ib)* and the character *(qd)* were the forces that raised, shaped, and channelled man's thoughts, desires, inclinations, and actions, including his understanding of right and wrong. In short, the Egyptian discovered his inner-directedness. The autobiographical inscription then became the most effective vehicle of self-expression.

17) Djari, a follower of king Wahankh Intef II, displays the new mixture of pride in his own qualities and devotion to the king. On one of his two Theban tomb stelae (Cairo JE 41437, TPPI no. 18; Schenkel, MHT no. 72) he tells of the mission for which the king chose him because of his "knowing matters, speaking well, being weighty in council, and calm in combat"; he also recalls his good standing in his home-town, a theme which harks back to the kingless time. His second stela (Brussels E.4985, TPPI no. 19; Schenkel, MHT no.73) is wholly concerned with the services he rendered "at home" and ends with the formula:

pr.n(.i) m pr(.i)
h3.n(.i) m is(.i)
n sp iwt ẖt im

I went from my house,
I descended to my tomb,
without incurring blame.

18) Rediu-khnum of Dendera, a contemporary of Djari but of higher rank and specifically a servant of queen Nefrukayit (CG 20543, Schenkel, MHT no. 81; Lichtheim, Autobiograohies, no. 18 & pl. I) relates his long years of service in the refined style which now comes into flower. The compounded epithet (e.g. *nb-šfyt, mꜥr-inm, rẖ-ẖt*) gives body to the new observation of "character"; and the active roles of heart and character are summed up in a pithy phrase: *in ib(.i) sẖnt st(.i) in qd(.i) rdi w3ḥ(.i) ḥ3t,* "It was my heart that advanced my rank, it was my character that kept me in front".

Another feature of the new style was that the self-laudation - the description of one's perfect character - became integrated with the career narration, so that the distinction between the two aspects of autobiography was effaced. To the scribes who developed the new style, combining narration and self-description must have been a challenge requiring rhetorical skill. Note for example how Rediu-khnum's narration of his good management is highlighted by pointing to his character in poetic metaphors:

ink wnnt sr ꜥ3 n ib.f
ḥn bni n mrwt (line 16)

I am truly a great-hearted noble,
a sweet lovable plant.

Similarly in lines 19/20:

ink rẖ sw ẖnt rmṯ
ẖt šps ir.n nṯr

I am a knower of himself as leader of men,
a costly timber made by the god.

19) The Theban stela of the chamberlain *Ḥnwn*, who served kings Intef II and III and Mentuhotep II (Cairo JE 36346, TPPI no. 24; Schenkel, MHT no. 375) is unfortunately a fragment. Of particular interest for us is that in line 7, between two lacunae, there occurs the phrase *mḏd.n(.i) m3ꜥw nw ꜥnẖ[w]* ... which Schenkel rendered, "Ich befolgte das, was die Lebenden für richtig halten." Here then Maat appears as the noun *m3ꜥw* "Richtigkeit" (Wb. 2, 23) and the expression "rightness of (or, for) the living" is noteworthy. Henun ends with the quatrain:

nn isft prt m r3(.i)
nn ḏwt irt.n ꜥwy
ink ir qd.f
mrrw rmṯ m ẖrt-hrw nt rꜥ nb

There was no falseness that came from my mouth,
no evil that was done by my hands;
I am a maker of his character,
one beloved of people each day.

20) The Theban Intef son of Tjefi, an official of Mentuhotep II, employed choice words to describe himself on his elegant stela (MMA 57.95, Fischer, JNES 19, 1960, 258-268; Schenkel, MHT no. 380; Lichtheim, Autobiographies, no. 20). Here is part of line 6 (i.e.

line 4 on the tablet, inside the raised border; and line 10, on the border):

ink wʿ n nb.f
šw m isft
ḏd mdt r wn.s m3ʿ
rḫ mdt sṯp ṯs
m33 w3 ḫmt ḥnt
rḫ st rd.f m pr-nswt

I am the sole one of his lord,
one free of wrongdoing,
who tells a matter rightly;
who knows speech, chooses words,
sees far, plans ahead,
and knows his station in the king's house.

iy.n(.i) m niwt(.i)
h3.n(.i) m sp3t(.i)
ir.n(.i) mrrt rmṯ ḥsst nṯrw
rdi.n(.i) t n ḥqr ḥbsw n ḥ3yt
im3ḫw Ini-it.f

I have come from my town,
I have descended from my nome,
having done what people love and gods praise;
I gave bread to the hungry, clothes to the naked -
the honored Intef.

Note the phrase "having done what people love and gods praise", which, as we found in text 14, has replaced "having done Maat for its lord".

21) The Abydene chief priest *Rwḏʿḥ3w* rounded off the account of his priestly functions by a brief characterisation of the "good man" (stela BM 159, Faulkner, JEA 37, 1951, 47-52; Schenkel, MHT no. 495; Lichtheim, Autobiographies, no. 29). The closing quatrain is the same as that of text 19:

ink mr.f nfrt msḏ.f ḏwt
iwty sḏr.n rmṯ špt r.f
nn isft prt m r3(.i)

nn ḏwt irt.n ʿwy
ink ir qd.f
mrrt rmṯ m ẖrt-hrw nt rʿ nb

I am a lover of good, a hater of evil,
with whom none stayed angry overnight.
There was no falseness that came from my mouth,
no evil that was done by my hands;
I am one who made his character,
one beloved of people each day.

Earlier in his text Rudjahau displayed his self-confidence by comparing himself to Thoth, Ptah, and Khnum *(Ḏḥwty m wḏʿ mity Ptḥ snnw H̱nmw).* This did not prevent his being "one guided by Thoth" *(sšmw Ḏḥwty).* Inner-directedness left room for divine or human guidance, even though a hardy soul might attribute all his competence to his own good natural endowment, unaided by parental teaching, as did the minor Abydene priest Mentuhotep (stela Cambridge, Fitzwilliam Museum E 9.1922; Petrie, Tombs of the Courtiers, pls. xvi, xxii-xxiii; Lichtheim, Autobiographies, no. 27 & pl. IV). He had been an orphan:

22) qb šsp t r tr.f
idn.n n.f sḫr.f mwt m ḫnt
it ḥr ir gm.k s3.i

nfr qd sb3.n bi3t.f
mi ẖrd ḫpr m-ʿ it
iw sk.(w)i grt w3.kwi r nmḥ

A cool one who got bread in time,
whose conduct replaced him a mother at home,
a father who said, "Take note, my son".

One well-disposed and taught by his nature,
like a child grown up with a father,
but behold, I had become an orphan!

* * *

Those of the Hatnub graffiti that are dated to the nomarchs of the Hare nome Ahanakht and Nehri I (Anthes, Felseninschriften von Hatnub, Graffiti 10-13 & 14-32) I propose to date as H.O.Williams did (in JEOL 28, 1985, 80ff.) as belonging to the latter part of the 11th dynasty. Their texts make significant contributions to the genre "self-portrayal" and they contain remarkable references to Maat.

23) Graffito no. 10 (Anthes, Hatnub Gr. 10, p. 25), dated to year 20 of the nomarch Ahanakht, is a self-presentation of his son, the scribe *H̱nmw-iqr*:

> ḏdt.n sš H̱nmw-iqr
> ink sš n ḫrt-ib
> qb-ẖt d3r-srf
> dw3 [s]w3.f ḥr.f
> šw m šnt nṯr
> iy.n.i ꜥ3 r ḥt-nbt r int šs
> r ir(t) mnw n Wnwt nbt wnw
> ḥr-tp snb ꜥḥ3-nḫt ꜥnḫ wḏ3 snb
>
> Says the scribe Khnum-iqer:
> I am a scribe who pleases,
> cool-bellied, calm-tempered,
> who salutes the passerby,
> and is free of profanation.
> I came here to Hatnub to fetch alabaster,
> to make monuments for Wenut, mistress of Wenu,
> for the health of Ahanakht - life, prosperity, health!

A praise of the highly valued quiet virtues: calmness, self-control, friendliness, politeness.

24) Graffito no.12 (Anthes, Hatnub, Gr. 12, pp. 28ff.) dated to year 13 of the nomarch Ahanakht, is the self-presentation of the nome official *Ḏḥwty-nḫt-ꜥnḫ*. Scribe, priest, and physician, he had major administrative duties which he describes thus (lines 6-18):

> iw ir.n(.i) m3ꜥt m sšm.i
> ḏꜥr(.i) ib ḥsb(.i) rdiw r ḫwd
> ir.n.(.i) ḥsst n rmṯ nb
> rḫw mi ḫmw n sṯn.i

ink mrwt(y) n sp3t.f
n sw3(.i) ḥr ḏ3r n h3bw
ink dmi nḏm n wḥwt.f
ʿpr n 3bwt.f nn 3hw.s
ink s3 n i3w it n ẖrd
ṯsw nḏsw m swt nb
iw sm.n(.i) ḥqr wrḥ(.i) ẖs3
iw di.n(.i) ḥbsw n nt(y) ḥ3w
iw ḥk3.n(.i) ḥr inḏ šnt.n(.i) sṯ
ink gr qrs sb n k3.f
iw wp.n(.i) mdt r m3ʿt.s
rdi.n(.i) pr snnw ib.sn ḥtp
iw sš.n(.i) bw-nfr ḫt sp3t.i
ir.n(.i) mrt.n nb.i

I have done rightness in my conduct,
when I probed the heart and assessed a payer by (his) wealth,
doing what is praiseworthy for every person,
known and unknown without distinction.
I am the favorite of his nome,
I did not pass over the need of a petitioner;
I am a pleasant abode for his kindred,
who provides for his kin, that it wants not.
I am son to the aged, father to the child,
protector of the poor in every place.
I have fed the hungry, anointed the unkempt,
I have given clothing to the naked.
I have exorcised the ailing face and fought the smell,
I am also one who buries the departed.
I have judged a case by its rightness,
and made the trial partners leave contented.
I have spread goodness throughout my nome,
and have done what my lord desired.

An excellent description of doing Maat in its typical context, that of public service, where the efficient and honest administrator proves his worth by absolute rectitude in assessing taxes, by benevolence to the weak and poor, and by judging litigation through a procedure aimed at conciliation.

The graffiti that are dated to the nomarch Nehri I (nos. 14-32) divide into two types: those written by officials on their own behalf, and those written by scribes in the shape of self-presentations of their superiors, the nomarch Nehri and his two sons, *Ḏḥwty-nḫt* and *K3y*. I quote two of the latter type, graffiti 23 and 24, both written by a scribe named Ahanakht. No. 23 is styled as the self-presentation of the nomarch's son Thothnakht, no. 24 as that of Kay. The two sons governed the Hare nome jointly, with some division of functions as indicated by their differing titles.

25) Graffito 23 (Anthes, Hatnub, Gr. 23, pp. 52f.) of Thothnakht, lines 1-3:

sḏ3wty bity smr wᶜty imi-r3 ḥm-nṯr
wᶜb ᶜ3 n Ḏḥwty s3ṯ n ir m3ᶜt
mn-rd twr-ᶜwy ḥby m wsḫt
ḥry-tp ḥt-nṯr mi qd.s
sḫnt.n Ḏḥwty st.f
s3.f ḏs.f n wn-m3ᶜ
ms n psḏty Rᶜ
qrḥt spyt ḫt t3 pn
rmṯ nbt wsšw
nḏs qn n mit(y).f
nb qd ᶜ3 ḫpš ...

Chancellor of Lower Egypt's king, sole companion, chief priest,
great web-priest of Thoth, who libates to the "Maat-doer",
firm-footed, pure-handed, festive in the hall.
Chief of the entire temple,
whose seat Thoth placed in front;
his own son in truth,
born of the two Enneads of Re.
Sole ancient nobility in this land -
all other people are base -
valiant citizen without his peer,
man of character, strong-armed.

Thothnakht then recalls that he saved the town "on the day of plunder", an event told at greater length by his brother Kay (in graffito 24), and he ends by describing his generosity and friendliness. Altogether, a portrayal of "the prince" in his pride and benevolence.

26) Graffito 24, of Nehri's son Kay, (Anthes, Hatnub, Gr. 24, pp. 54ff.) is even more elaborate; here are portions of lines 3-9:

(3) ḥḏ-ḥr nfr-bi3t
pḫ3-ẖt šw m snkt
nty t3 pn ẖr mrwt.f
ḥʿ.n rmṯ nṯrw m ḫsfw ẖntyw.f
....
s3 Ḏḥwty n wn m3ʿ
wtwt k3 m3ʿt
dw3 n ḥr.f r pr.f
r dw3 k3.f rʿ nb
....
(5) iw ir.n(.i) m3ʿt spd r wšm
iw nḥm.n(.i) m3r m-ʿ wsr
iw snf.n(.i) ẖ3rt iwtt hi.s
iw šd.n(.i) nmḥy iwty it.f
iw ṯs.n(.i) ḏ3mw.s n ẖrdw
n mrwt ʿš3 ḫprw.s
iw grt ḏ3mw.s ʿq n nḏsw ḥms m prw.sn
n mšʿ.sn m rk snḏ n pr-nswt
(7) iw nḥm.n(.i) niwt.i hrw ʿw3
m-ʿ ḥrt mrt nt pr-nswt
ink grt ḫnt.s hrw ʿḥ3.s
nh3t.s m šdt-š
s3 ḥq3 n wnt
(9) ḫwd ʿ3 ḥr qd

(3) Generous, good-natured,
open-hearted, free of glumness,
whom this land holds in affection,
whom men and gods hail when his statues approach.
....
Son of Thoth in very truth,
begotten of the Bull of Maat,
whom he worships in his house,
so as to praise his ka each day.
....

(5) I have done rightness razor-sharp!
I have rescued the weak from the strong,
I succoured the widow bereft of her husband,
I raised the orphan bereft of his father.
I marshaled (the town's) young men
in order to increase its forces -
its youths had become burghers who sat in their homes,
not having campaigned since the palace became feared.
(7) I saved my town on the day of plunder
from the dread terror of the palace!
I was its wall on the day of its combat,
its rampart in the marshland!
Son of the Hare nome's ruler,
(9) one wholly rich and great!

Here is the perfect ruler and administrator who has all the requisite virtues: skill, courage, benevolence, and justice, so that he "did Maat" *spd r wšm*. If the word *wšm* meant "ear of grain" (Anthes, p. 55; Wb. 1, 374; Faulkner, Dict. 70) it should have the plant determinative and not the harpoon-head. Chances are that it meant a sharp and pointed blade in a variety of materials. My free rendering of *spd r wšm* as "razor sharp" is meant to stress what this vivid image conveys: doing Maat encompassed the gentle deeds of charity and the "sharp" actions of rescuing the weak and of defensive combat.

As for the epithet "son of Thoth", borne by the nomarch Nehri and by his two sons, Anthes (Hatnub, p. 58) reflected on what he considered a very remarkable claim to divine descent: "bemerkenswerte Prätention unmittelbar göttlicher Abstammung". I take a different view. The language at this time abounds in rhetorical devices: pictorial expressions, metaphors, rare words, and hyperbole. Such terms as "son" and "father" were used metaphorically. The scribe Thothnakht of text 24 had called himself "son to the aged, father to the child". As priests and governors of the temple of Thoth, the nomarch and his sons could call themselves "sons of Thoth" without thereby claiming divine descent, just as the Abydene high priest Rudjahau (text 21) called himself "Thoth in judgment, the like of Ptah, the second of Khnum", without implying divine status.

The four Hatnub graffiti have yielded four distinctive portrayals of character: the nomarch's son who, rather than flaunting his rank, wished to be known as pleasant, kind, and modest. The responsible nome official who carried out his duties in an exemplary Maat-observing manner. And the two princely nomarch's sons who, with pride in their ancient lineage and devotion to the great god Thoth who dwelled in their midst, ruled the Hare nome in the fullness of Maat-oriented beneficence.

These self-presentations show that the basic meanings of Maat - Right-Truth-Justice - are the same as they were in the 6th dynasty. What has been added is a great advance in thinking about experiences and formulating conclusions. Thus, the range of actions defined as doing Maat was enlarged, and the ability to perform the works of Maat was now seen as grounded in the character.

The Egyptian's strong sense of selfhood and personal worth brought forth both the quest for immortality and an ethic of responsibility toward his fellow human beings, a responsibility which translated quite specifically into fair-dealing and beneficence. Practiced in the privacy of family life, these virtues were called "goodness"; but on the larger stage of public life they were defined as "doing Maat".

3. Justice

A. Autobiographical Stelae

27) The stelae of the steward Mentuwosre, erected as a royal gift in year 17 of king Sesostris I (MMA 12.184; Sethe, Les. no. 19; Hayes, Scepter, I, 299; Lichtheim, Autobiographies, no. 44) typifies the quality product by which the high officials now memorialized themselves as followers of Osiris in the context of Abydene worship. Such memorials strove to emphasize the moral personality so as to justify the wish for admittance to the entourage of Osiris in the afterlife. In carefully constructed, rhythmically balanced, sentences ("I am ... I did...") the official declared that he had acted in accordance with the moral norms:

... I am a brave second in the king's house ...
... I am one loved of his kindred, close to his kin ...
... I am father to the orphan, support of widows ...
... I am one who listens rightly *(r wn m3ˁ)*
and leans not to him who can pay.

28) In years 24/25 of Sesostris I, another royal steward, Intef son of Sitamun, erected a cenotaph at Abydos with four handsome stelae (Simpson, Terrace, ANOC 4.1-4 & pls. 10-11). Two of them are in the Louvre (C 167 & C 168) and two in Cairo (CG 20542 and CG 20561). The Louvre stelae are badly damaged. James Burton copied their texts at Abydos when that of C 167 was still complete, and Rosalind Moss published his handcopies in Griffith Studies, 310ff. The two Cairo stelae bear offering texts and afterlife wishes, while the Louvre stelae presented the man's career and his moral personality. Here are lines 7-9 of Louvre C 167 (except the end of line 9 where a new section begins):

ink b3k mry nb.f
ḏd m3ˁt nn sw3 ḥr ḥr.f
ḫrp-ib wnwt 3st
grg-ḥr m irt ḫt m k3b ẖnmmt
rdi ḥ3w ḥr ḏddt n.f
š3 ˁrq.f m ḫt nb
sḏm ir.f mi ḏddt
smnḫ mi ntt ib r.s
sḏmw hnw š3w irw

w3ḥ-ib iqr-ṯsw
d3r-srf šw m ḥnw
m3ᶜty iwty wᶜ(3)
wn-ib r wẖdw sfnw
s-n-mty ᶜq3-ib mnḫ-sšrw

I am the servant his lord loves,
who speaks truth without evasion,
is forceful in the fleeting hour,
and keen to act among the people.
Who does more than told to do,
whose skill is apt for every matter,
who, hearing, acts as ordered,
performs according as desired.
Considerate hearer, able doer,
thoughtful and eloquent,
calm-tempered, free of anger,
a righteous one who does not plot evil.
Heedful to the pained and suffering,
man of rectitude, upright, effective in action.

What we are witnessing here is how the earlier build-up of character study and rhethorical skill reaches its culmination in the classical style of the reign of Sesostris I. Note also the appearance of the term *m3ᶜty*, "righteous".

29) In year 39 of Sesostris I, the chamberlain Intef son of Sent erected an Abydene cenotaph with three tall stelae and a statue (HTBM II, 22-24; Simpson, Terrace, ANOC 5.1-4, pls. 12-13). Again, the texts are complementary, the tallest stela (BM 572) relating the chamberlain's multiple tasks, the two others (BM 562 & 581) presenting his moral personality. On BM 562 Intef describes his all-round goodness *(nfrw)* and like Intef son of Sitamun he calls himself *s n mty*, "man of rectitude". Of Maat he speaks thus (lines 11-12):

n ir.i iwyt r rmṯ
msḏḏt nṯr pw
ir.n.i m3ᶜt mrt.n nswt

I did no wrong to people,
it is hateful to the god,
I did the right beloved of the king.

And on stela BM 581 Intef declares:

ink sḏmw sḏm m3ʿt ...
ink ʿq3 mity iwsw
mty m3ʿ mi Ḏḥwty

I am a hearer who hears the truth ...
I am exact like the balance,
truly straight like Thoth (lines 13 & 17)

30) The two stelae of the Abydene chief priest Wepwawet-aa, dated to year 44 of Sesostris I (Leiden V4 & Munich Gl.WAF 35; Simpson, Terrace, ANOC 20.1-2) share phrases with those of Intef son of Sent. He too "did no wrong to people, it is hateful to the god"; and he was *mty m3ʿ r gs rmṯ*, "truly straight with people" (Leiden V4, lines 8 & 10).

31) The large stela of the vizier Mentuhotep (CG 20539), he too an official of Sesostris I, shows clearly that it was the judicial function that called forth the most emphatic statements of Maat doing. On the recto Maat is named seven times. In addition to being priest of Maat, the vizier was: *s n m3ʿt ḫnt t3wy / mty m3ʿ mi Ḏḥwty / snwf m shrt t3wy ... w3ḥ-ib r sḏm mdwt / mity nṯr m wnwt.f ... dd s r wn.f m3ʿ ... siʿr m3ʿt r ʿḥ,* "Man of right before the Two Lands / truly straight like Thoth / his second in contenting the land ... patient in listening to speeches / equal of the god in his hour ... who puts a man in his right ... who raises Maat up to the palace".

32) Similarly, near the end of the 12th dynasty, the official *Rmny-ʿnḫ* (CG 20571) tells he was:

mry nb.f m3ʿ n st ib.f
rḫ st.f m pr-nswt
siʿr m3ʿt n nb.f
smi n.f ḫrt t3wy

Truly loved by his lord, and trusted,
one who knew his place in the palace,

who raised Maat up to its lord,
reported him the state of the land.

In the two texts we encounter the phrase "raising up Maat to the palace" (or, "to its lord") and we recall that much earlier, at Dendera (texts 11-13) the tomb owners spoke of "having raised up Maat to the great god, the lord of sky". What had meant offering one's Maat to the sungod from whom Maat had issued now means the royal official's reporting to the king on the responsible performance of his duties. And this is the sense in which the phrase was used throughout the New Kingdom.

33) Another theme that points forward to the New Kingdom was sounded by the chamberlain Semti the Younger, in the reign of Amenemhet II. On his Abydene stela (HTBM II, 8-9 no. 574; Sethe, Les. no. 16; Lichtheim, Autobiographies, no. 41) he ends with this appeal:

rmṯ im3 ibw n mꜥḥꜥt.i
ḏ3t ḏrt n srḫ.i
ḏr ntt n ir.i ḏ3t
ḫnm.n.i nṯr m m3ꜥt
wn.i im b3.kwi 3ḫ.kwi
m smt ḥq3t nḥḥ
ir.i ḥpt h3 r nšmt
sn.i t3 n Wp-w3wt

People, be kind to my monument,
gentle to my memorial!
For I have not done wrong;
I gladdened the god with right,
so as to be yonder ensouled, transfigured,
in the desert, mistress of eternity,
to take the rudder in the Neshmet,
and kiss the ground to Wepwawet!

Here, the connection between doing Maat on earth and a blessed afterlife as its reward is clearly made. And in such prayers Middle Kingdom piety attained its most urgent expression. In general, the devotional attitude found words in maxims such as:

n wnt ꜥnḫ n ḫm nṯr

There is no life for the godless.
(Barns, Five Ramesseum Papyri, Pap. II, pl. 8, p. 13 n.6)

B. Tomb Inscriptions

Given the small number of currently known private tombs of the Middle Kingdom, and their poor state of preservation, it is not surprising that Maat statements are scant. Those that occur come from highly placed personalities - nomarchs and a vizier - and all are significant.

34) In his tomb at Beni Hasan, Amenemhet, nomarch of the Oryx nome in the reign of Sesostris I, recorded two brief statements of his rightness, phrased in the third person in conjunction with an offering formula and with his titulary, i.e. as epithets in a non-narrative context:

nn wn ḥnt m ẖt.f
ḏd.f m mdt m3ʿt

No greed is in his body,
what he speaks is truth. (Urk. VII, 18.2-3)

ḏd m3ʿt wp.f snw
šw m ḏd grg

Who speaks truth when he judges two men,
who is free of speaking falsehood. (Urk. VII, 19.18)

The two statements bring out clearly what many other Maat phrases have already shown: far from being a blanket term for virtuous behavior, Maat meant specifically veracity and fair dealing. As I pointed out in my Autobiographies (text 60) the nomarch Amenemhet wished to be remembered in particular for a different virtue, that of graciousness or benignity: *im3-ʿ*, a term which he kept adding to his name and titulary. It is all part of the striving for nuance in the description of character, which is so marked in the autobiographies in the latter part of the 11th and first half of the 12th dynasties.

35) At Siut, Djefai-hapi, governor of the 13th nome of Upper Egypt in the reign of Sesostris I, reviewed his good government (Urk. VII,63.9-16):

iy.n.i m niwt.i m sp3t.i
ir.n.i mrrt rmṯ ḥsst nṯrw
iw wp.n.i snw r ḥtp.sn
shrw.i -------
[n rdi.i] šps ḥmt r ḥnwt.s
n mrwt irt m3ʿt
sḥtp.n.i nṯr.i m mrrt.f
iw.i sḫ3.i spr.i r nṯr hrw pf n mny
----
smn hpw.f ḫt sp3t.f
imi-r3 ḥm nṯr n wp-w3wt nb s3wt

I have come from my town, my nome,
having done what people love and gods praise;
I have judged between two to their contentment,
I appeased --------
[I did not let] a servant woman be valued above her mistress,
for the sake of doing right.
I satisfied my god with what he desired,
for I was mindful I would reach the god on that day of
landing.
---------..........
One who maintained his laws throughout the nome,
the chief priest of Wepwawet, lord of Siut ...

Djefai-hapi's understanding of right-doing included the proper maintenance of class distinctions: a maid must not be honored more than her mistress. Otherwise, his right-doing revolved around satisfying "his" god, Wepwawet, lord of Siut; and he was mindful that he would meet the god after his death.

36) At Aswan, Sarenput II, nomarch of the first nome of Upper Egypt, probably in the reign of Sesostris III, made a similar statement about doing right for "his" god; and he varied the "I-came-from-my-town" formula so that it acquired the sense which was fully developed in the New Kingdom: instead of coming "<u>from</u> one's town" one now went "<u>to</u> the land of eternity" (Urk. VII, 8.2-3):

iy.n(.i) r t3 pn m-ḫt i3wt
n itw imiw ẖrt-nṯr
ir.n(.i) m3ʿt n nṯr.i

I have come to this land after old age,
to the ancestors in the graveyard,
having done right for my god.

37) Again at Beni Hasan, the nomarch Khnumhotep II, in the reign of Amenemhet II, included a major account of royal performance of Maat in his own great autobiography. Relating his appointment to the nomarchy by king Amenemhet II, he recalls that this royal act duplicated the appointment of his grandfather Khnumhotep I by king Amenemhet I, after the king had pacified the region (Urk. VII, 27):

m iyt ḥm.f dr.f isft
ḫʿw m Itmw ḏs.f
smnḫ.f gmt.n.f wst
iṯt niwt m snnwt.s
di.f rḫ niwt t3š.s r niwt
smnḫ wḏw.sn mi pt
rḫ mw.sn r ntt m sšw
sip r ntt m iswt
n ʿ3t n mrr.f m3ʿt

As his majesty came he expelled wrongdoing:
Risen like Atum himself,
he restored what he found in ruins,
what one town had snatched from another.
He made town know its borders with town,
their markers made firm like the sky,
their waters known as found in writing,
assigned according to old records,
because he so greatly loved Maat.

This incisive description of royal might, engaged in setting things right, introduces the political dimension of Maat doing as exercised by kingship.

38) Very little is preserved of the inscriptions in the Theban tomb of Antefoker, vizier of Sesostris I (TT 60, Davies-Gardiner, Tomb of Antefoker). A band of hieroglyphs extends across the north wall above scenes of hunting, food preparation, etc. It contains the vizier's titulary and some epithets: he was *mḥ ib n nswt m irt m3^{c}t*, "trusty of the king in doing justice", and he reaffirms it: *ir.i m3^{c}t n nb.i*, "I did justice for my lord" (pls. vi-vii & x).

The tomb of Antefoker had been a splendid one, and it was visited in the early part of the 18th dynasty by scribes who recorded their visits in a total of 36 hieratic graffiti (transcribed and translated by Gardiner, op. cit., pp. 27-29 & pls. xxxv-xxxvii). One of the longest and best preserved is no. 15 of a scribe named *R^{c}-ms-nfr*. He wrote an offering prayer in his own behalf and described himself thus:

38a) ^{c}q3-ib iqr-sḫrw
šw m isft rdi s3.f r bw-ḏw
ir m3^{c}t r mtr.s
sš m3^{c}ty m ẖt mwt.f
sš R^{c}-ms-nfr m3^{c}-ḫrw ...

Straightforward, trustworthy,
one free of wrong, who turns his back on crime,
who does right as befits;
a scribe righteous from his mother's womb,
the scribe Ramose-nefer, justified ...

The phrase "righteous from his mother's womb" makes the point that this man's virtue was born with him; it was innate. The same claim had already been made in text 1, where *Wr-ḥww* declared he had not angered anyone "since my birth". Thus from early on, there had been the realisation that people were born with moral qualities - it was not all a matter of education. The insight was stated dramatically by the priest Mentuhotep (text 22), the orphan who had educated himself by means of his own good nature. The discovery of the heart as teacher and guide - man's inner-directedness - had been the consequence of the basic understanding of the self as a being endowed with moral qualities, which were nurtured by education and experience, i.e. by the reasoning heart. This two-pronged fundamental understanding had been completed by the qualifying observation that some persons were born with evil inclinations. That insight yielded the paradigm of the foolish and evil son on whom the Instructions in Wisdom, from Ptahhotep to PInsinger, poured their scorn.

C. Didactic Literature

39) The Instruction for King Merikare (P. Petersburg 1116A(=P), etc., ed. Volten, 1945; Helck, 1977) has four passages on Maat, all of them weighty.

1. The authority of the sage (P 34-35)

iw n.f m3ʿt ʿtḫti
mi sḫrw n ḏdt tpw-ʿw

Right comes to him distilled
in the condition of sayings of the ancestors.

2. How to prevent corruption (P 42-43)

sʿ3 wrw.k ir.sn hpw.k
nn nmʿ.n ḫwd m pr.f
nb ḫt pw tm g3w
n ḏd.n šw3 m m3ʿt.f

Advance your nobles so that they uphold your laws,
one rich at home will not be partial,
being wealthy he has no need,
the poor man does not speak justly.

3. Speak and do Maat (P 45-47)

ḏd m3ʿt m pr.k
snḏ n.k wrw ntyw ḥr t3
mty n nb ʿq3-ib
in ḫnt dd snḏ n s3 pr
ir m3ʿt w3ḥ.k tp t3
sgr mrw m m3r ḫ3rt
m nš s ḥr ḫt it.f
m ḥd wrw ḥr išt.sn

Speak truth in your house,
that the nobles of the land may respect you;

uprightness befits the master,
the front of the house puts fear in the back.
Do justice, then you endure on earth:
calm the weeper, harm not the widow,
drive no man from his father's property,
despoil not the nobles of their wealth.

4. Doing Maat is your monument (P 127-128)
siqr ḥt.k nt imnt
smnḫ st.k nt ẖrt-nṯr
m ᶜq3 m irt m3ᶜt
rhnt ib.sn pw ḥr.s

Endow your house of the west,
equip your place in the graveyard,
by being straight, by doing justice,
it is what men's hearts rely on.

Here, nobly phrased, is the gist of Maat thinking as taught by the sages and applied to kingship: Truth telling; honest administrators carrying out the laws; justice and benevolence for all.

40) The justice due to the common man was most impressively worked out in the Tale of the Eloquent Peasant. Robbed of his goods, a peasant pleads his case in the royal residence before a magistrate who is so enchanted by the poor man's eloquence that, at the king's suggestion, he feigns indifference in order to make him continue his pleading. When after nine increasingly indignant speeches the despairing peasant falls silent, the magistrate does him full honor, enacts the right judgment, and all is well. The nine speeches have to be read in full to appreciate the verve, skill, and poetic imagery with which changes are rung on the basic two-faceted thought: People live by Maat - right-truth-justice - as much as by the air they breathe, and dispensing Maat is the foremost duty of the magistrate:
Speak Maat, do Maat, for it is mighty,
it is great, it endures, its worth is tried,
it leads one to reveredness. (Bl, 320-322)

During the stable reigns of the 12th dynasty, the thinking about past times of trouble, when the state had been beset by dynastic strife and local warfare, produced a number of literary works which grappled with the phenomena of turmoil on the national scale. Two of these literary works, the Prophecies of Neferti and the Instruction of King Amenemhet, have a recognizable core of historical facts.

41) Though disguised as the prophecies of a sage speaking in the time of the long-past Old Kingdom, the Prophecies of Neferti were designed to be understood as an account of the turmoil and lawlessness that gripped the nation when the 11th dynasty foundered, a turmoil overcome when Amenemhet I took the crown and restored order. A glimpse into these disturbances is provided, as we have seen, by the autobiography of the nomarch Khnumhotep II (text 37). And just as the nomarch viewed the restoration of order as the king's doing Maat, so the sage Neferti, lamenting in an oracular style how men crave blood and laugh at distress, and how beggars become rich men, ends by predicting the future king's pacification of the land as the return of Right and the expulsion of Wrong - the thin prophetic disguise allowing past and present readers to recognize in the pacifier king Amenemhet I, the founder of the 12th dynasty:

Then a king will come from the South,
Ameny, the justified by name ....
Then Right will return to its seat,
while Wrong is driven out.
(iw m3ᶜt r iyt r st.s
iw isft dr sy r rwty)

42) The Instruction of king Amenemhet I, composed as the testament of the king to his son Sesostris, is the gloom-laden counterpart of the Prophecies of Neferti. Where the earlier work had hailed the eventual triumph of Maat through the reign of Amenemhet I, the testament of Amenemhet I focusses on the attempt on his life and is a deeply pessimistic discourse on human ingratitude and treachery. While the word Maat does not occur, the Instruction teaches that the right order can be destroyed and evil can triumph.

43) In the Complaints of Khakheperre-sonb the author dispenses with an audience and addresses his laments on the state of the land to his heart (BM 5645, rt. 10-11):

ink pw ḥr nk3 m ḫprt
sḫrw ḫpr ḫt t3
ḫprw ḫpr nn mi snf
dns rnpt r snw.s
sh3 t3 ḫpr m ḥḏn ...
rdi.tw m3ʿt r rwty
isft m ẖnw sḥ
ẖnn.tw sḫrw nṯrw
wn.tw mẖrw.sn
wnn t3 m snmn
irtyw m st nbt

I meditate on the events,
the conditions throughout the land;
what happens is not like yesteryear,
one year is more toilsome than the other.
The land founders beset by dissent ...
Maat is cast outside,
Isfet is in the council hall;
the plans of the gods are disturbed,
their arrangements are neglected.
The land is in confusion,
mourning is everywhere ...

Internalized as an address to the heart, the whole lamentation is characterized by the absence of factual details. Yet it makes its point: Maat has been routed by Isfet.

44) The internalization of the lament provides a link between Khakheperre-sonb and the artistically much superior work known as the Dispute of a Man with his Ba (or, Man Weary of Life). The second of the four superb lyrics that conclude the Dispute deals with the Man's accusation that the norms of decency have been overturned and virtues replaced by corresponding vices: greed, insolence, and hatred are ruling everywhere (P. Berlin 3024, stanzas 1, 4, 12):

To whom shall I speak today?
Brothers are evil *(bin)*,
Friends of today do not love .

To whom shall I speak today?
One is content with evil *(bin)*,
Good *(bw nfr)* is cast to the ground everywhere.

To whom shall I speak today?
There are no righteous *(m3^{c}tyw)*,
The land is left to evildoers *(irw isft)*.

In the work as we have it - the beginning is missing - there is no recognizable political dimension. Thus it looks like a meditation on evil as the willed product of human depravity. Very significant is the appearance of the term m*3^{c}tyw*. We have encountered the *m3^{c}ty*, the "righteous man" in text 28. As yet not in frequent use, it is a word that will become a key term in the ethic of the individual person.

Together, the six works here named, and of course also the very difficult "Admonitions of Ipuwer", pondered the problems of good and evil and did so from three points of view:

I. The standpoint of the individual person who seeks redress of wrong from the jurisdiction of the magistrate (Eloquent Peasant).

Ia. The individual person who despairs of life because he sees all around him the perversion of the moral standard (Man Weary of Life).

II. The king who counsels his successor on statecraft, the sum of which is truth, justice, benevolence, and piety (Merikare).

IIa. The king who, mindful of the same statecraft, has encountered treason (Amenemhet).

III. Officials speaking as sages, who condemn rebellion, lawlessness, and civil war, summed up as the reversal of the social order and the expulsion of Maat by Isfet (Neferti, Khakheperre-sonb, Ipuwer). Their specific political and propagandistic concern is to exalt kingship as being the only effective form of government.

In his new large volume entitled Ma'at (1990) and his latest article, "Weisheit, Schrift und Literatur im alten Ägypten" (1991), Jan Assmann has expounded the view that, in the Middle Kingdom, Egyptian thought developed a two-fold and contradictory anthropology. In the book "Ma'at" (pp. 58ff.) he draws the picture of the inner-directed person who knows and performs Maat through the prompting of his heart, a performance which centers on reciprocity, solidarity, and beneficence. In the later chapters, however, especially from pp. 213 onward, he presents a "negative anthropology" the textual basis of which is said to be found in those lamentations of the sages, the "Klagen" in which the overturn of the social order is deplored (i.e. Neferti, Khakheperre-sonb, Ipuwer):

> "Da die Gerechtigkeit im menschlichen Herzen nicht angelegt ist, muss sie von aussen kommen. Nach ägyptischer Vorstellung kommt sie von oben, von Gott, der sie in der Form des Königtums auf Erden einsetzt." (pp.216ff.)

In the article "Weisheit" (1991) the contradiction is summed up succinctly:

> "Die ägyptische Anthropologie geht von einem dilemmatischen Menschenbild aus. Das Dilemma liegt in der widersprüchlichen Verbindung der folgenden beiden Sätze:
> 1. Der Mensch ist auf Gemeinschaft angewiesen.
> 2. Der Mensch ist von Natur zur Gemeinschaft unfähig.
> Die ägyptische Lösung dieses Problems ist der pharaonische Staat, der nichts Natürliches hat, sondern eine göttliche Institution darstellt. Was die Klagen beschreiben, ist eine Welt ohne Staat. Der Staat ist die Bedingung dafür, dass in der Welt überhaupt Maat herrschen kann." (p.487).

I have reviewed the texts of the "Klagen" for the alleged negative view of man as a being incapable of Maat, and have found no evidence. Despite all their propagandistic hyperbole, the "Klagen" texts nowhere claim that man is by nature incapable of doing right. Outside of the Instructions, which beginning with Ptahhotep deal seriously with the problem of man's inclinations toward evildoing, one can find a small number of statements in Coffin Texts and elsewhere which focus on man's capacity for evil. There is the wellknown passage in Coffin Text Spell 1130 (CT VII, 463f-464c) which I cite in Assmann's translation (Ma'at, p. 215):

> Ich habe jedermann gleich seinem Nächsten geschaffen.
> Ich habe verboten, dass sie Isfet tun sollten.
> Aber ihre Herzen haben mein Verbot übertreten.

Then there is the passage in the "Admonitions of Ipuwer" where the sage, lamenting the overturn of the social order, wishes that the creator-god had abstained from creating mankind (12.1ff.):

> If only he had perceived their nature in the first generation!
> Then he would have smitten the evil, stretched out his arm against it, would have destroyed their seed and their heirs!

A related idea is expressed in the tale of the "Destruction of Mankind", where the sungod, perceiving that mankind is plotting against him, decides to destroy it but eventually relents.

Although these three texts express drastically man's potential for evildoing, they do not go beyond the basic recognition of man's dual nature, his capability for good and evil, which was expounded in all the literary genres: Instructions, Autobiographies, Schooltexts, Tales, etc. The thoroughly negative view that "die Grossen fressen die Kleinen" (Assmann, Ma'at, 214ff.) did not exist in ancient Egypt. On the contrary, the one text that alludes to this "law of nature" exempts mankind by declaring that man lives on bread:

> Falcons live on (small) birds, jackals by roaming,
> pigs on hill-country, hippos on marshes,
> mankind on grain, crocodiles on fish ... (CT 80, II.42)

Recognizing his innate capacity for good and evil, this ancient man, this bread eater, formulated a normative ethic which centered on the concept of Maat, the primordial rightness by which the gods lived and which it behooved man to uphold in his daily behavior.

4. Ethics and Piety in 18th Dynasty Autobiographies

The appearance of gods is the major innovation in the representational scheme of 18th dynasty private tombs and stelae. Men and women are now depicted worshipping the gods, and in the texts the gods are invoked more directly and more frequently than had hitherto been done. Furthermore, 18th dynasty autobiographies formulated detailed visions of a personal afterlife lived in the celestial regions where the gods dwelled.

45) The great stela of the royal tutor Paheri in his tomb at El-Kab is the perfect paradigm of the new approach (Urk. IV, 111-123; Sethe, Übers., 55ff.; Lichtheim, AEL II, 15-21; reigns of Thutmosis I & II). The four-part text includes a lengthy offering formula, an exalted vision of life in the beyond; a recital of virtuous conduct, and an emphatic appeal to the living. In dwelling on his excellent character Paheri remarked:

> rḫ.kwi nṯr imi rmṯ
> si3.i sw rḫ.i pf3 r pn
>
> I knew there is a god in man,
> aware of him, I knew this from that. (Urk. IV, 119.15)

In his appeal to the living he impressed upon his visitors that bending the hand in the gesture of offering was also a form of Maat doing:

> qʿḥ.tyfy nb m ḏrt ḫpr.f m sḫrw m3ʿt
> Whoever will bend the hand will be in the condition of Maat (121.12)

46) Craftsmen of the top rank are well represented by 18th dynasty monuments. On his tomb stela at Hierakonpolis the chief sculptor *Ḏḥwty*, in the reign of Thutmosis I, speaks thus (Urk. IV, 131):

> imi-r3 gnwtyw ḥs.n nṯr.f m nḫnw.f
> ḫrp n nswt rs-tp ḥr k3wt
> wḥʿ-ib ḥr irt mnḫwt
> hr-ib r imitw srw
> dm.tw rn.f ḥr qdw.f
> iwty wn.f ḫr nb.f
> n pr.n isft m r3.f

m3^{c}-ib r imitw špsw
iw ir.n.i mrrt rmṯ ḥsst nṯrw
di.sn mn ḥt.i n nḥḥ
rwḏ rn.i m r3 n rmṯ

Chief sculptor, his god's favorite since his youth,
royal controller who oversees the works;
skilled in doing excellent work,
modest among the nobles.
Whose name was spoken for his qualities,
without blame before his lord;
no falsehood issued from his mouth,
truthful among the grandees.
I have done what people love and gods praise -
may they let my house last forever,
may my name remain in the mouth of men!

Two well-rounded quartets outline the artist's professional and moral worth *(wḥ^{c}-ib - hr-ib - m3^{c}-ib)*, and the concluding tristich requests the appropriate rewards (note the alliteration in the last line).

47) The high officials of Hatshepsut were equally unstinting in their selfpraise. Here is the favorite minister Senenmut on a statue from the Mut temple at Karnak (Urk. IV, 410.10-411.4):
ink wr wrw m t3 r ḏr.f
sḏm sḏmt w^{c} m w^{cc}w
imi-r3 pr n [Imn] Snnmwt m3^{c}-ḫrw
ink mḥ-ib n nswt n wn m3^{c}
ir ḥst nb.f m ẖrt-hrw
imi-r3 iḥw n Imn Snnmwt
ink [wp] m3^{c}t tm rdi ḥr gs
hrr nb t3wy ḥr tpt r3.f
r3 nḫn ḥm-nṯr m3^{c}t Snnmwt

I am greatest of the great in the whole land,
who hears hearings alone in privacy,
Steward of Amun, Senenmut, justified.

I am the king's trusty in very truth,
who does what his lord praises daily,
Overseer of herds of Amun, Senenmut.

I am the judge of right who is not partial,
whose pronouncement pleases the lord of the two-lands,
Mouth of Nekhen, priest of Maat, Senenmut.

Note the symmetrical composition in three tristichs, each one ending with his name and one of his titles.

48) A chief steward of Hatshepsut, whose name has been erased, speaks of his role (Urk. IV, 456.15ff.):

mḥ ʿnẖty Ḥr m m3ʿt
wstn nmtt m pr-nswt
r3 md n nbt t3wy
r shrr m t3 r ḏr.f

Who fills the ears of Horus with truth,
who steps freely in the palace;
mouth that speaks for the lady-of-the-two-lands,
so as to content the whole land.

Note the expression "fill the ears of Horus with Maat"; it became a set phrase in the 18th dynasty (exx. Urk. IV, 961.13; 1172.13; 1189.8; 1465.19; 1882.4). It implies speaking confidentially to the king and in an advisory capacity, rather than mere reporting.

49) Hepusonb, overseer of Hatshepsut's building works at Karnak, employed the old I-came-from-my-town formula in the altered version which became standard in the 18th dynasty (see text 36) on a long autobiographical statue inscription from Karnak (Urk. IV, 484.1ff.):

iw.i iy.kwi r niwt.i nt nḥḥ
r sp3t.i nt ḏt
ir.n.i mrrt rmṯ ḥsst nṯrw nbw
šms.n.i Ḥr nb ʿḥ
mḏd.n(.i) rdit.n.f m ḥr.i
n wn.i ḥr sp n nb t3wy
nḏr.n(.i) mtrt.n.f ẖr.i

n iw sp.i m stp-s3
n srḫ.twi m-m šnyt
n gm wn.i m r3w-prw
nn bs pf sḥ3w.n(.i) r rwty
iy.kw(i) m ḥswt nt ḫr nswt
ḥtp.kw(i) m imnt nfrt
b3.i m pt h̲3t.i m mḥt
ꜥb.n nṯr ir ḥr mw.f

I have come to my town of eternity,
to my district of everlastingness,
having done what people love and all gods praise.
I followed Horus, lord of the palace,
I carried out what he assigned to me;
I did not neglect the concern of the lord-of-the-two-lands,
I attended to his instructions.
No mistake of mine occurred in the palace,
I was not accused by the courtiers;
I was not found at fault in the temples,
there was not a secret rite that I revealed outside.
I have come with the king's favor,
and now rest in the beautiful west,
my Ba in heaven, my corpse in the graveyard,
the god befriends him who acts on his water.

Observe again how the essence of Maat doing is now encompassed by the phrase "having done what people love and gods praise"; and it is explicated in terms of loyal service to king and god. Note also the use of *sp* in its two opposite senses: positive, as the affairs of the king *(sp n nb t3wy)* and negative, as not having been faulted *(n iw sp.i)*.

50) As for the divine rewards of right action, Hatshepsut's vizier Ahmes-Ametju defined them succinctly (Urk. IV, 492.5ff., TT 83):
iw nṯr [ḏb3.f] isft n ir sy
m3ꜥt n iy h̲r.s
iḫ di.tw n.i m3ꜥt mi irt.i sy
ḏb3.tw n.i nfrw m šs nb

The god will repay wrong to its doer,
and right to him who brings it:
May I be given right according as I did it,
may goodness be repaid me with everything good!

51) *S3-tp-iḥw*, Hatshepsut's governor of the Thinite nome, envisaged the rewards of rightdoing both in terms of a transfigured existence in the beyond and a lasting memory on earth (Urk. IV, 518.7ff., on a statue from his Abydene tomb):

3ḫ m pt wsr m t3
m3ʿ-ḫrw ḫnt ẖrt-nṯr
wḥm ʿnḫ m-ḫt qbḥ
šbw pw n iwty ḏwt.f
m3ʿty pw šsp sw
ḥsb.t(w).f ḫft imiw b3ḥ
wnn rn.f mn m mnw
n ḥtm.n irt.n.f r t3

Spirit in heaven, power on earth,
justified in the necropolis,
and revival after being death-cold:
these are the gifts to the faultless man.
A righteous one is he who receives them,
he will be counted among the ancestors,
his name will remain as monument,
his deeds will not perish on earth.

52) Intef, herald of Thutmosis III and governor of the Thinite nome and the oasis country, had a large stela in his Theban tomb (TT 155) with a long text that gathers the main autobiographic themes in four major sections (Louvre C 26, Urk. IV, 964-975): 1. Offering formula and Appeal to the living. 2. Official duties, enumerated in the participle style, and including an unusual description of Intef's role as suppressor of rebels and all kinds of criminals. 3. Portrayal of his many social virtues and kindnesses. 4. Assertion of the truth of his statements and summary of his service to the king.

As *sš iqr* and governor of the Thinite nome, Intef must have been versed in Middle Kingdom literature including the autobiographical texts of Abydene cenotaphs. His self-portrayal reads like a compendium of all the good character traits which the Middle

Kingdom scribes had worked out, plus some additions of 18th dynasty vintage. Deeds of justice and charity are emphasized: he had "sought after Maat" *(pẖr m-s3 m3ꜥt)* and consequently he was, among other things, *šw m isft, mnḫ n nbw.f, ꜥq3-ib nn grgw im.f, šs3 m w3t nbt,* "free of wrongdoing, effective for his lords, straightforward without falsehood, and skilled in every way". Thus equipped, he was *mrw m3r, it nmḥw, sšmw n tfn, mwt snḏw, ibw n 3t, mkty mn,* and more: "servant of the needy, father of the poor, guide of the orphan, mother of the timid, shelter of the battered, succour of the sick". Most significantly, Intef - here too an heir of Middle Kingdom thinking - attributed his virtuous actions to the promptings of his heart (Urk. IV, 974):

in ib.i rdi iry.i st m sšm.f ḫr.i
iw.f n.i m mtr mnḫ
n ḥḏ.n.i ḏdt.f
snḏ.kwi r tht sšm.f
rwḏ.kwi ḥr.s wrt
mnḫ.n.i ḥr rdit.n.f iry.i
iqr.n.i m sšm.f
is grt m3ꜥ --- in rmṯ tp r3
nṯr pw iw.f m ẖt nbt
w3ḏ pw sšm.n.f r w3t nfrt nt irt
mk.wi m mitt iry

It was my heart that made me do this as it guided me,
it was for me an excellent instructor,
and I did not neglect its prompting,
being afraid of straying from its guidance.
I flourished greatly on account of it,
I excelled through what it made me do,
and became worthy by its guidance.
⸢True is [what] people [tell] by saying:⸣
"A god it is who is in every body,
blessed is whom he guides to the good way to act";
lo, such a one was I.

The lacuna after *is grt m3ꜥ* is unfortunate. I have placed *tp r3* after *in rmṯ,* rather than in front of *nṯr pw,* as was done in Urk. IV, 974. For it is not so much the "saying" of a god that operates in man but the god himself. Compare Paheri's statement (text 45) *rḫ.kwi nṯr imi rmṯ, si3.i sw rḫ.i pf3 r pn.* What Paheri had said succinctly Intef says with the loquacity that begins now, in the reign of Thutmosis III.

Intef's whole discourse on the heart as teacher is built on Middle Kingdom foundations. Rediu-khnum (text 18) had said: "It was my heart that advanced my rank, it was my character that kept me in front." And among the maxims of the fragmentary Ramesseum Papyrus No. II there is the saying: *[in] ib sꜥš3 qdw / sb3w qn r mst bi3wt,* "It is the heart that multiplies traits, a mighty teacher for shaping qualities." (J.Barns ed., Five Ramesseum Papyri, pl. 8, p. 13, n. 5).

The Middle Kingdom had worked out the concept of Maat doing from three angles: that of the king; that of society; and that of the individual person. The 18th dynasty writers worked with the same three aspects and added one new element: the strongly felt presence of the gods. We have followed the high officials in their expressions of loyal service to the king, of just and compassionate behavior toward the people, and of their devotion to the gods, declared in adoring recognition and in prayer. We now turn briefly to the summit of Maat doing in the office and person of the vizier.

53) The tasks of the vizier Weser are summarized with clarity and succinctness by his scribe and steward Amenemhet in the latter's tomb (TT 82, Urk. IV, 1044f.; reign of Thutmosis III):

sš Imn-m-ḥ3t m3ꜥ-ḫrw ḏd.f
ink b3k šms nb.f
mnḫ-ib ir ḏdt.f
di.n.f pr.f dmḏ r ḫt.i
ḏbꜥwt.f nb ẖr sḫr.i
tp-rs ḥr ip ḫt.f
n mh.n.i ḥr ḫrp k3wt.f

iw ir.n imi-r3 niwt ṯ3ty Wsr
ḥsst k3 ꜥnḫ nswt m ẖrt-hrw nt rꜥ nb
siꜥr.n.f m3ꜥt n nb.s
mrr.f ḥm.f r trwy
nis tnw wnwt ḥr spw.f nbw mnḫw

iw ir.n imi-r3 niwt ṯ3ty Wsr mrrt nṯrw nbw

m irt hpw smnt tp-rd
m irt r3w-prw.sn
m smnḫ ḥtpw-nṯr.sn
m wpt šbw.sn
m ḥnq n.sn m3ꜥt mrrt.sn

iw ir.n imi-r3 niwt ṯ3ty Wsr mrrt pꜥt rḫyt
nḏ m3r ḥnꜥ wsr
nḫ ḫ3rt iwtt hnw
snḏm ib im3ḫw i3w
di.n.f ẖrdw ḥr st itw
di.n.f t3 nb m ḥtpw

The scribe Amenemhet, justified, says:
I am a servant who follows his lord,
one willing who does as told;
he placed his whole house under my staff,
all his seals under my care.
Alert in overseeing his affairs,
I was not slack to control his works.

The mayor of Thebes and vizier Weser
did what the king's live ka favors daily:
He raised up Maat to its lord,
his majesty's ever beloved.
reporting every time on all his effective deeds.

The mayor of Thebes and vizier Weser did what all the gods
love:
Applying laws, establishing rules,
organizing their temples,
furnishing their offerings,
allotting their foods,
and offering them the Maat they love.

The mayor of Thebes and vizier Weser did what nobles and
folk love:
Protecting the poor and the rich,
succouring the widow lacking a family,
pleasing the revered and old;

he placed sons on the fathers' seat,
and put the whole land at ease.

This is an excellent summary of the vizier's threefold Maat doing: toward the king, the gods, and the people.

54) The long texts of the vizier Rekhmire add much interesting detail but no new perspectives. Rekhmire's autobiography describes his performance largely in poetic images: he raised Maat to the height of heaven, and made her beauty circle the breadth of the land (Urk. IV, 1077.13). He suppressed the violence of evil characters, drove away the rapacious, and had the liar hung upside down (1078.2 & 16). The "installation" speech of the king (1087ff.) is of course a most important document, and it tells much about the vizier as representative of Maat in a sequence that culminates in the sentence:

ẖr [wp] m3ᶜt ẖr ḥ3t rmṯ nbt ṯ3ty pw
He who does justice for all people he is vizier. (1092.8)

55) As for the vizier Ramose, before he served Akhenaten, he had inscribed his tomb with a prayer to Osiris in which he announced his arrival in the hereafter (TT 55, Urk. IV, 1776):

iy.n.i m ḥtp km.n.i ᶜḥᶜw
m ḥswt nt nṯr nfr
iw ir.n.i mrrt rmṯ
hrrt nṯrw ḥr.s
iw ir.n.i ḥsst nswt n rk.i
n ḥḏ.i wḏt.n.f
n ir.n.i isft r rmṯ
iw ir.n.i m3ᶜt tp t3
iw.i rḫ.kwi ḥss.k m3ᶜ-ib
tm irt spw n ḏ3t

I have come in peace at lifetime's completion
in the favor of the good god;
I have done what people love,
and what gods are pleased with.
I have done what the king of my time favored,
and did not neglect what he commanded.
I did no wrong to people,

I have done right on earth!
I know you favor rightmindedness,
and not committing crimes.

Coming from a vizier, this declaration is rather humble; but it is in keeping with the new tone of piety. We are tracing the growth of piety and observing its relation to thoughts on Maat, and to the expectation of divine rewards. Citing several more texts will give body to what is clearly a growing trend.

56) Still in the reign of Thutmosis III, the scribe Ahmes, a minor official, inscribed his palette with two short prayers to Amen-Re and Thoth, respectively. The prayer to Thoth reads (Urk. IV, 53):

ḥtp di nswt D̲ḥwty ḥq3 sšw
di.f ḥswt.f n ir ḥr mw.f
mrwt n tm mhy ḥr.f

A royal offering to Thoth, master of writings:
May he give his favor to one who acts on his water,
and love to one who forgets him not!

Here, in simple and lucid phrasing, is a man's personal approach to the deity, steered by a sense of reciprocity: human loyalty invites divine favor.

57) *Sn-nfr,* mayor of Thebes in the reign of Amenhotep II, prayed thus to Osiris (on his group-statue from Karnak CG 42126, Urk. IV, 1435.18ff.):

sb.i ꜥḥꜥw m ḥswt nswt nfr
wd̲.n.k n.i rdi.n.k sw n.i
m ḥtp nfr nn šnn im.f
spr.kwi r niwt nt nḥḥ
st nt wnn im.s
di.k wn.i m-di ḥsyw
ḥtp.i ḥr t n dd.k

I have spent a lifetime in the king's good favor
which you ordained for me and granted me,
in perfect peace without affliction.
Now that I have come to the town of eternity,

the abode where one shall be,
grant me to be among the favored,
and to be sated by the bread of your giving!

Note that the god is addressed in the second person, and that it is the god who is said to have granted the king's favor. Now the divine favor is besought for the afterlife.

58) The fragments from the tomb of the royal scribe Siese (Urk. IV, 1924ff., reign of Amenhotep III) add up to a long prayer to Osiris and other gods. Having served his king with devotion, Siese prays for a blessed afterlife as reward for his earthly rightness, and he does so in tones of poetic fervency (Urk. IV, 1928.4-6):

spr.kwi r iw n m3ᶜtyw
nn bt3.i tp t3
irw n.i mnywt nḥḥ nᶜyt d̲t

Now that I have come to the isle of the righteous
without a crime of mine on earth,
make for me a mooring-post of eternity, a landing-post of everlastingness!

59) At Memphis, Amenhotep, steward of royal domains in the reign of king Amenhotep III, inscribed his numerous monuments with self-presentations detailing his activities, accomplishments, and righteousness (Urk. IV, 1793-1812), his principal text being on a statue which stood in a temple erected by Amenhotep III. Here are some excerpts from it:

ir.n.i m3ᶜt n nb t3wy grḥ mi hrw
iw.i rḫ.kwi ᶜnḫ.f im.s
bwt.i mdt bšt3

I did right for the lord-of-the-two-lands night and day,
for I know he lives by it,
and I abhor rebelliousness. (1795.2-4)

ḥr ntt ink s pw m3ᶜ tp t3
rḫ ntr.f sᶜ3 nfrw.f
ir 3ḫt n ḥmw pr.f
n dr.i s m i3wt.f

n ʿwn.i ky m ẖt.f
n iṯ(.i) ẖt kywy m grgw
bwy pw sp n ʿwn-ib

For I am a righteous man on earth,
who knows his god and exalts his goodness,
and is helpful to the servants of his house.
I did not drive a man from his office,
I did not rob another of his possessions,
I did not seize another's goods by lies,
I abominate rapacity. (1799.7-13)

In the end, after promising punishment to those who would steal the offerings destined for his statue, and rewards to those who would safeguard their presentation, he concludes with the following quatrain (1801.1-5):

ḥr ntt ink s pw mty m3ʿ
iw rdi.n.i t n ḥqrw
mw n ib
ir.n.i hrrt rmṯ ḥsst nṯrw

For I am a man who is truly straight:
I have given bread to the hungry,
water to the thirsty,
and have done what pleases people and what gods favor.

We recognize the final tristich as an old acquaintance which, since the First Intermediate Period has functioned as a summary of Maat doing (texts 14 & 20) and with minor variations is widely used in 18th dynasty self-presentations, from which it was taken over into chapter 125 of the Book of the Dead.

60) At Abydos, the same steward Amenhotep erected a statue on which he prays to Osiris (HTBM V, 38, no. 632; Urk. IV, 1802-1803):

iy.n.i ẖr.k nb w-pqi
snmḥ.i k3.k rʿ nb
di.i n.k i3w sq3.i tw
sw3š.i nfrw n ḥr.k
di.tw n.i prt-ẖrw t ḥnqt iḥw 3pdw
šs mnẖt snṯr qbḥw

irp irṯt wrḥt tpy mḏt
m sfẖw n wpt nṯr
šsp sšdw m w3g m w3ḏt ḥr ins
ẖnd.i nšmt m b3 iqr
nn tny r šmsw Ḥr
ink m3ᶜty bwt isft
n gm.tw wnt

I have come to you, lord of U-Peqer,
to beseech your ka every day,
to praise you and exalt you,
to adore your face's beauty!
May I get voice-offering of bread-beer-beef-fowl,
salve, cloth, incense, cool water,
wine, milk, prime ointment, unguent,
that are offered to the god's brow,
receive wrappings on the Wag-feast of green cloth and red linen,
and step into the Neshmet as a worthy Ba,
not distinct from the servants of Horus.
I am one righteous who abhors evil,
no fault of whom is found!

Here we can observe how the old offering formula and other requirements of the funerary ritual have been shaped into requests addressed directly to Osiris. They form part of an integrated vision of the resurrected and justified dead person joining the company of Osiris.

61) At Thebes, the sage Amenhotep son of Hapu, outstanding minister of Amenhotep III, multiplied his prayers to the gods of Thebes on his Karnak statues. On the statue of the "80-years'-old" (CG 42127, Urk. IV, 1827ff.) speaking to Amen-Re, he declares his righteousness:

ntk is Rᶜ nn ḥr ẖw.f
di.k wn.i m-m ḥsyw
iryw m3ᶜt ink m3ᶜ

n rdi.n.i ḥr gs
n sm3.n.i m ir bw-ḏw

For you are Re beside whom there is none:
Grant me to be among the favored
the doers of right - I am righteous!
I was not partial,
nor allied with the evildoer. (1827.12-16)

The text is discussed for its bearing on the Negative Confessions of BD 125 in Study 2 (text 19). Here it is meant to round off the sampling of the conjunction of ethics and piety in 18th dynasty autobiographies, which now, in the reign of Amenhotep III, attain their most nuanced expressiveness.

At this very time, Akhenaten's revolutionary disavowal of all gods except the sungod drastically reduced the scope of autobiographical inscriptions of royal officials. They now consist of adulations of Akhenaten, hymns to the sundisk, and self-presentations limited to assertions of efficiency and kindness, and above all, loyalty to the king and to his teaching. That teaching declared that on earth Akhenaten alone was the fount and dispenser of Maat. The courtiers possessed Maat by virtue of having been taught by the king.

62) Akhenaten's chief courtier, the 'divine father' Ay, speaks of his Maat in his tomb inscriptions (Urk. IV, 1997.13-16):

ink mty m3ʿ šw m ʿwn
pḥ rn.i ʿḥ ḥr 3ḫ n nswt
ḥr sḏm sb3yt.f irt hpw.f
tm šb mdwt ḥḏ bit

I am truly straight, free of greed,
my name reached the palace for serving the king,
for hearing his teaching and doing his laws,
without changing words or neglecting conduct.

And in the parallel inscription (Urk. IV, 1999.3-9):

ink m3ʿ n nswt n sḫpr.n.f
ʿq3 n nb t3wy 3ḫ nb.f
m33 nfrw.f ḫʿʿ.f m ʿḥ.f

iw.i m ḥ3t srw smrw
tpy nswt n šmsw nb.f
di.f m3ᶜt m h̲t.i bwt grg
ᶜnḫ.i m dw3 k3.f
ss3.i m ptr.f

I am one true to the king who raised him,
straight to the lord-of-the-two-lands, useful to his lord,
who sees his beauty when he rises in the palace,
I preceding the nobles and courtiers.
The king's first one in following his lord,
he placed truth in my body and loathing of lies,
so that I live by adoring his ka,
and am sated by seeing him.

63) Of lesser rank, hence expressing himself more modestly yet in the same general vein, here is the chamberlain Tutu addressing future visitors of his tomb at al-Amarna (Urk. IV, 2017.2-6):

ink b3k n Wᶜ-n-Rᶜ
p3 ḥq3 ᶜnḫ m m3ᶜt
šms.i sw iw dw3.f
r ḥs.i n ir.i prt m r3.f
bw sdḫ.i ḥr sp n sᶜd̲3
m wpt nb n ḥm.f
iw(.i) m r3-ḥry n t3 r d̲r.f

I am a servant of Sole-one-of-Re,
the ruler who lives by Maat;
I served him mornings when he rose,
and was praised for doing what he ordered.
I was not reproved for any mistake
in any task for his majesty,
in my role as chief speaker for the whole land ...

64) Though preoccupation with the afterlife had been suppressed, it sometimes surfaced. In his Amarna tomb, the chief physician *Pnt̲w*, after a brief hymn to Re-Harakhti-Aten, permitted himself a request to the sungod for some modest and typical afterlife favors (Sandman, Texts, p. 49):

di.k ḥtp.i m st.i nt nḥḥ
h̲nm.i tpḥt nt d̲t
pr.i ᶜq.i m-h̲nw ḥwt.i
nn h̯ni b3.i m mrrt.f
stwt.i r dd ib.i m mnw sk ir.n(.i) tp t3
swri.i mw ḥr m3ᶜ n š.i rᶜ nb nn ibw

Allow me to rest in my place of eternity,
joined to the cave of lastingness,
and to go out and come in to my tomb,
my Ba not held back from its wishes,
and stride as my heart desires in the grove I made while on earth,
and drink water by the bank of my pool every day without fail.

65) When the death of Akhenaten ended the great upheaval, the general Haremhab was decorating his Memphite tomb. The furnishings included a large stela showing him adoring the standing triad of Re-Harakhti, Thoth, and Maat. Below the scene is a prayer in three parts; the long first part is addressed to Re-Harakhti, the two short ones to Thoth and Maat, respectively (HTBM VIII, no. 551, p. 33 & pl. xxviii; Urk. IV, 2094ff.). The prayer to Re ends thus:
dw3.i tw nfrw.k m irty.i
h̯pr 3h̯w.k ḥr šnbt.i
siᶜrw.i m3ᶜt h̯r ḥm.k h̲rt-hrw nt rᶜ nb

I worship you, your beauty in my eyes,
your rays touching my chest,
I raise up Maat to your majesty daily. (Urk. IV, 2097-2098)

The prayer to the goddess Maat is a fine lyric (2098.11-15):
i3w nt M3ᶜt nbt mḥyt
swnt fnd̲w n ᶜnh̯w
ddt t̲3w n ḥr-ib wi3.f
di.t h̯nm iri-pᶜt Ḥr-m-ḥb t̲3w mss pt
mi h̯nm nbt pwnt h̯nm.s m mr n ᶜntiw

Praise to Maat, mistress of northwind,
opener of noses of the living,

giver of breeze to one in his bark:
Let prince Haremhab inhale sky-born breeze,
as Punt's mistress inhales its breath at myrrh-lake!

66) Two door panels in the tomb of Haremhab were inscribed with prayers to Osiris and Re (HTBM VIII, nos. 550 & 552, p. 30f. & pl. xxvii; Urk. IV, 2099-2202). Addressing Osiris, Haremhab begs admission to his entourage (2100):

iy.n.i n.k ^{c}.wy m i3w n nfrw ḥm.k
di.k wi m šmsw.k mi 3ḫw sšmyw d3t
^{c}nḫyw m m3^{c}t r^{c} nb
ink w^{c} im.sn bwt.i isft
ir.n.i m3^{c}t tp t3 nn mkḥ3.s

I come to you, my arms hailing your majesty's beauty:
Place me in your following like the spirit-leaders of Dat,
who live on Maat each day!
I am one of them, I abhor wrong,
I did right on earth unfailingly.

Clearly, the rejection of Akhenaten's teaching was rapid and vehement. And as all the gods returned to their seats, so did the original Maat, the principle of right-truth-justice, with the added nuance that the personification of Maat was now favored.

67) In these years of restauration, the 'chief scribe of Amun' Neferhotep inscribed his Theban tomb with a hymn to Re in which he adores Re as owner of Maat (TT 49, ed. N. de G. Davies, pl. xxxvii, 6-18 & p. 54; reign of Ay or Haremhab). Anthes concluded his study of the Maat des Echnaton with this hymn, in order to emphasize the rapid return to traditional Maat thinking. Identified as a "Maat-Litanei", the text is included in Assmann's Sonnenhymnen in thebanischen Gräbern (Text 62, pp. 89-90, and reference to parallel versions in BIFAO 49, 131ff. & 150ff., i.e. from the temple of Seti I at Qurnah):

i R^{c} ḥtp m m3^{c}t
ẖnm.n m3^{c}t m ḥ3t.f
i R^{c} wbn m m3^{c}t
ḥtp.n m3^{c}t nfrw.f
i R^{c} mnḫ m m3^{c}t

smn n.f m3ʿt m wi3.f
i Rʿ wsr m m3ʿt
ʿnḫ.f im.s rʿ nb
i Rʿ msiw m3ʿt
ḥnk.tw n.f m3ʿt
dd.k m3ʿt ḫnt ib.i
siʿr.i s(y) n k3.k
iw.i rḫ.kwi ʿnḫ.k im.s
ntk iriw ḏt.s
ink ʿq3 šw m grg
nn ir sp snnwt
nṯrw nbw m3ʿty
šsp.tn sš n Imn Nfrḥtp m3ʿ-ḫrw m ḥtp m ḥtp

O Re who sets with Maat,
Maat is joined to his brow.
O Re who rises with Maat,
Maat embraces his beauty.
O Re, effective through Maat,
Maat is secured to his bark.
O Re mighty through Maat,
whereon he lives every day.
O Re who made Maat,
and whom one offers Maat:
You placed Maat in my heart
that I may raise her up to your ka!
I know you live by her
and it is you who made her body.
I am a straight one free of lies,
who does not practice deception.
Gods, lords of the two Maats,
May you receive Amun's scribe Neferhotep, justified, in peace, in peace.

The litany hails the sungod as the maker of Maat who possesses in his daughter a forceful helpmate for his daily sailing across the sky, a journey that ensures the order of the world. That same helpmate resides in the heart of man.

5. Ramesside Ethics and Piety

A. The Officials: "How good to sit in the hand of Amun"

68) ink smr n sḫpr.n.f
sb3wt.f m ẖt.i
sḫrw nb ip ḥr ib.i
šs3.kwi m nn ir.n.f n.i

I am a companion raised by him,
his teaching is in my body;
the plans of the lord are mustered in my heart,
I am skilled through what he did for me.

It sounds like a courtier of Akhenaten speaking, but it is the vizier Paser who served kings Seti I and Ramses II. He is receiving rewards from Seti I, who is enthroned and attended by the goddess Maat. The scene is in the Broad Hall of Paser's tomb (TT 106, KRI I, 292.14f.). Now full of lacunae, the text is recognizable as a fulgent praise of the king, ending in an address to the spirits residing in the netherworld (KRI I, 293.5f.):

k3 ḏd n.i imiw d3t
iy.wy iy.wy m ḥtp
iw ir.n.k m3ʿt n nb w3st
w3ḏ.f n.k imntt

May those in Dat say to me:
"Come, come in peace,
for you have done right for Thebes' lord,
and he will green the west for you!"

Elsewhere in the Broad Hall the vizier recalls his rise to the vizierate and attributes his eminence to his right-doing:

pḥ.n.i nn ḥr irt m3ʿt n nṯr.i
I reached this by doing right for my god. (KRI I, 299.15)

69) On a much damaged stela, Huyshery, treasury scribe of the temple of Seti I at Qurnah, addresses the gods and future generations (KRI I, 332.16-333.2):

ḏd.i n.tn rmṯ n m-ḫt ḫpryt ḥr s3.i
ink wᶜ iqr qbḥ -------
rdiw m3ᶜt m ib.f
nn wni sp.s
pr.n.i m ẖt 3bḫ s m ib.i -------
rḫ.kwi ḥtp nṯr.i ḥr.s
ᶜnḫ.f im.s rᶜ nb
in wᶜ iqr mty m3ᶜ
nn sm3.n.f m -------

I say to you, future people coming after me:
I was one worthy, cool -------
who had put Maat in his heart
without neglecting her occasion.
Since I left the womb she was joined to my heart -------
I know my god is pleased with her
and lives by her every day.
So says one worthy and truly straight,
who did not consort with [the evildoer].

In text after text, the officials of Seti I and Ramses II built up the connection between their right-doing and their hopes for recognition and reward in the hereafter. And observe here how Huyshery explained his right-doing by his having Maat in his heart, both because he had placed her there and because she was joined to his heart since his birth. If this phrasing is somewhat clumsy, it nevertheless expresses the sound intuition that moral behavior results from an innate disposition as well as from reasoning and learning.

For a preliminary summary of this twofold recognition turn back to text 38a. The third major element in the Egyptian's understanding of his moral selfhood is the element present in rudimentary form since the Old Kingdom which came to full fruition in the New Kingdom: the conviction that the gods desired, and also inspired, man's Maat doing.

With king Seti I's large scale temple building at Abydos, the sacred city of Osiris was once again in focus as a major gateway into the beyond. Hence the following "Hymn to Abydos" - the genre "hymns to cities" being a Ramesside innovation.

70) The hymn to the sacred city of Abydos, known in four copies (as published by Clère in ZÄS 84, 1959, 86-104), is now dated to the reign of Seti I by Kitchen in his edition, KRI I, 357-360. The hymn appears as a complete text on the stela of the priest Horemwia reproduced here (see Illus. 1), and is partly preserved on three broken lintels, two of which give additional verses not found in Horemwia's version. Horemwia's text is an excellent example of how a hymn which existed in varying versions would be shaped into a coherent unit so as to fit the space of a particular monument. Horemwia's stela, now in Berlin, must have come from an Abydene tomb or cenotaph, as would have the three lintels in Berlin, Leiden, and Vienna.

In the upper part of the stela, Horemwia kneels before the enthroned Osiris behind whom stand Horus, Isis, and Nephthys. The hymn, written in six lines below the scene, is structured anaphorically and written stichically, each stichos representing a whole verse consisting of several sentences. Verses 1 and 2 are shorter than verses 3-6, and the larger number of words in lines 3-6 is clearly visible in the more crowded carving.

Two of the lintel versions address the hymn not to the town of Abydos but to its god, Osiris. For all details the reader is referred to Clère's important study.

The stichic writing being clearly visible on the photograph, I transliterate directly into the verse form dictated by the anaphoric pattern. Line 1 begins with *it-nṯr Ḥr-w3ḏ Ḥr-m-wi3 ḏd.f*:

i3w n 3bḏw mi ḥ^{c}y Ist
ms s3.s Ḥr m-ẖnw 3ḫ-bit

i3w n 3bḏw mi ḥ3y Ist
pr s3.s Ḥr m3^c-ḫrw
sḫr ẖ3bty-nik ḥr it.f Wnn-nfr

i3w n 3bḏw m prt ^{c}3t
nty ḥr-tp t3 m ršwt dw3tyw m ḥb
šsp.sn ṯḥw n nfrw.f
mrwt.f m ib n ḥr nb

i3w n 3bḏw m w-pqr
šsp.n.f m3^c-ḫrw ib.f nḏm

imw-ḥt.f m ḥb ib.sn 3w
m3.sn wr pn m m3ᶜ-ḫrw

i3w n 3bdw m d3 m nšmt
iw p3 nb 3bḏw ḥtp m ᶜḥ.f
ẖnm.n.f iwᶜ n pr.f n ḏt
nṯrw hr-ib ḥr ḥtpw.sn

i3w n 3bdw t3 n m3ᶜt
iw pn n m3ᶜtyw šw m grgw
w3ḏ.wy m3ᶜ-ib nty m ẖnw.s
pḥ.f imi-wrt iw.f m3ᶜ-ḫrw

Hail to Abydos as Isis rejoiced:
Born was her son in innermost Chemmis!

Hail to Abydos as Isis rejoiced:
Horus her son came forth triumphant,
the snake-fiend felled for his father Onnophris!

Hail to Abydos in great procession:
those on earth in joy, the adorants in feast,
as they jubilate to his beauty,
love of him in each one's heart.

Hail to Abydos in the district of Peqer:
Triumph obtained his heart rejoices,
his servants are festive, their hearts at ease,
seeing this great one in triumph.

Hail to Abydos as one sails in the Neshmet:
the lord of Abydos comes to rest in his palace,
having taken possession of his house of eternity,
and the gods are content with their offerings.

Hail to Abydos, land of Maat:
isle of the righteous, free of lies!
Blessed is the rightminded within it,
he has reached the west as one true of voice!

As Clère observed, the hymn has two parts, the first devoted to the triumph of Horus, the second to the death and vindication of Osiris, as celebrated at Abydos; and the principal acts of the festival as known from Middle Kingdom texts are alluded to in an order which had clearly been maintained unchanged through the centuries: the "great procession" during which Osiris met his death, the burial at Peqer, the return of Osiris on the Neshmet bark, and his reinstallation in the temple of Abydos. As for Abydos as the "isle of the righteous", we have encountered the expression in the prayer of Siese (text 58).

71) The chief sculptor Userhat, owner of the lintel Leiden K.9 which has one of the four copies of the Abydos hymn, had inscribed the door jambs belonging to the lintel with two prayers to Osiris and two prayers to Re. The two prayers to Osiris have a distinct division of topics. The left jamb has an offering prayer and a self-presentation; the text on the right jamb requests afterlife blessings. Here is the self-presentation on the left door jamb (KRI I, 361.5-8):

> i nṯrw imy 3bḏw nbw ʿnḫ tp t3
> msddyw grgw isft ʿnḫyw m m3ʿt
> ink m3ʿ ir ḥr mw.tn
> n sm3 ib.i m ḏw-qd
> n šm.i ḥr w3t nt sh3
> n sḏd.i ḥnʿ q3-ḫrw
> bwt.i pw ẖnn mdwt.f
> n hnn.i n ḏdt.f nb
> iw.i rḫ.kwi bwt nṯr.i
> ir.i ḥr mw n wḏ.f

> O gods of Abydos, lords of life on earth,
> who hate lies and wrongdoing and live by rightness:
> I am a true one who acts on your water,
> I did not consort with the evil man.
> I did not follow the path of hostility,
> I did not converse with the loud-voiced;
> I abhor the tumult of his words,
> and did not assent to any of his sayings.
> I know what my god abhors,
> and I act on the water of his precept.

72) To the same Userhat belonged a handsome stela of unusual autobiographical interest (Leiden V.1, KRI VII, 27-29). On it Userhat tells with great emotion how, though of humble origin, he had been noticed by the king and chosen, favored, and promoted to the rank of chief sculptor. He then took part in the production of statues of gods; and it was he who provided the divine images with their shrines. The king rewarded him with the "gold of favor". He concludes by swearing in the name of Ptah, lord of Maat, that all he has told is the truth.

73) Amenemopet, royal scribe and overseer of workmen at Deir al-Medina, had a seated statuette group of himself and his wife. Carved in wood in the most elegant style, its base and dorsal pillar are inscribed with carefully thought-out prayers. Those written on the base are addressed to: Amen-Re, Mut, Khons, Thoth, Re-Harakhti-Atum, Ptah, and Osiris; the dorsal pillar has, on its right half, a prayer addressed jointly to Osiris, Thoth, and Hathor, and on its left a hymn to Amen-Re (Berlin 6910, Aeg. Inschr. II, 63-71 = KRI I, 386-388, and see PM I^2, tombs 215 & 265). In the prayer to Thoth, on the base, Maat epithets are heaped on the god (KRI I, 386.15):

> Ḏḥwty nb iwn šmᶜ
> ṯ3ty wp m3ᶜt ḥsb m3ᶜt
> mr m3ᶜt dd m3ᶜt n ir m3ᶜt ...
>
> Thoth, lord of southern On,
> Vizier who decides Right, reckons Right,
> loves Right, gives Right to the doer of Right ...

74) The prayer to the triad Osiris-Thoth-Hathor (KRI I, 387.9ff.) reads:

> Ḥtp-di-nswt Wsir Ḫnt-imntt
> Wnn-nfr nswt ᶜnḫw
> nṯr ᶜ3 nb nḥḥ
> sḥtpy.i nṯr špsy ḥtp ḥr m3ᶜt
> Ḏḥwty nb mdwt nṯr
> sš šs3 n psḏt
> tm iṯ-in m sp.f
> ṯ3ty wpp m3ᶜt
> n irr m ḫmt.f m nṯrw rmṯ

di.i i3w n Ḥt-Ḥr ḥry-tp w3st
nbt pt ḥnwt idbw
di.sn ᶜq ḥsy pr mrw
ẖr ḥsw n nb nṯrw
r3.i wḏ3 nn in sp.f
r pḥ.i i3wt m ḥsw ḥm.f
wni ḏw ẖnm ršw
sbi ᶜḥᶜw ḥtp
n k3 n wᶜ iqr mrr nṯr.f
sš nswt nw imi-wrt Imn-m-ipt m3ᶜ-ḫrw ...

A royal offering to Osiris Khentamenthes,
Wenennofer, king of the living,
great god, lord of eternity!
May I please the noble god who is pleased with right,
Thoth, lord of divine words,
skilled scribe of the Ennead,
who wavers not in his concern.
Vizier who judges right,
and acts not in ignorance of gods and people!
May I praise Hathor, lady of Thebes,
sky's mistress, queen of the Two Banks!
May they grant: entering praised, leaving beloved,
in the favor of the lord of gods,
my speech sound, not causing blame,
till I reach old age in his majesty's favor,
shunning evil, embracing joy,
passing life in peace -
for the ka of one worthy who loves his god,
the royal scribe of the westside Amenemopet, justified ...

75) The concluding hymn to Amen-Re (left half of dorsal pillar, KRI I, 387.15ff.) reads:

ḫy p3 ḥmsi nfr ḥr-ᶜ Imn
p3 sbb n gr šd nmḥw
dd ṯ3w n mrr.f nb
wḏ.n.f i3wt nfr ḥr imnt w3st
n k3 n sš nswt imi-r3 pr.wy-ḥḏ m st m3ᶜt Imn-m-ipt, m3ᶜ-ḫrw
ḏd.f
i nṯr.i nb nṯrw

Imn-rʿ nb nswt t3wy
imi n.i ḏrt šd wi
wbn n.i iry.k sʿnḫ.i
mtwk p3 nṯr wʿ iwty snw.f
Rʿ pw wbn m ḥrt Tmw ir rḫyt
sḏm snmḥw n iʿš n.f
nḥm s m ʿ sḫm-ib
in Ḥʿpy n wnm.sn
sšmw nfrw n irt nb

wbn.f ʿnḫ rḫyt
ʿnḫ ib.sn m33.sn
rdiw ṯ3w n nty m swḥt
sʿnḫ rmṯ 3pdw
ir ẖrt pnw m b3b3w.sn
ḏdft pwyw mitt iry
di.f qrst nfrt ḥr ḫt i3wt
iw.i wḏ3.kwi m ḏrt.k
n k3 n sš nswt Imn-m-ipt m3ʿ-ḫrw
snt.f nbt-pr Ḥt-Ḥr m3ʿ-ḫrw ḏd.tw Ḥwnr

How good to sit in the hand of Amun,
protector of the silent, savior of the poor,
who gives breath to all he loves!
He has assigned a good old age in the west of Thebes
to the ka of the royal scribe and overseer of the Double House
of Silver in the Place-of-Truth, Amenemopet, justified.
He says:
O my god, lord of gods,
Amen-Re, lord of Thrones-of-the-two-lands!
Give me a hand, save me,
rise for me to make me live!
You are the one god who has no second:
Re who rises in heaven, Atum maker of people,
hearer of prayers of one who calls to him,
who rescues a man from the violent one,
who brings Hapy, that people may eat,
good guide of every being!

When he rises people live,
their hearts live by seeing,
who gives breath to one in the egg,
nourishes people and birds,
provides for mice in their holes,
for worms and fleas likewise.
May he give a good burial after old age,
I being hale in your hand:
to the ka of the royal scribe Amenemopet, justified,
and his wife, the lady Hathor, justified, called Hel.

King Amenhotep I, deified, had become the patron saint of the workmen of the Theban necropolis; and his worship had spread upward to the ranks of middle-level royal officials. Two stelae of officials on which Amenhotep I is adored in nearly identical phrases were published by Wente in JNES 22, 1963, 30ff. The texts of these two, and a third parallel one, are now available in KRI III, 187; III, 239; and III, 247. Here are the principal lines, addressing king Amenhotep I in his role of divine judge, from the stela of Nahihu, high steward of the Ramesseum (KRI III, 187.6-9):

76) inḏ ḥr.k p3 s3 Imn
mw nṯry pr m ḥʿw.f
p3 ṯ3ty wp m3ʿt
gmḥ.f r ḥ3ty bwt.f grg
ntk nṯr n mḥ ib im.f
nẖw n šms sw
ršwy nty m ḥs(t).k
n pḥ sw ḏw

Hail to you, son of Amun,
divine seed issued from his body;
vizier who determines right,
as he looks at the heart and abhors falsehood!
You are a god in whom one trusts,
protector of one who serves him;
happy is he who is in your favor,
no evil shall befall him!

The partnership of man and god in Maat doing here takes the form of assigning the doing to the deified king in his role as judge, as was also done in prayers to Thoth or Amun. But naturally, men's declarations of their own Maat doing had greater scope and urgency; and now, at the beginning of the Ramesside age, they were most intense.

77) Tjia, treasury chief of the Ramesseum, inscribed a free standing block stela with prayers on all four sides, addressed respectively to Re-Harakhti, Atum, Osiris, and Sokar. In the prayer to Atum, Tjia declares (KRI III, 366.16):

> ink wꜥ iqr nfr bit
> w3ḥ-ib r irt m3ꜥt
> mty m3ꜥ tm rdit ḥr gs
>
> I am trustworthy, good natured,
> intent on doing right,
> one truly straight who is not partial.

In the prayer to Sokar, Tjia says (KRI III, 367.12-14):

> iy.i m niwt.i m ḥsw nswt
> iw ir.n.i mrr k3.f
> iw.i rḫ.kwi bwt nṯr
> n iry.i isft
> iw di.i t n ḥqrw
> mw n ibw
> ḥbsw n ḥ3wty
>
> With the king's favor did I come from my town,
> having done what his ka desired.
> Knowing what the god abhors,
> I did no wrong,
> and I gave bread to the hungry,
> water to the thirsty,
> clothes to the naked.

When one compares the texts of these six Ramesside officials with those of their 18th dynasty colleagues, one observes a direct continuation of the 18th dynasty trend of piety and an intensification of that trend. The changes in phrasing add up to a significant increase in intimacy with the gods, as when Huyshery (text 69) speaks of the Maat whom "he had put in his heart" as the personal goddess rather than the concept of rightness. Or when, in the prayer of Userhat (text 71) observance of right-doing and personal devotion to the gods are linked with the utmost precision: Userhat has acted rightly because he knew it was what his god wanted him to do. In speaking of their right-doing, the 18th dynasty officials showed an awareness of the distance between man and god. The Ramesside officials appeal to the gods more directly and more intimately, asking them to be witnesses of their Maat doing, and to act as their guides and protectors in this life and in the hereafter. The Ramesside age added to Maat thinking the clearest tones of personal piety, and it did so in three distinct voices: those of officials; of the craftsmen of Deir al-Medina (who appear in the next section); and of kings.

The great temple of Seti I at Abydos, with its numerous depictions of royal devotion including scenes of the offering of Maat, is a major monument to royal piety. To sound the royal note, here is a prayer of king Seti I on a stela from his mortuary temple at Qurnah; it is just one verse from his hymn to the sungod (the text was published by Stadelmann & Osing, MDIK 44, 1988, 246f.):

78) ir irrw ḥr wḏ n nṯr.f
n wh.n šsp wᶜ n irr.f
ntk it.i di m ib.i
irt.n.i ḫft wḏt.n.k

As to him who acts by command of his god,
no palm's width of his actions will fail.
You are my father who inspires my heart,
what I did accorded with your command.

Except for the royal privilege of calling the god "my father" (rather than "our father") a high Ramesside official could have spoken thus.

B. The Craftsmen: "A house filled with foods"

When Erman published Denksteine aus der thebanischen Gräberstadt (Sitzungsber. Akad. d. Wiss. Berlin, 1911) and coined the term "persönliche Frömmigkeit", he had assembled eleven stelae. The group was augmented to thirteen when Gunn translated and discussed them in "The Religion of the Poor in Ancient Egypt" (JEA 3, 1916, 81-92). What impressed both scholars was the penitential aspect of some of the prayers. In Gunn's words: "... we find the very spirit of that self-abasing and sorrowful appeal, conscious of unworthiness, which Matthew Arnold ... called the Hebraic attitude as opposed to the Hellenic..."

Now that the workmen's village of Deir al-Medina has been excavated, published, and studied for more than fifty years, and now that the texts are readily accessible in Kitchen's great assemblage (KRI), it can easily be determined that the penitential texts, which aroused so much interest and are so often cited, are very few in number. Those known to Erman and Gunn were exactly four (all dating to the reign of Ramses II):

1. Berlin stela 20377 of Nebre (KRI III, 653ff.) who recalls a crime committed by his son Nakhtamun and extols the mercy of Amun who forgave it. Thus it is the innocent man who is speaking.
2. Stela of Neferabu, Turin 50058 (KRI III, 772f.) on which this skilled craftsman who built a fine tomb at Deir al-Medina speaks of an unspecified "transgression" *(p3 sp n h3i)* against the goddess Peak-of-the-West who, when he implored her, cured his malady and thereby signified forgiveness.
3. The same Neferabu, on British Museum stela 589 (KRI III, 771f.) relates that he swore a false oath by Ptah, Lord of Maat, whereupon the god struck him with blindness. He now prays for mercy. This is the verso of the stela. On the recto Neferabu prays to Ptah "that my eyes may behold Amun every day, as is done for a righteous man *(m3ᶜty)* who holds Amun in his heart". Neferabu did the same on the stela he dedicated to the Peak-of-the-West: in the scene above his main text he declared that he had been "a just one on earth" *(m3ᶜty tp t3)*.
4. Stela of Huy, Turin 50044 (KRI III, 795) on which Huy declares that he swore a false oath by Thoth-the-Moon, who thereupon made him see his might *(ᶜ3w pḥty.f)*. He now asks for mercy.

A fifth example is the Deir al-Medina stela 320 of Qen (KRI III, 687) who also swore a false oath and now prays for mercy *(ḥtp)*. There may be a few more stelae of the confessional type; but they are not likely to change the overall impression that confessions of sin were the exceptions proving the rule that an enduring stone monument was not the right place for recording one's faults and failings. Hence Neferabu's insistence that, despite his confessed crime, he had been a righteous man!

The bulk of the monuments of Deir al-Medina craftsmen, whether votive stelae set up in the small temples of the village, or stelae, statues and shrines from their tombs, carry prayers that may be divided into two groups: those that pray for help or mercy *(ḥtp)* in cases of illness, blindness, or other distress, and those that pray in a positive vein for a happy life and a good burial.

79) An example of the latter type is the prayer of the "great craftsman" Karo, inscribed on the top of the base of his wooden statue which came from his tomb, Deir al-Medina 330 (MMA 65.14: Fischer, Orientation of Hieroglyphs, I, pp. 137-140 = KRI VII, 410f.; cf. PM I² Pt. II, p. 711. Reign of Ramses II):

ḥtp di nswt Imn-rᶜ nb nswt t3wy
ḥtp di nswt Mwt nbt pt
ḥtp di nswt Ḫnsw-m-w3st Nfr-ḥtp nb 3wt-ib
di.sn ᶜnḫ wḏ3 snb spd-ḥr nb ḥsw mrwt
ᶜḥᶜw nfr sm3 m snb nḏm-ib ršw rᶜ nb
irty.i ḥr m33 ᶜnḫwy ḥr sḏm
r3.i mḥ m m3ᶜt rᶜ nb
mi irt n m3ᶜty dd Imn m ib.f
n k3 n gr m3ᶜ nfr bit
n k3 n ḥmww wr m st m3ᶜt Knr3 m3ᶜ-ḫrw

A royal offering to Amenre, lord of Thrones-of-the-two-lands,
a royal offering to Mut, mistress of sky,
a royal offering to Khonsu-in-Thebes Neferhotep, lord of joy:
May they grant life-haleness-health, all keenness, favor, love,
a good lifetime endowed with health, gladness and joy, daily,
my eyes seeing, ears hearing, my mouth filled with truth, daily;
as is done for a righteous man who holds Amun in his heart,
for the ka of the truly silent and good-natured,
for the ka of the great craftsman in the Place of Truth, Karo, justified.

On the dorsal pillar, Karo added a request to Amenre for:

qrst nfrt ḥr-ẖt i3wt
sm3-t3 n smt ḥsyw
ḥr imntt wrt n w3st

A good burial after old age,
landing in the desert of the praised ones,
in the great west of Thebes.

Essentially the same prayer, with varations, is inscribed on many stelae, statues, and shrines of Deir al-Medina craftsmen and workmen whose only title was that of "Servant in the Place of Truth". Able to build and furnish good tombs for themselves and their families, these craftsmen pray for a lifetime in health and happiness, and for a good burial with afterlife blessings, all this in requital of their having been "righteous" *(m3ᶜty)*. Thus every average person (including women) could now approach the gods directly with requests for this life and the afterlife. (See in particular the mass of Deir al-Medina craftsmen's and workmen's inscriptions in KRI III, 576ff.).

80) One of those craftsmen whose only title was "servant in the Place of Truth" was the man Iry-nefer. He built a good tomb for himself which included several stelae (TT 290, PM I^2, 372f., KRI III, 714ff.). His stela no. 4 seems to me especially appealing (BM 814 = KRI III, 718f.). It shows him adoring the Hathor cow in a naos, and below the scene is this prayer:

rdi i3w n Ḥt-Ḥr ḥri-tp w3st
nbt pt ḥnwt nṯrw
sn t3 n t3 ḥ3t nṯrw
di.i n.s i3w r q3 n pt
sw3š.i nfrw.s iw.s iy.ty m ḥtp
mn.ty ḥr st.s mḥ.s t3 m nfrw.s
di.s n.i pr mḥ m ḏf3w
n dd.s r nḥḥ n ḏt
in sḏm-ᶜš m st m3ᶜt Iry-nfr
wḥm ᶜnẖ nfr m ḥtp

Giving praise to Hathor, lady of Thebes,
mistress of sky, queen of gods!

Kissing earth to the foremost of gods,
I give her praise to the height of sky!
I worship her beauty when she comes in peace,
when in rest on her seat she fills the land with her beauty!
May she grant me a house filled with foods
as her gift for ever and always!
Says the servant in the Place of Truth Iry-nefer,
may he live again in good peace.

C. Tales of Maat

Ramesside writers created such new literary genres as Love Songs, Praises of Cities, and Allegorical and Satirical Tales. Two of the Tales are especially significant for Maat: "Truth and Falsehood" and "The Contendings of Horus and Seth":
1. Falsehood *(grg)* denounces his older brother Truth *(m3ᶜt)* to the Ennead and tries to kill him. Though blinded, Truth escapes. And when he has raised a son, the son becomes the avenger, and Falsehood is punished by the gods.
2. Horus and Seth have been contending for many years before the tribunal of the Ennead, each claiming the kingship of Egypt in succession to Osiris. The Ennead tends to agree that Right is on the side of Horus; but Re-Harakhti, King of Gods, cannot make up his mind to award the kingship to the young and weak Horus rather than to the older and mightier Seth. It is Might against Right. Eventually, the gods are persuaded by a threatening letter from Osiris in the netherworld, who reproaches them for letting Maat sink into the netherworld by failing to award the kingship to Horus. Then they all agree to give the kingship to Horus, and Re-Harakhti conciliates all parties by proposing that Seth shall dwell with him in the sky and be allowed to thunder. Thus Right wins over Might, and Confrontation gives way to Conciliation.

6. The Theban Clergy of Amun: "I know the god acts for the right-minded"

The high-ranking priests of Amun of Thebes, who served the kings of the 22nd and 23rd dynasties, and married daughters of the royal house, are well known owing to the preservation of their excellent statues by the Karnak Cache. The new and useful edition of the most important pieces by K. Jansen-Winkeln (Ägyptische Biographien der 22. und 23. Dynastie, hereafter abbreviated as J.-W.) makes them easily accessible. Their powerful portrait sculptures bear texts of matching forcefulness, styled in a manner both incisive and sophisticated: the phrasing is choice, ornate, and complex. We focus on their prayers for divine rewards in this life and in the next, prayers sturdily supported by declarations of right-doing.

81) CG 42206 is a seated statue of Nakhtefmut, fourth prophet of Amun (J.-W., A 2, pp. 25ff. & 441ff.). On the back of the seat, the priest extols Amenre, whom he calls "our father", "a mother", "protector and helper" (p. 444.6-7):

di i3wt sm3 m snb
wsrt 3bẖ m nḏm-ib
nty ḥr mw.f n n.f ḥ3
wᶜb n.f n mrḥ
ḥnk n.f m3ᶜt rᶜ nb
n ḥ3w-ib m rk.f
mr.k ḥm.k mi mr.f tw
sw3ḥ.k s(w) m pr.k n sk

Who gives old age endued with health,
and force imbued with joy!
One who is on his water has no want,
he who is 'pure' for him without fail,
and offers Maat to him daily,
has no sorrow in his lifetime!
May you love your servant as he loves you,
may you keep him in your house unendingly!

82) To the same Nakhtefmut belonged the stelephorous statue CG 42208 (J.-W., A 4, pp. 44ff. & 453ff.). The reign is that of Osorkon II.

The bulk of the text consists of Nakhtefmut's prayers and requests to Amenre to protect his daughter from being deprived of the property he has bequeathed to her. In the end, he reminds the god of his faithful service to him and requests to spend his old age in peace in the temple (p. 456.2ff.):

ḥnk.i n.k m3ᶜt bwt.i isft
ḥri.i r s3d wᶜb.k kni m grg
bw sḏw.i ḥr nb n imi-irty t3
....
iw.i rḫ.kwi prw ir 3ḫw
wḏ3t gm s msw ḥr-s3 dw3
iw.k r dit n.i isw m i3wt ᶜ3t nfrt
m33 Imn m-mnt mrr ib.i
iw šms.i nsyw ᶜḏ.kwi m nšn.sn

In loathing of evil did I offer you Maat,
and shunned soiling your pureness by false complaints.
I did not slander anyone to the captain of the land,
....
I know the profit of doing what is helpful:
A storehouse for the children who come after.
May you give me the reward of a good great age:
Daily seeing Amun as my heart desires,
and serving the kings while safe from their wrath.

83) CG 42210 is a cube statue of Harsiese, son-in-law of king Harsiese, made by his son Djed-khons-efankh (J.-W., A 5, pp. 63ff. & 462ff.). On the right side, the son addresses the Ennead of the temple, asking them to safeguard the offerings destined for his father (p. 465.4-6):

imi ḏrty.fy ḥr 3bt.tn
mk wᶜb ᶜwy
imi n.f r3.f mḥ m ḏf3w
mk ḏd m3ᶜt
m wšr.f swri m qbḥ.tn
mk mr tḫ
ḥr nty ir ḥtp.tn ḥr m3ᶜt[1]-ib tp-t3
mr nṯr.f iwty mity m ḫnw.f

---

[1]The *t* is redundant.

Place his hands on your offerings:
Behold one pure of hands!
Let his mouth be filled with food:
Behold a speaker of truth!
Let him not lack drink of your libation:
Behold a lover of drunkenness!
For as you are pleased with the truthful on earth,
so will his god love one free of duplicity!

84) CG 42226 is the cube statue of the priest of Amun, Hor, who also held the post of royal letter-writer, and other administrative offices in the reign of Petubastis, wherefore his Maat doing had a wide scope (J.-W., A 11, pp. 136ff. & 506ff.). Here are parts of cols. 3, 5-7 of the text on the back (p. 510):

h3b.kwi m wpwt nt nb t3wy
r smnḫ kmt n nb.f
rḫ.n.f is 3ḫ.i ḥr tp t3
... ...
pḥ.n.i i3wt n gm wn.i
km.n.i ʿḥʿw.i n nḏm-ib
ḏr-ntt fq3.tw iqr ḥr mnḫ.f
mrwt n ḫm-ṯs
di.i m3ʿt wrty m t3
p3t.f ḥtp.f ḥr.s

I was sent on missions of the lord-of-the-two-lands,
to organize Egypt for its lord,
for he knew my usefulness for the land.
... ...
I reached old age without being faulted,
I completed my lifetime in gladness;
for the good man is rewarded for his virtue,
and there is love for one who is blameless.
I made Maat great in the land -
his offering that contents him.

On the base is this verse (p. 511.3-4):

ḏr ḫms.n.i m3ʿt ḥr tp t3
mrwt.s pẖr ḥ3.i

iry.i wʿb.s snṯr.i sw im
nḏ.n.i ḥr.s m wrt.s

Since I befriended Maat on earth,
her love enveloped me;
by purifying and censing her,
I guarded her in her greatness.

85) CG 42227 is a second cube statue of the same Hor (J.-W., A 12, pp. 150ff. & 515ff.). Evidently designed as a pair, A 11 gives his autobiography, while A 12 has a prayer for his afterlife with self-justifications that stress his righteousness (p. 516.8-9):

ḥnk.i n.f m3ʿt mrr.f
p3t.f tfy m ʿntyw
ti ḏd.i dw3 pw iw.f
fq3.tw iqr m ir.n.f

When I offered him the Maat he loves,
that loaf of his which is myrrh,
I used to say, "On the morrow that comes
the good man is requited for his deeds."

86) CG 42228 is the seated statue of the lady *Šb-n-spdt*, daughter of the king's son Nemrat, and granddaughter of Osorkon II. The husband Hor who dedicated her statue may be identical with the Hor of A 11 and A 12, presented above. The finely carved statue has a significant text, and one in which a woman - highborn but not a queen - was accorded a Maat epithet. On the left side of the seat the lady prays for an afterlife in the company of the sungod as the reward of her virtue (p. 522.9):

iqrt mitt.i špst rḫ r3.s
s3t nswt iqr-bi3 wʿb-ʿ.wy m ḫt nb

One virtuous like me, noble lady who knows her speech,
king's daughter, good-natured, pure-handed withal.

On the back of the seat (p. 524, line 4 & cols. 5-6):

iqr-mdw ḫnmw.s iry m ʿntyw
Skilled in speech whereof the fragrance is myrrh.

wnn.i ḥm ḥr tp t3 wd.i m3^{c} n bw nb
While I dwelled on earth I spoke truth to all.

The dearth of women's Maat statements confirms the obvious: Maat doing was eminently an activity of persons in public life, and, except for temple service, women did not hold office. Thus, the testimony of having been truthful is the only aspect of Maat doing accorded to the noble lady.

87) CG 42231 is the cube statue of the priest of Amun, Horakhbit (J.-W., A 17, pp. 193ff. & 542ff.). On the front is an address to the living, and the beginning of his autobiography. The address begins thus (p. 543):

i wnw nty r ḫpr
iw.sn ḥr-s3 rnpwt
imi prw n šms Imn
r ḏd m3^{c}t mrr.f

O people who will be,
as they come after years:
Give an extra in serving Amun
by speaking the truth he loves!

We had the term *prw* in text 82, where I translated it as "profit". The range of meaning suggested by the two occurrences is: "extra - surplus - profit". Later in the same address Horakhbit declares (p. 545.5-9):

ink pw m3^{c}-ib n nṯr.f
šw m th-nmtwt
iw ṯs.i s3 n gs.wy.i
ḫft wḏ3 itw.sn r ḥrt
iw ir.i 3ḫt n snw.i
ḏb3.n.i nty m iwty
mr.n.i m m3^{c}ty nb
rdi s3 r th-w3t
ink it n nty m g3ḥ
tm wni r m3r ḥr m3^{c}t.f
iw ir.n.i mrr nb nṯr
iwty ḥr.wy m rmṯ

I was one truthful to his god,
one free of errancy.
I advanced the son(s) of colleagues,
when the fathers had gone to the grave.
I was helpful to my comrades,
and provided for one in need.
I cherished every righteous one,
who turned the back on transgression.
I was a father to the weary,
one who did not shun the pauper in his right.
I have done whatever the god loves,
and had not two faces to people.

In the sentence *tm wni r m3r ḥr m3ᶜt.f,* the expression *ḥr m3ᶜt.f* is somewhat ambiguous. Jansen-Winkeln (p. 196) rendered, "einer der nicht wegen seiner (eigenen) Gerechtigkeit an einem Elenden vorüberging", and commented (n. 21) "d.h. der sich nicht pharisäerhaft gebärdete". That interpretation assigns an unparalleled, hence unlikely, negative sense to Maat. I take the sentence to mean that the speaker, being "father to the weary", did not ignore the pauper's rightful claim to assistance.

88) CG 42229 is a stelephorous statue of Nakhtefmut with cartouches of Osorkon III (J.-W., A 18, pp. 205ff. & 552ff.). This priest was also vizier, hence his Maat doing had broad authority (p. 553.8-11):

ink m3ᶜt[2]-ib n rdit ḥr gs
n nfr.i n ir bw-ḏw
di.i wn pr-wnḫ ḥr mty
mi sšm.f n-ḏr ir sḥn
ḥnk.i m3ᶜt n nṯr nb
tfnn.sn ḥr ir.n.i
wd.i hpw m snt r isyw
st-r3.i n ṯ3w n ᶜnḫ

I am rightminded without partiality,
I am not kind to the evildoer.
I restored the *pr-wnḫ* exactly,

---

[2]Redundant *t* as in text 83.

so that it functioned as when established.
I offered Maat to all the gods,
so that they rejoiced at my actions.
I issued laws in accord with old writings,
my verdict was breath of life.

89) CG 42232, a cube statue of Nespekashuty, bears the cartouches of Shoshenq III (J.-W., A 19, pp. 210ff. & 556ff.). In two highly stylized quatrains this priest of Amun describes his appointment to the vizierate as having occurred at the beginning of the king's reign (p. 557, left and right):

šsp nswt ẖkr n Ḥr
iw.i ḥnʿ.f mi Ḏḥwty
ḥms.i ḥr tm3 m ḥwt wrw 6
wp.i s.wy r wn ḥtp.sn

When the king received the badge of Horus,
I was with him like Thoth;
seated on the mat in the six great houses,
I judged two men to their contentment.

šsp.i m3ʿt m ẖkr.s m ʿḥ
di.i (s)rf n Ḏḥwty ḥr.s
ḏsr.i s imitw šnbty
imn.tw r ḥr nb

When I received Maat in her badge in the palace,
I gave leisure to Thoth by it;
I secluded her between my breasts,
so that she was hidden from all sight.

90) Cairo JE 37512 is a statue of the vizier Hor, son of Iutjek (J.-W., A 20, pp. 216ff. & 561ff.). The strongly archaising features of the sculpture, and of the literary style, have made the dating problematic. Kees (ZÄS 83, 1958, 137) weighed several factors without reaching a firm conclusion: "Bleibt also die Wahl zwischen den geordneten Verhältnissen in der 1. Hälfte der 22. Dynastie bis in die Zeit Osorkons II. oder ein Ausweichen in die sehr unübersichtlichen Jahre ganz am Schluss der 22. und der 23. Dynastie bis zum Einbruch der Äthiopen, wo dann die zahlreichen Veziere unter

den Vorfahren des Montemhet unterzubringen sind." The inscription begins with a long address to posterity which concludes as follows (p. 562.1-4):

ṯ3ty Ḥr m3ꜥ-ḫrw k3.tn ḫft th.tn
n k3.i ḫw tn m bw nb
it im(3) n iwty sw
mwt n ng3w
n sqsn.i ky m mr-ḫt
nn ḥwtf(.i) dnit m r3-pr
psš.n.i ps(n) ḥnꜥ wꜥbw iww r nmtwt.sn
nn ḏd.i m ib.i sr r.i
sḫ3.n.i wi m wꜥ m iryw-nṯr
iw sw3ḥ.n.i mnw n bit nfrt
rḫ.n.i 3ḫ n ḥnty
ptr qsn r.tn tm.tn ir.f
nfr irt n ir.n.f
im.tn ḏd m-tr ḫpr ḫr.f
sḫ3.tw k3.f
iw šfd ḥr ḏd 3ḫ n ir.f
ṯ3w n r3 3ḫ n sꜥḥ
mi ntt r isyw
n ḥtm.n b3.f m-ꜥb nṯrw r nḥḥ ḥnꜥ ḏt

"Vizier Hor, justified", shall you say when attacked,
to my ka that protected you everywhere -
a father kind to the have-not,
a mother to the needy!
I did not deprive anyone by greed,
nor did I steal a portion from the temple;
I shared the loaves with the priests on their rounds,
and did not say "Master" to myself in my heart,
for I recalled I was one of the servants of the god.
I have erected a monument to good character,
knowing it would serve for eternity!
Behold, it will harm you not to act,
it is good to act for one who acted!
Do not say, "What was done by him,
that his ka should be remembered?"
The book says, "It is good for the doer,
breath of the mouth helps the blessed";

also according to ancient writings:
"His Ba, among the gods, will never perish!"

The son Iutjek comments (p. 563.1-2):
iw ir.i m3ᶜt n nb m3ᶜt
m3ᶜty wḏ3 m3ᶜt
Imn-rᶜ nb nswt t3wy
f3i pt irt[3] itn im.s
rḫ.n.i rdi.n.f (w)i n.k
ḥr ir.k n.f m3ᶜt ... ...

I did right for the lord of right,
the righteous who determines right,
Amenre, lord of Thrones-of-the-two-lands,
who raised the sky
and made the sundisk in it;
for I knew he gave me to you,
because you did right for him.

91) On his cube statue CG 559 (J.-W., A 1, pp. 9ff. & 433ff.) the priest Djedkhons-efankh concluded the main portion of his autobiography with the sentence (p. 436.14):
rḫ.kwi irr nṯr n m3ᶜ-ib
I know the god acts for the rightminded.

An "emphatic" statement which may well be read as the credo of Maat thinking in the New Kingdom and thereafter.

On the dorsal plinth, Djedkhons-efankh added an account of his liberality toward needy persons, and he ended thus (p. 437.6):
iw.i rḫ.kwi n šps.ti m iwḥ
in nṯr ir n ib.f

I knew one is not enriched by theft,
the god does what he wishes!

Note the statement on the "free will" of the deity. Far from being arbitrary, the divine will implements Maat by denying success to the rapacious man.

---

[3]Redundant *t*, or read *ir.tw*.

7. "Principium Sapientiae Timor Domini"

92) On the front of his seated statue Cairo JE 36711, Harwa, high steward of Amenirdis, recorded his moral portrait (Gunn-Engelbach, BIFAO 30, no. II, pp. 796f., text A, lines 10-14):

ink wr ḥsw r gs nswt
ḫnt st m pr ḥnwt(.i)
n mdw.n(.i) ky r gs.sn
n sk.n(.i) nb sp
sb3.n wi ib(.i) r hr
sšm.n.f wi r mnḫ-ib
ḏd.n(.i) m m3^c ir.n(.i) m m3^c
iw.i rḫ.kwi m hrw spr

I was greatly favored at the king's side,
and foremost in the house of my lady;
I did not malign anyone to them,
nor did I harm an unfortunate man.
My heart taught me contentment,
and guided me to excellence;
I spoke truly, I acted justly,
for I knew of the day of arrival.

Harwa's Maat thinking combines two traditional ideas: his heart has taught him, i.e. he is "inner-directed", and he expects to face the divine judgment, called "day of arrival". In text 35 (Djefaihapi) we had "that day of landing" *(hrw pf n mny)* in the same sense. On his statues VI and VII Harwa added the concept of "divine reward" to that of "divine judgment" (BIFAO 30, 806 & BIFAO 34, 137 &139, lines 8-9):

ir.n.i nw iw.i rḫ.kwi f3t.sn
isw.sn ḫr nb ḫt

I did these things knowing their weight,
and their reward from the Lord of Things.

Regarding the so often maligned "archaism" of Late Period inscriptions, it is worth observing how the skilled scribes made their planned and pondered choices from the vocabulary and phraseology of the Middle and New Kingdoms. In terms of Maat thinking, their method yielded, as we shall see, a coherent end-piece.

93) On his naophorous statue in Lyon, Nakht-hor-heb, an official of Amasis, has an autobiography with considerable factual interest. Having been made inspector of ports in the Delta, Nakht-hor-heb found that the temples in those outlying regions were in disrepair and lacked funds. Thereupon, on his own initiative, he devised the means to restore them. He also paid special attention to the temple of Neith at Sais. Here are lines 10-21 (Tresson, Kêmi 4, 1931/33, pp. 126ff. & pls. vii-ix; Posener, Douanes (1947), 121ff.; R. El-Sayed, Documents relatifs à Sais, p. 256):

ḥḥ.n.i 3ḫw n nṯrw m ib.i ḏs.i
smnḫ.n.i wḏḥw.sn m bw nb
wḏ.n ḥm.f rdi wn.i im m ḥq3.sn
wḏ wi ḥm.f m imi-r3 ʿ3w ḫ3swt w3ḏ-wr
gm.n(.i) ḥtpwt nt nṯrw pr(w) m bw pn tš
mn sw ḥr ib.i wr
ḥḥ.n ib.i sḫr nb n s3ḫ.sn
wnn(.i) ḥr smn sn r nḥḥ m wḏ.n ḥm.f
stn.n(.i) wḏḥw Nt s3w ḫnt.sn
n ir.n ky ẖr ḥ3t ḥntw m ib.i
wr sqr.f rʿ nb

In my own heart did I seek what would serve the gods,
and I endowed their offering-tables in every place
in which his majesty had appointed me their controller.
His majesty having made me overseer of portals of foreign sea-lands,
I found the offerings of the gods exhausted in that borderland,
and it grieved my heart greatly.
Then my heart sought all means to refit them,
and I established them forever at his majesty's command.
I singled out among them the offering-table of Neith of Sais,
no one previously having done what my heart devised,
so that its provisioning was ample every day.

Then he turns to the goddess (lines 24-28):

mwt nṯr nt ir ḥ3t pḥ

mt ir.n(.i) mn r nḥḥ
ir sp nfr r sw3ḥ.f
di ir s3 rᶜ Iᶜḥ-ms ḥb-sd ḥr st Ḥr
di sb.f wi m ḥtp m i3wt ᶜ3t nfrt
ḥs.k(wi) šw m ṯs.f
iḫ ḏd iy ḥr-s3
šms(w) Nt r im3ḫwt

Mother of god who made beginning and end!
Behold, I have done a work for eternity,
do you the good deed to make it last!
Grant the Son-of-Re Ahmes a jubilee on the Horus throne,
grant that he guide me in peace to good great age,
as one praised and free of his reproach!
May he who comes hereafter say:
"A servant of Neith till veneration day!"

Three things are noteworthy here. First, the stress laid on the ancient virtue of personal initiative. Second, the man's close attachment to "his" goddess, Neith of Sais. Third, the respectfully remote attitude toward the king. It is from the goddess that Nakht-hor-heb requests the continuing benevolence of the king! The king remains the center of power, but he is not the bearer of spiritual authority and comforting protection.

Among the biographical Serapeum stelae of priests who served the Apis there are two that use Maat-oriented terms to describe the priests' devotion as practiced in their nightly vigils and fasting during the Apis burial ceremonies, including the seventy day period of embalming. These are the stelae designed by the letters M and O in Vercoutter's publication, Textes biographiques du Serapéum de Memphis. Vercoutter dated them as Persian and Saito-Persian, respectively.

94) Stela SIM. 4030 (Vercoutter, text M, pp. 82ff. & pl. xii) has the usual scene of an Apis bull being adored, in this case by a kneeling shaven-headed man wearing a short kilt. Below is a coarsely carved 8-line text. Here are major portions of lines 3-8:

ink ḥm ir m3ᶜt nb.f
n ky ṯnw r.i
sḏr.i rs.kwi ḥr ḥḥy 3ḫwt nb n wᶜbt

sḫm.n.i k3t nb m ḥt-nbw
… …
s nb ḥr [dw3] nṯr ḥr
ḥsy pw n nṯr niwty.f
mr sw nṯr.f ḥr <irt>.f nb
isw ir skm ʿḥʿw
[m nḏm-ib] m-m im3ḫw
ẖrdw.f m-ḫt.f n sk

I am the servant who does his lord's Maat,
none other is better than I;
I lay awake devising what would serve the Wabet,
I guided all the work in the gold-house.
… …
Everyone [praised] god saying:
"A favorite of his town-god,
his god loves him for all he <has done>.
The reward: completing life [in gladness] among the revered,
his children after him unendingly."

The burial ceremonies of Apis were, as Vercoutter has explained, performed by the lower ranks of the priesthood of Ptah, with some participation of priesthoods from other towns. The strenuous service entailed vigil and fasting; and it was by taking part in the hardships of the service that priests and other persons were entitled to erect stelae for themselves in the Serapeum. Sometimes a high ranking official would join in the ceremonies and would leave a stela recording his participation.

95) Such a stela is SIM. 4112 (Vercoutter, text O, pp. 93ff. & pl. xiv). In lines 5-10 of the 17-line inscription, the many-titled official Wahibre-merneith outlined his moral portrait:
ink sʿḥ iqr ḫnt sp3wt
w3ḥ-ib rḫ bw-nfr
mʿr-spw iqr-sḫrw dns
ʿpr m rḫ gm ṯs m g3w.f
š3w ⌜qsn⌝ gm-gr ḥss m qi.f
ḏd nfr wḥm nfr

irt[4] ḥsst nṯr.f
irt[5] ḥsst nb.f
ir mr rmṯ
s m3ᶜ pw mr nṯrw nbw

I am a worthy noble, a leader in the nomes,
a thoughtful one who knows the good;
successful, resourceful, weighty,
knowledgeable, who finds the missing word,
a solver of problems, discreet, dignified.
Who speaks the good, repeats the good,
does what his god praises,
does what his lord praises,
does what people love:
A man of right, beloved of all the gods.

Once again the stress is on the ancient virtues of the responsible administrator who acts with efficiency and fairness because he knows what people require and what the gods wish to see done.

96) The naophorous statue of the priest Djedher, found at Heliopolis and now in Bayonne, was dated by H. de Meulenaere to the reign of Nectanebo I (BIFAO 61, 1962, 29ff.). Djedher identifies himself as a priest of Horus and Hathor, and a royal chamberlain. The inscription ends on the dorsal pillar and consists of three columns. In column 3 he addresses Hathor:
šfyt(t) ẖtmt ḥr ib(.i)
ir.n(.i) mr k3.t rᶜ nb
ink m3ᶜ-ib bwt grg
ir.n.i mrr rmṯ ḥsw nṯrw
ink im3-ib nfr-qiḥ n s nb
isw ẖr.t sq3i ᶜḥᶜw(.i)
m nḏm-ib m-m ḥsww nswt
mryt.i ḥr-ib n nb t3wy
qrst nfrt ---

[4]Redundant *t*.
[5]Redundant *t*.

My heart engraved with awe of you,
I did what your ka loves daily.
I am one truthful who abhors lying,
I did what people love and gods praise,
I was gracious and benign to all.
Your reward: to prolong my lifetime,
in gladness among the king's favorites,
love of me in the heart of the lord-of-the-two-lands,
and a good burial ---

Here, yet another royal official, one living in the final peaceful decades of the last native dynasty, affirms the key virtues of the traditional ethic - honesty and beneficence - and the traditional rewards besought from the gods.

97) The great stela of Somtutefnakht in Naples is of unusual historical interst on account of its allusions to the destruction of the Persian empire by Alexander the Great, even if to us moderns the overly discreet Egyptian manner of reporting great historical events is frustrating. The entire account of this man's life is cast in the form of an address to his god, Harsaphes, lord of Heracleopolis Magna, to whom he recalls the constant guidance and support which he received from the god (Tresson, BIFAO 30, 369ff.). In lines 5-7 he specifies his Maat doing and his piety:

ink ḥm.k ib.i ḥr mw.k
mḥ.n.i ib.i im.k
n sẖpr.n.i niwt wpw niwt.k
n wš.n.i m rdit b3w.s ḫr ḥr nb
ib.i ḥr ḥḥy bw m3ᶜ m pr.k rᶜ nb
ir.n.k n.i m nfr.sn n ḥḥ n sp

I am your servant, my heart is on your water,
I filled my heart with you.
I sustained no town except your town,
I failed not to place its might before all.
My heart sought what is right in your house every day,
and you gave me its reward a millionfold!

Lines 10-14 recall the great events:

You protected me in the combat of the Greeks,

when you repulsed those of Asia.
They slew a million at my sides,
and no one raised his arm against me.
Thereafter I saw you in my sleep,
your majesty saying to me:
"Hurry to Hnes, I protect you!"
I crossed the countries all alone,
I sailed the sea unfearing;
knowing I had not neglected your word,
I reached Hnes, my head not robbed of a hair.
As my beginning was good through you,
may you make my end complete,[6]
giving me a long life in gladness!

Once again, observe how Maat doing and piety are interwoven, and how close and trusting is the relationship between man and god.

98) In its very eclecticism, the sumptuous family tomb of Petosiris, high priest of Thoth at Hermopolis Magna, provides an outstanding summation of Egyptian moral thought in the Late Period. In his principal autobiographical inscription Petosiris reviewed his achievements as controller of the temple of Thoth. The whole text being addressed to future visitors of the tomb, Petosiris included a teaching on life-after-death, and a summation of the benefits which the god Thoth had bestowed on him (Lefebvre, Tombeau de Petosiris, inscr. 81, v. 1, 136ff., v. 2, 53ff.). Lines 16-24 read:

imntt dmy n iwty wn.f
dw3 nṯr n s pḥ sw
nn spr s nb r.s
wpw ib.f ʿq3 m ir(t) m3ʿt
n ṯnw wšw r bw3w
wpw gm.n.tw m iwty wn.f
iwsw ḥnʿ qdt m-b3ḥ nb nḥḥ
n šw n tm ḥsb.t(w).f
Ḏḥwty m ʿʿn ḥr mḫ3t
r ḥsb s nb m irt.n.f ḥr tp t3

---

[6]So with O. Perdu, RdE 36, 1985, 110.

wn.i ḥr mw n nb ẖmnw ḏr msw.i
sẖr.f nb wn m ib.i

The west is the abode of the blameless,
praise god for the man who reached it!
There is no man who attains it,
unless his heart is exact in right-doing.
Poor and rich are not distinguished,
only that one be found blameless.
Scale and weight being before eternity's lord,
none is exempt from being reckoned.
Thoth as baboon upon the balance
will reckon each man for his deeds on earth!
I was on the water of Khnum's lord since my birth,
I had all his counsel in my heart.

The admonition to be mindful of the Last Judgment is as forceful as the famous one in the Instruction to Merikare. And it shows that, over the span of two millennia, the basic understanding of Maat doing and its rewards had not changed.

99) While some ideas recur, each member of Petosiris' family has a distinctive speaking role. Here is Sishu, the father of Petosiris (Lefebvre, inscr. 116, v. 1, 158, v. 2, 83). Cols. 4-6:
iy.n.i dy r niwt nt nḥḥ
iri.i bw nfr tp t3
mḥ.i ib.i ḥr w3t nṯr
ḏr rnp.i r mn min
sḏr.n.i b3w.f m ib.i
dw3.n.i ḥr ir(t) mr k3.f
ir.n.i m3ᶜt bwt.n.i isft
iw.i rẖ.k(wi) ᶜnẖ.f im.s ḥtp.f ḥr.s
ir.n.i wᶜb 3b k3.f
n ẖnms.n.i ẖm b3w nṯr
rhn.n.tw n ir ḥr mw.f
n iṯ.i ẖt n rmṯ nb
nn ir.i sp ḏw r s
niwtyw nb ḥr dw3 nṯr n.i
ir.n.i nn iw.i sẖ3 spr nṯr m-ẖt nn
iw.i rẖ.k(wi) hrw n nbw m3ᶜt

r pẖ3.nw ẖr wḏ[c]
dw3 nṯr n mr nṯr
spr.f ḥt-k3.f n iyw

I came here to the town of eternity,
having done the good upon earth,
having filled my heart with god's way,
from my youth until this day.
I lay down with his might in my heart,
I arose to do his ka's wish,
I did right - despising wrong -
knowing he lives, and is pleased, by it.
I was the priest his ka desires,
I did not befriend one who knew not god's might,
but trusted one who acts on his water.
I did not rob another's goods,
I did no harm to any man,
all citizens praised god for me.
I acted thus, mindful of reaching god after this,
knowing the day of the lords of Maat,
when they separate in judgment!
One praises god for the lover of god,
he will reach his ka-mansion unharmed.

By now, all these formulations are familiar to us - with one exception, the term "Day of the Lords of Maat", to denote the Judgment of the Dead. I cannot cite a parallel for it. It is an impressive term that adds overtones to the usual formulations, "day of arrival", or, "day of judgment". Altogether, what one learns from the speech of Sishu is that it is an incisive summation of Maat thinking which reaffirms the basic ethical norms that had been outlined in the Old Kingdom, emphatically formulated in the Middle Kingdom, and modulated in the New Kingdom, the modulation consisting of the full integration of moralty and piety. The saying from Proverbs 1.7 and 9.10 (also Psalm 110/111), which heads this chapter, was cited by Lefebvre in his annotations to the speech of Sishu (v. 1, p. 160). I find it a perfect paraphrase of the interconnection between Egyptian wisdom thinking and piety, as worked out in the New Kingdom and maintained to the very end of pharaonic history.

Egyptian autobiographies reflect the teachings of Egyptian Wisdom Literature. For surveying that literature the reader is now well served by H.Brunner's new anthology, Altägyptische Weisheit, Lehren für das Leben (Zürich 1988). Now, in some current views on Egyptian Maat thinking, the "Wisdom of Amenemope" (the date of which is Ramesside or slightly later) appears especially significant, in particular chapter 20 with its somewhat baffling Maat saying:

ir m3ᶜt f3t ᶜ3t n nṯr
di.f sw n mr.f

As for Maat, great gift of god,
he gives it to whom he wishes.

In his Strasbourg lecture "Der freie Wille Gottes" (SPOA, 1963) Brunner drew from the saying two radical conclusions: 1. that it signified a view of God's free will which entailed unpredictability and even arbitrariness; 2. that by this saying the classical Maat thinking of the older wisdom literature, namely a generally available and teachable Maat, was set aside: "Das Maat Denken der älteren Weisheit ist aufgehoben" (p. 109). Brunner's thesis was vigorously opposed by Sainte Fare Garnot (ibid., pp. 118-120), and I have always thought (and said so in Late Eg. Wisdom Lit., 133f.) that Garnot's objections and suggestions were justified and should be taken into account. To some extent, a blending of the two views has come about in Brunner's pondered "Einführung" in the new volume cited above (see especially pp. 56ff.). At the same time, however, Jan Assmann has carried Brunner's original formulations to their logical conclusion by stating that the Amenemope passage signified "the disappearance of the concept of Maat", and the "replacement of wisdom by piety" ("State and Religion in the New Kingdom", Yale lecture, YES 3, 1989, 55ff., especially pp. 72-77). So also in the concluding chapter of his Collège de France lectures, Maât, l'Egypte pharaonique et l'idée de justice sociale (Paris 1989), and most recently in his Ma'at (Munich 1990), pp. 252ff., as "Ausgänge aus der Ma'at": "... Wenn der Wille Gottes an die Stelle dieser Ordnung tritt, verschwindet die Ma'at." (p. 252)

The sources here assembled do not support the thesis of the absorption of wisdom by piety and the concomittant disappearance of the concept of Maat. The texts cited in chapters 4-7 have formulated ever more emphatically that thinking about Maat was linked to thinking about the will of the gods. That will was not viewed as hidden, or unpredictable, or arbitrary; quite the contrary. The texts affirm over and over that a man knew what the god wished him to do. A man's heart taught him to distinguish right from wrong, and taught him that right-doing was what the gods desired.

As for the Maat saying of Amenemope, it should be read in the context of the chapter; the context is a stern warning to shun bribes, so as to be able to make correct judgments. It is followed by warnings against falsifying documents. Thus the Maat saying need be no more than the observation that not everyone is willing or able to judge fairly and act honestly. Moreover, to think of one's virtue as a "gift of god" was a popular notion current at all times. Amenemope's Maat saying should be placed alongside such statements as that of Rediu-khnum (text 18) who called himself "a precious timber made by the god", and that of Djedkhons-efankh (CG 559, J.-W., A 1, pp. 11 & 434.3-4):

Khnum fashioned me as one competent,
an adviser of excellent counsel;
he made my character superior to others,
he steered my tongue to excellence.

And consider PInsinger 13/4-5 where divine giving is combined with divine withholding:

Shame is the gift of the god in whom one trusts.
(or: Shame is the gift of the god <to> him whom one trusts).
He does not apportion it to the evil man, nor to the impious one.

In sum, the autobiographical voices here assembled have told in an ever swelling chorus that Maat thinking - the core of Wisdom - functioned in close alliance with piety. Wisdom and piety were partners in the endeavor to formulate and teach the right kind of living. Barely sketched in the Old Kingdom ("Doing the right thing is what the god desires", text 4) the partnership reached maturity in the New Kingdom and continued in full strength in Late Period autobiographies and wisdom texts.

The Maat thinking in the two major Late Period Demotic Instructions, Ankhsheshonqi and PInsinger, is entirely in keeping with the overall development. In Ankhsheshonqi, Maat in the form of *mt.t* $m3^{c}t$ occurs twice, in the sense of "justice" and "truth", respectively (5/5 & 13/15). Consider the saying in 5/5:

"If Pre is angry with a land, he makes justice cease in it."

Along with the lines that precede and follow, this is the description of a nation's perdition when its Maat has been destroyed.

In PInsinger $m3^{c}t$ and *mt.t* $m3^{c}t$ together appear six times, and the adjectives $m3^{c}$ and $m3^{c}y$ "true" and "justified", five times.

I had a deplorable lapse of memory when I wrote in my Late Egyptian Wisdom Literature (p. 39) that Maat is not used in Demotic Instructions. I wrote this sentence before I had indexed the occurrences of Maat (on pp. 58 & 172-174). It is unfortunate that this error of mine has now been compounded by Assmann's citing it (in his Ma'at, p. 254, n.39) as circumstantial support of his theory of the disappearance of Maat. But more significant than the perhaps somewhat perfunctory use of the term Maat in the Demotic Instructions is the fact that, to the very end of pharaonic history, Instructions and Autobiographies, by their insistent and detailed precepts and prohibitions, upheld the principle of man's personal initiative, responsibility, and accountability for doing right.

In conclusion, the reader is invited to reflect on the distance that separates, and the congruence that unites, ancient Egyptian thinking about Maat and the thoughts of this 18th century philosophic poet:

God in nature of each being founds
Its proper bliss, and sets its proper bounds:
But as he framed a Whole, the Whole to bless,
On mutual Wants built mutual Happiness:
So from the first, eternal ORDER ran,
And creature linked to creature, man to man.
(Alexander Pope, Essay on Man, III.109-14)

II

AUTOBIOGRAPHIES AND "NEGATIVE CONFESSIONS"

When Drioton published the stela of Baki, Turin Museum no. 156, (in Recueil Champollion, 1922, pp. 545-564) he viewed its text as a major source for the "Negative Confessions" of Book of the Dead chapter 125, and hence as significant evidence for the connection between the moral self-portraits of autobiographical inscriptions and the creation of the Negative Confessions. To him these Confessions were an isolated block of ethical thinking in the mass of magical spells that constitute the Book of the Dead; they possessed a "doctrine morale élevée" and thus were an "îlot de dogmatique très pure perdu dans une mer immense de textes magiques". His aim, then, was to reconstruct the path by which these ethical statements had entered the BD. However, apart from the famous passage on the Judgment of the Dead in the "Instructions for Merikare" his harvest of bridge-building texts was very meager, and he wondered why this should be so.

Spiegel, in Die Idee vom Totengericht (1935) took up the same question from a different angle. His argument was designed to show that the concept of a judgment of the dead was originally a purely ethical one, with judgment rendered by the sungod Re, the upholder of justice. It was the growth of the Osirian faith that fostered a magical reinterpretation of the judgment, such as dominates in the Book of the Dead. The Negative Confessions, he argued, derived directly from the moral self-presentations of Middle Kingdom autobiographies and thus preserved the ethical character of the judgment: "Dieser Ursprung der sog. Konfessionen des 125. Kapitels aus der Idealbiographie des Mittleren Reiches, der sich in ihrer Struktur zeigt, lässt sich nun auch formal beweisen..." (p.60). Though coherent and plausible, Spiegel's reasoning was yet not based firmly, because his harvest of terms and phrases relevant to the Confessions as found in BD 125, though larger than Drioton's, was still very scant. His main witnesses were the same as Drioton's: the stela of Baki (for which he gave a good translation) and the passage on the judgment in Merikare. In addition he cited the tomb text of Pepinakht (Urk. I, 132) and the stela of Mentuwosre (Sethe, Les. no. 19) as Old and Middle Kingdom witnesses for the growth of ethical self-presentations in autobiographies.

The third scholar who dealt with the text of Baki, Varille (in BIFAO 54, 1954, 129-135 & pl.) provided a much needed photograph of the stela, reproduced here (Illus. 2). Varille was not concerned with the relationship of Baki's declarations to the Negative Confessions of BD 125, for to him Baki was a mystic whose ethic was shared by other 18th dynasty officials. He also disputed Drioton's dating of the stela to the early 18th dynasty and argued that the stela belonged in the reign of Amenhotep III (both scholars having observed the erasure of the name of Amun in the offering formula, which provided the terminus ante quem) on the grounds that it showed "le même style épigraphique et la même technique de gravure" as the stelae of Ptahmes, Surer, and Sobeknakht, all three from the reign of Amenhotep III.

I have looked at the three stelae (Ptahmes, ed.Varille, BIFAO 30, 497ff.; Surer, ed. Chevrier, ASAE 50, pl. 12, and Sauneron, ASAE 52, 145, also Urk. IV, 1896; Sobeknakht, Dyroff-Poertner, Grabsteine, II, München 1904, pl. XII, 17); they seem to me entirely unlike the stela of Baki. All three have the ornate and crowded iconography typical of the reign of Amenhotep III. The surfaces are filled with multiple adoration scenes, and figures of relatives, the whole divided into many registers, whereas Baki sits quite alone, his left arm clasped on the chest, in the upper left corner, separated from the offering table by three text columns of the offering formula. In fact, the bareness of Baki's iconography is most unusual, though it does agree with the peculiar vagueness of his text, which fills the lower portion in fifteen lines.

The stela of Baki was translated three more times: by Daumas in Etudes carmélitaines, 31e année, 1952, pp. 105-107; by Roeder in Ägyptische Religion, 4: Reformation, Zauberei und Jenseitsglauben (1961), pp. 243-250; and by Assmann, Maât (1989), pp. 91-93, and Ma'at (1990), pp. 154-156. I reexamine the stela's iconography, text, and dating later in this study. First I want to consider Drioton's question posed nearly seventy years ago, to which, as far as I know, no answer built on a textual documentation ample enough to carry conviction has yet been given: What is the connection between the moral self-laudations of Autobiographies and the Negative Confessions of BD 125? The question could also be phrased: Is there a connection between the two? For I have gained the impression that the existence of a connection is not generally assumed. Nor do the current standard translations of the Book of the Dead, those of Barguet, Faulkner, and Hornung, discuss the literary origins and affinities of BD 125.

The principal formal difference between the Negative Confessions (or, Declarations of Innocence) of BD 125 and the moral self-laudations of private autobiographies is that the latter are predominantly phrased as positive statements of good character and right action, whereas the former are disclaimers of wrongdoing. Keeping this difference in mind, we shall observe the gradual appearance in autobiographies of disclaimers of wrongdoing, i.e. of negatively phrased self-praises. We shall also follow up the concept of the Judgment of the Dead as found in autobiographical and other sources since the 11th dynasty.

As I showed in my Autobiographies (p. 62f.) the Ny Carlsberg 963 stela of Intef speaks of the Judgment in the context of afterlife wishes belonging to the "Abydos Formula":

May he arrive at the divine council,
at the place where the gods are,
may his ka be with him, his offerings before him,
his voice found true in the reckoning of the excess:
"Tell your wrong and it will be removed from you
with all you have told."

This looks like an ethical approach to the judgment: vindication will be obtained by a confession of faults. Yet the fact that this advice to the deceased is embedded in ritual afterlife wishes, and the existence of Coffin Text phrases in which the dead person speaks of purifying himself of his faults (spells 296 & 306), or of having them removed by the gods (spells 44, 73, 335) suggest the close proximity of the magical approach to vindication. See Grieshammer's thorough discussion in his Jenseitsgericht in den Sargtexten (1970), pp. 46ff., and 56ff. For a strictly ethical view of the Judgment one turns to the famous passage in the Instruction to King Merikare (P.St.Petersburg 1116A, 53ff.):

The Court that judges the distressed,
you know they are not lenient
on the day of judging the poor man,
in the hour of doing their task.
etc.

Thus, at the beginning of the Middle Kingdom, the concept of a judgment of the dead is documented in three kinds of literary sources. 1. in the didactic genre: Merikare; 2. in Autobiographies: stela of Intef; 3. in mortuary literature: Coffin Texts. The approach to the judgment is wholly ethical in Merikare; more or less ethical in the stela of Intef; and largely magical in the Coffin Texts. But even the magical practice had an ethical basis, as Grieshammer rightly stressed: "Wir halten also fest, dass die Sargtexte zwar noch keine negativen Konfessionen kennen, dass ihnen die "Ableugnung" genereller negativer Qualitäten ... und die Notwendigkeit, der Maat gedient zu haben, als Voraussetzung für ein seliges Dasein im Jenseits durchaus vertraut sind." (Jenseitsgericht, p. 63)

Negative Declarations from Autobiographies in the Old and Middle Kingdoms

1) Tomb inscription of Hetep-her-akht(i) (Urk. I, 50.1f.; also Urk. I, 69; and see Maat study, texts 3 & 4):

ir.n(.i) is pw m išt(.i) m3^{c}
n sp iṯy(.i) ḫt nt rmṯ nb

I have made this tomb from my rightful means,
and never took the property of anyone.

2) Tomb inscription of Seshem-nefer (Urk. I, 57.15f.; Maat study, text 2):

wn(.i) ḏd(.i) ḫr nswt 3ḫ n rmṯ
n sp ḏd(.i) ḫt nb ḏw r rmṯ nb
ḫr ḥm n nb(.i)

I used to tell the king what serves people,
I never told an evil thing against people
to the majesty of my lord.

3) Tomb inscription of Nekhebu (Urk. I, 219.6f.):

ink d̲d nfrt wḥm nfrt
n sp d̲d(.i) ḫt nb d̲w r rmt̲ nb

I am one who speaks the good, repeats the good,
I never said an evil thing against people.

The three two-part statements are representative of the Old Kingdom manner of combining a positive statement with a negative one in such a way that the negative declaration is the reverse of the positive one and thereby serves to complement it. There are some variations to this pattern, for instance a negative declaration might appear in isolation. Basically, however, the rule holds that negative declarations directly match the positive ones. But altogether, there are far fewer negative declarations than positive ones.

In the 11th dynasty, when autobiographies turned into character studies, and the moral vocabulary grew by leaps and bounds, new sequences of positive and negative declarations were formulated. The chamberlain Henun ended his self-portrait with this quatrain (TPPI no. 24; Maat study, text 19):

4) nn isft prt m r3(.i)
nn d̲wt irt.n ʿwy
ink ir qd.f
mrrw rmt̲ m h̲rt-hrw nt rʿ nb

There was no falseness that came from my mouth,
no evil that was done by my hands;
I am one who made his character,
one beloved of people each day.

Denials of having done wrong are interspersed. Here is Intef son of Tjefi (MMA 57.95; Maat study, text 20):

5) ink wʿ n nb.f
šw m isft
dd mdt r wn.s m3ʿ
I am the sole one of his lord,
free of wrongdoing,
who puts a matter rightly.

In the Hatnub graffito no. 10 (Maat study, text 23) we had the four-line portrait of a sweet-tempered man:

6) ink sš n ẖrt-ib
qb-ẖt d3r-srf
dw3 sw3.f ḥr.f
šw m šnt nṯr

I am a scribe who pleases,
cool-bellied, calm-tempered,
who salutes the passerby,
and is free of profanation.

In addition to *šw m isft* and *šw m šnt-nṯr,* we have encountered (in Maat study, text 26) *šw m snkt,* "free of glumness".

In the late 11th and early 12th dynasties the portrayals of good moral character reach their peak, and do so in phrasing that remains eminently positive; that is to say, denials of wrongdoing continue to be used sparingly although there is an overall increase. The denials are mainly blanket denials of all wrongdoing:

7) I am one who loves good, hates evil,
with whom none stayed angry overnight.
No falsehood came from my mouth,
no evil was done by my hands.
(Rudjahau, BM 159; Lichtheim, Autobiographies, no. 29)

7a) I committed no crime against people
- a thing hateful to the god -
I buried the old ones of my town ...
(Wepwawet-aa, Leiden V 4; Autobiographies, no.31)

The steward Mentuwosre (MMA 12.184; Autobiographies, no. 44) added a threefold negative declaration to his long statement of positive accomplishments; each of the three embodies a major theme of Egyptian morality:

8) n isq.i s m mẖnt
n ds.i s n wsr r.f
n ꜥḥꜥ.i ḥr n nḏwyt

I hindered no man at the ferry,
I maligned no man to his superior,
I paid no heed to calumny.

One generation later, in the reign of Amenemhet II, the chamberlain Semti the Younger (HTBM II, 8-9, no. 574; Maat study, text 33) in appealing to future visitors to be kind to his monument, made the specific connection between his right-doing on earth and his hope for a blessed life in the beyond:

9) Be gentle to my memorial!
for I have not done wrong,
I gladdened the god with right,
so as to be yonder ensouled transfigured,
in the desert, mistress of eternity,
to take the helm on boarding the neshmet,
to kiss the ground to Wepwawet!

* * *

The 18th dynasty writers took over many features of the 12th dynasty autobiographies. In addition, they developed two themes which began to take shape at the end of the Middle Kingdom: large visions of the life-after-death, and every individual person's direct approach to the gods.

Afterlife Wishes and Self-Justifications in 18th Dynasty Autobiographies

10) Stela of the scribe Weser (Brussels E 2162, Limme, Stèles, p.25 & pl.; early 18th dynasty). Couple seated at offering table, sons carry libations. Below, text in seven lines. Good workmanship. The offering formula invokes the triad Osiris-Hathor-Anubis:

May they grant 1000 bread, 1000 beer,
1000 beef, 1000 fowl, 1000 ointment & clothing,
1000 incense, 1000 unguent, 1000 loaves, 1000 foods,
1000 of all things good and pure
in food and plant offerings,
that sky gives, earth produces,
and Hapy brings from his hole;

to drink water at the river's edge,
inhale sweet breeze of the westwind,
come and go as living Ba
to get what is given on earth
at every feast of the living,
for the ka of the scribe Weser, justified.
He says:

iw.i iy.kwi r niwt <nt> nḥḥ
r smyt nt ḏt
n srḫ.t(w).i n gm.tw wn.i
n ḏd.i grg r ky

I have come to the town of eternity,
to the desert of everlastingness,
not having been accused, not having been faulted,
not having lied to another.

11) Final section of the great stela of the granary chief Ineni in the portico of his tomb (TT 81, Urk. IV, 61-62. Reigns of Amenhotep I - Thutmosis III):

ḏd.i n.ṯn rmṯ sḏmw
ir.ṯn bw nfr ir.n.i
ir <n>.ṯn mitt
sbt.i ꜥḥꜥw m ḥtp n ḫpr bt3w.i
rnpwt.i m nḏm-ib nn šntyw.i
nn srḫ.i nn kt.i nn ḏbꜥw.i
ink sḫm sḫmw n ḫpr sk.i
mnḫ-ib n nb.f šw m bg3
ink sḏm ḏdt.n ḥry-tp.f
n bq ib.i r wrw imiw ꜥḥ
iw ir.n.i mrrt nṯr niwty
šw.i m ḏ3t-r3 ḥr ḫt nṯr
ir skk rnpwt m ḥsy
wnn b3.f ꜥnḫ r-ꜥ nb-r-ḏr
rn.f nfr m r3 ꜥnḫw
sḫ3.t(w).f 3ḫ.f n ḏt

I speak to you, people, listen!
If you do the good I did,
the same will be done for you!

I passed the span of life in peace, without a crime,
my years in heart's delight, without an enemy,
without accuser, unfaulted, unreproached.

I was a leader of leaders, I failed not,
one devoted to his lord, who tired not;
I was one who heard his master's word,
and was not arrogant to the great men of the palace.
I have done what my town-god desired,
and did not covet his possessions.

He who passes the years as a praised one,
his Ba will live at the side of the all-lord;
his good name in the mouth of the living,
he is remembered and blessed forever!

12) In a ceiling inscription of his tomb the same Ineni invokes the day of judgment (Urk. IV, 66-67):

ink sʿḥ gr ⌜spẖ⌝-ib[7]
šw m sẖm-ib
wnn rn.i mn ḥr bi3wt(.i)
r-ḏ3wt irt.n(.i) tp t3
s3ẖ.tw n3(.i) m-ẖt mny
m-m irw 3ẖt
wnn ẖrw(.i) m3ʿ m wsẖt
ink is m3ʿ-ẖrw tp t3

I am a noble, silent, ⌜modest⌝,
free of violence;
may my name endure through my conduct,
in accord with my actions on earth!
May my Ba be potent after death,
among those who rendered service;

---

[7]Sethe, Urk. IV, 66 Übers. read "*spẖ-ib,* bescheiden (?)", a reading which did not get into the Wb.

may my voice be found true in the Hall,
for I was one true-voiced on earth!

This brief evocation of the judgment is significant; for in the first half of the 18th dynasty such allusions are still rare, whereas large visions of a hale life in the beyond now abound in the autobiographies.

Thus Paheri on his great tomb stela at El-Kab (reigns of Thutmosis I-II) has an expansive vision of his free roaming in the beyond, to which he added an allusion to the judgment phrased in such a way as to brush it aside (Urk. IV, 116.9-10):

13) ẖnm.k wsḫt nt m3ᶜty
wšd tw nṯr im.s

You will reach the Hall of the Two Truths,
and the god within it will greet you!

Later, speaking of his excellent standing at court, he passes a hypothetical judgment among the living (the sentence has been mistranslated sometimes through not recognising its hypothetical character):

dd.kwi ḥr mḫ3t
pr.[n.i] [s]ip.kwi mḥ.kwi wḏ3.kwi

Were I to be placed on the balance,
I would come out judged whole and sound.
(Urk. IV, 119.10-11)

As we move forward in the 18th dynasty, we shall observe that autobiographical denials of wrongdoing become increasingly prominent.

Here are the self-presentations of a father and a son, the two viziers Ahmes-Ametju and Weser.

14) On the ceiling of the portico of his tomb the vizier Ahmes-Ametju had a four-part set of afterlife wishes and self-justifications much of which is now destroyed (TT 83, time of Hatshepsut/Thutmosis III; Urk. IV, 490-492). Part A, after some half-destroyed afterlife wishes reads:

n ḥw.f it.f
n sḥwr.f mwt.f

iw ir.n.f ḥsst nswt
m h̲rt hrw nt rʿ nb
bwt.f grg n ir.f sw
n wnm.f bwt nt̲rw
drp.tw.f ḫr nt̲rw ḥr ḫ3wt Rʿ
rʿ nb d̲t r nḥḥ

He did not beat his father,
he did not revile his mother,
he has done what the king praises
in the course of every day.
He abhorred lying, he did not do it,
he did not eat what the gods abhor:
May he be nourished with the gods from Re's altar,
every day and for all time!

Note that the two quatrains are spoken in the third person, as if said by a tribunal that is granting the desired justification. Do these "negative confessions" not come close to the tone and manner of BD 125?

15) Stela of the vizier Weser in Grenoble (probably from TT 131; PM I^2, 247, reign of Thutmosis III; Urk. IV, 1030-1033). The text has three parts: offering formula, career narration, appeal to the living. The career narration tells of his priestly functions which preceded his appointment to the vizierate (Urk. IV, 1031, and see the improved text and translation of the section in J.-M. Kruchten, Les annales des prêtres de Karnak, p. 188f., from which I profited):

ink sʿḥ iqr
iw ir.n(.i) wʿb ʿq m ḥt-nt̲r nt Imn
di.n(.i) md̲t r ḥʿw nt̲r
sh̲kr.n(.i) Imn-Min
iw rmn.n(.i) Imn m ḥb.f
t̲s.n(.i) Min r rdw.f
n q3(.i) rmn m pr nb ksw
n f3(.i)-ʿ m pr f3-ʿ
n q3(.i) ḫrw m pr nb sgr
n d̲d(.i) grgw m pr nb m3ʿt
n nm.i m wʿbt n i(t)-nt̲r
n d̲3(.i) r3 ḥr ḥtpw-nt̲r.f

iw ir.n(.i) wꜥb ṯs(w)
sḏm sḏmt wꜥ m wꜥꜥw
n pr.i ẖr mdwt pr nswt
sḫnt.n iqr(.i) st(.i)
bs.kw(i) r i3wt ṯn mnḫt
r imi-r3 niwt ṯ3ty Wsr

I am a worthy noble:
I have been a priest who enters the temple of Amun;
I gave oil to the god's body,
I adorned Amun-Min.
I carried Amun in his feast,
I raised up Min on his platform.
I did not stand tall in the house of the lord of bowings,
I did not raise the arm in the house of the arm-raiser,
I did not lift the voice in the house of the lord of silence,
I did not tell lies in the house of the lord of Maat.
I did not steal from the kitchen of the 'divine father',
I did not covet his divine offering.
I also served as ranking priest,
who hears what is heard alone in privacy,
and I did not reveal palace affairs.
My worth advanced my position,
so that I was inducted to this potent office
of mayor-of-the-city and vizier - Weser.

Here we have a striking set of "negative confessions". But does it advance our understanding if the declarations are cited as examples of "fruits défendus", as Montet did in his contribution to the Strasbourg Colloquium, Les sagesses du proche-orient ancien (1963)? Surely there were taboos, and surely the Papyrus Jumilhac, adduced by Montet, is a significant source for them. But what the vizier Weser is saying amounts to stating basic rules of propriety in temple service. He formulated them with effective rhetoric as the negative and unacceptable opposites to the required behavior. Nor do the proscribed actions have to do with ritual purity; the vizier is saying that he did not shout, lie, and steal!

As before, the ethical declarations continue to be formulated primarily in positive terms, but they are accompanied by an increasing number of negatively phrased statements. And more often than not, the place in the autobiography in which negative declarations appear is that part in which entry into the hereafter is visualized; or they are clustered in addresses to the gods and appeals to posterity.

16) On the great stela of Menkheper (Urk. IV, 1190-1200) there are several clusters of negative declarations. Here is the final one, which is appended to the "arrival at the graveyard" (Urk. IV, 1199):

iy.n.i r niwt.i nt ẖrt-nṯr
nn rqy.i tp t3
n dr(.i) iwʿw ḥr nst.f
nn sm3r.i
nn iṯ(.i) ḫt nt ḥwrw

I have come to my town of the graveyard,
without having rebelled on earth.
I did not drive an heir from his seat,
I did not cause poverty,
I did not rob the poor.

17) Also in the context of arrival at the graveyard, the architect *P3-ḥq3-mn* employed a triple negative declaration to recall his loyalty to the king (TT 343, Thutmosis III - Amenhotep II; Urk. IV, 1470):

iw.i iy.kwi r niwt.i nt nḥḥ
r smt.i nt ḏt
iw šms.n.i nṯr nfr
n iw sp n sk.i
n srḫ.i
n gm wn.i
ḥs [wi] [mr] wi nb.i ḥr mnḫ.i

I have come to my town of eternity,
my desert of everlastingness,
having followed the good god,
without a failure of mine;
I was not blamed,
no fault of mine was found,
my lord praised and loved me for my excellence.

A different context for denials of wrongdoing is offered by the tomb inscription of Amenemhet, first prophet of Amun (TT 97; Gardiner, ZÄS 47, 87ff.; Urk.IV, 1408-1411; reign of Amenhotep II [?]). Amenemhet addresses his descendants in a "teaching" and describes his youth when, taught by his father, he began to serve in the temple administration (Urk. IV, 1408-1409):

18) ḏd.f m sb3yt ẖr msw.f
ḏd.i swt di.i sḏm.tn ḫprt ẖr.i ḏr hrw tpy
ḏr prt.i m wʿrty mwt.i
wn(.i) m wʿb md n i3wt
m-ʿ it(.i) m wn.f tp t3
iw pr.i h3(.i) ẖr wḏ.f
n th(.i) prw n r3.f
n ḥḏ(.i) š3t.n.f ẖr.i
n mkḥ3.i ḥr wḏdt m ḥr.i
n stwt(.i) sw m gmḥw ʿš3w
ḥr.i m ẖr.i mdw.f ẖr.i
n sẖm.i m irt ḫmt.n.f
n rẖ.i ḥmt nt pr.f
n sḏ3m.i mtḥnt.f
n sḥwr.i wdpw.f
n ʿq.i ḥr.f m ʿḥ3
ḥs.n.f wi n gm.f wn.i

He spoke in a teaching to his children:
I speak to let you hear how I fared from day One,
since I issued from my mother's thighs;
I was priest and staff-of-old-age
to my father while he was on earth.
I came and went by his command,
and did not disregard his orders;
I did not damage what he assigned to me,
did not neglect what he enjoined on me;
I did not shoot many glances at him,
I faced down when he spoke to me.
I did not dare to act without his knowledge,
I did not sleep with a servant of his house,
I did not impregnate his concubine,
I did not revile his cup-bearer,

nor assault him by force.
He praised me for he found no fault with me ...

This "teaching" exemplifies how the genre Instructions *(sb3yt)* was adapted to autobiographical statements which in turn served as instructions. As for the denials of wrongdoing, they voice elements of the realistic traditional ethic.

19) The Karnak statue of Amenhotep son of Hapu that portrays him in his old age (CG 42127) was, by the favor of his royal master Amenhotep III, destined to be placed in the temple of Amun. Hence its text is wholly conceived as a prayer and address to Amun, in which the old man, heavy with years and honors, claims the favor of the god as due to a man fully deserving of it. (Legrain, Statues, I, pp. 78-80 & pl. 76; Urk. IV, 1827-1828; Varille, Inscriptions concernant l'architecte Amenhotep fils de Hapou, pp. 6-8 & pl. I). The main text is inscribed on the kilt. In line 3, where Varille's reading differs from Helck's and yields a better sense, I have adopted it. Here are lines 1-9 of the 11-line text:

(1) rpᶜt ḥ3ty-ᶜ sḏ3wty-bity sš nswt sš nfrw Imnḥtp s3 Ḥpw n km-wr ḏd.f
iy.n.i n.k r snm k3.k
r wnn m r3-pr.k
Imn p3wty t3wy
ntk nb n nty ẖr pt
(3) m nṯr ḥmmt
nty m pt ḥr sw3š nfrw.k
n wr.k r nṯr nb
i3w(.i) nfrw.k sḏm.k nis
ntk is Rᶜ nn ḥr ẖw.f
di.k wn.i m-m ḥsyw
iryw m3ᶜt ink m3ᶜ

(5) n rdi.n.i ḥr gs
n sm3.n.i m ir bw-ḏw
n rdi.i ᶜnẖ ḥr qsn.f
m nty r ẖt.i ḥr k3wt
n nis s pw m tp-m3ᶜ.i
mkḥ3.i r sḏm ḏd.f
n rdi(.i) irt ḥ3w

n ḫʿm.i (7) ir n.i
n rd.i ḥr.i r sḏm iwms
r sḏwy ky m ḥryw.f

iw qd.i mtr.f iryt n.i
iww m-b3ḥ ḥr nb
in m33 wi nḥ.t(y)f(y) mi qd.i
n wr ḫprwt n.i
mtr (9) n m3ʿt m i3w.i
pḥ.i rnpt 80 wr ḥsw ḫr nswt
iw.i r kmt rnpt 110

The prince, count, royal seal-bearer, royal scribe, scribe of recruits, Amenhotep son of Hapu, of the nome of Athribis, says:
I come to you to worship your ka,
and to abide in your temple,
Amun, oldest of the Two-Lands!
You are lord of what is under sky
(3) of gods and mankind.
Sky-dwellers acclaim your beauty,
for you are the greatest of gods!
I hail your beauty, hear the caller,
for you are Re beside whom there is none!
Grant me to be among the favored,
the doers of right - I am righteous!

(5) I was not partial,
nor allied with the evil-doer.
I did not swear at one in pain
of those under my control in building-works.
If a man called out at my side,
I did not neglect to hear what he said.
I did not impose extra work,
nor did I press (7) one who worked for me.
I did not pay heed to calumny,
so as to slander a man to his superiors.

My repute bears witness to the things done for me,
they are before all people.

He who sees me will pray to be like me
because of all that accrued to me.
Witness (9) to the truth is my old age:
having reached 80 years greatly favored by the king,
I may yet complete year one-hundred-and-ten!

20) Also in the reign of Amenhotep III, Haremhab, another scribe of recruits, inscribed his Theban tomb with an autobiography which is integrated with the weighing-of-the-heart scene in the netherworld, the scene that served as the standard vignette for the text of BD 125. The weighing on the scales, attended by the gods, is drawn on the tomb wall in such a way that the text columns of the autobiography loom behind the balance, as if the words were actually being weighed! Scene and text are located in the passage leading from the main hall into the inner room, where they follow after scenes of the funeral procession. The text in 17 columns, some of them damaged, consists of a prayer to Osiris; a self-presentation in which Haremhab summarizes his services to three kings and declares his moral soundness; and a concluding appeal to the gods for their grace and benignity. (TT 78, PM I^{2}, p. 155 (11); Urk. IV, 1589-1590; and see the full publication of the tomb by A. & A. Brack, Das Grab des Haremheb, Theben Nr.78, Mainz 1980, text 35, p. 51f. & pl. 65a & 90a). The text reads:

(1) rdi(t) i3w n Wsir Ḫnt-imntt
sn-t3 n Wnn-nfr nb 3bḏw
nṯr ꜥ3 nb pt
(3) di.i n.k i3w nṯr nfr pn
ḥs(w).k rꜥ nb
iw(.i) <m> šmsw nṯr nfr nb-t3wy ꜥ3-ḫprw-rꜥ di ꜥnḫ
s3.f mr.f nb-ḫꜥw Mn-ḫprw-rꜥ di ꜥnḫ
(5) s3.f mr.f nb-n-ḫ3st Nb-m3ꜥt-rꜥ s3 Rꜥ Imn-ḥtp ḥq3 w3st mr Imn
nn ḥḏ r ḏd.sn nb
n ḏd rmṯ iry ptr irt n.n
nn wn bt3w(.i)
n ḫpr srḫ(.i)
n iw (7) grg.i ḥ3.i ḏr mswt.i
wp.i ḥr irt m3ꜥt n nb ḏr
ink is w3ḥ-ib ḫr nṯr
wḏ3-ib wḏ3-r3 wḏ3-ḏrwt

imi wḏ3 ib.tn (9) nbw nḥḥ
3ḫw mnḫw nw ẖrt-nṯr
mtn iy.n(.i) m t3 pn ᶜnḫw
r wnn ḥnᶜ.tn m t3 ḏsr
ink wᶜ im.tn bwt(.i) (11) isft
iy.n.i ḥr mtn nfr n ᶜq3y-ib
n mrw (13) swḏ3 ᶜwt(.i) nbt
iḫ ᶜnḫ b3.i nṯry
ᶜ3 3ḫ špsy
Wsir ---
i nṯrw imiw pt
i nṯrw imiw t3
i nṯrw imiw d3t
i nṯrw nbw sqd
(15) ẖnyw Rᶜ
sṯ3yw nṯr ᶜ3 r 3ḫt.f
sᶜr.tn mdw.i n nb nḥḥ
m sprt n b3k n nb.f
di.f ḥtp(.i) m st(.i) n nḥḥ
tpḥt n ḏt ... ---

(1) Giving praise to Osiris Khentamenthes,
kissing earth to Wenennofer, lord of Abydos,
great god, lord of heaven!
(3) I adore you, o good god,
be you praised every day!
I was a follower of the good god, Lord of the Two-Lands,
Aakheprure, given life,
and his beloved son, Lord of Crowns, Menkheprure, given life,
(5) and his beloved son, Lord of foreign lands, Nebmaatre,
son of Re, Amenhotep, lord of Thebes, beloved of Amun,
without faulting an order of theirs,
no man of theirs having said, "what has been done to us?"
There was no crime of mine,
there was no accuser of mine,
no lie of mine (7) pursued me since I was born,
rather did I do right for the all-lord!
For I was steadfast before the god,
hale of heart, hale of mouth, hale of hands!

Be you pleased, (9) you lords of eternity,
and you worthy spirits of the graveyard!
Behold I have come from the land of the living,
to abide with you in the sacred land.
I am one of you, I abhor (11) wrongdoing,
I have come on the good path of uprightness,
that (13) all my limbs may be sound,
that my Ba may live as divine,
great, potent, and noble!
Osiris ---

O gods in heaven,
o gods on earth,
o gods in Dat,
o gods, lords of the voyage,
(15) rowers of Re,
who convey the great god to his lightland:
Raise up my speech to the lord of eternity,
the plea of a servant to his lord:
May he grant my resting in my place of eternity,
the cavern of everlastingness!
... ---

Viewing texts 19 and 20 together brings out the difference in tone and purpose. A high official's portrait statue destined for a temple was not the usual place for voicing one's hopes for the after-life. Rather did it serve to remind gods and men of one's worthy personality now abiding in effigy in the temple. The private tombs, on the other hand, became increasingly the focus for extended afterlife visions and wishes. And this being the time when the spells of the Book of the Dead were formulated, assembled, and illustrated by vignettes, it followed easily that individual BD spells and scenes were incorporated in the schemes of tomb decoration. Their occurrence in 18th dynasty private tombs has been surveyed most usefully by M. Saleh in his Das Totenbuch in den thebanischen Beamtengräbern des NR (1984); see also Chr. Seeber, Untersuchungen zur Darstellung des Totengerichtes im alten Ägypten (1976). Having first appeared in the subterranean parts of the tomb, in the second half of the 18th dynasty they are found increasingly in the upper rooms and passages. Hence we encountered the weighing of the heart scene in the tomb of Haremhab, joined to his autobiography. That means the union of the two spheres: the ethically conceived self-presentation, now much concerned with the idea of judgment, and the depiction of the judgment in the magical framework of BD 125.

21) The chief of granaries, Khaemhet, he too an official of king Amenhotep III, inscribed his Theban tomb with four spells from the Book of the Dead, numbers 110, 112, 113, and 117, that are designed to enable the deceased to roam freely in the regions of the beyond. They are placed in the passage connecting the outer hall with the inner room; and there also, on the right-hand side of the passage, is the tomb-owner's autobiography. It consists of three parts: First, a lengthy appeal to the living, addressed specifically to those able to read. Second, a self-presentation phrased in the third person instead of the usual first-person speech. It includes his coming before the divine tribunal in the "Hall of the Two Truths", undergoing the examination by means of the balance, and being found justified - the whole narrated in the past tense. Third, a sequence of prayers to several gods, also formulated in the third person and bearing the heading "recitation" *(ḏd mdw)*. Here are portions of parts 1 and 2 (TT 57, PM I^2, 113ff., esp. 118 (21)-(23); Varille, ASAE 40, 601ff.; Urk. IV, 1845-1849).

The Appeal (Urk. IV, 1845.8-1846.3):

ḏd.f ḥr rmṯ ḫprt(y).sn
ḥryw t3 m wrw kttyw
sš nb wḥʿw ḏrf
spdw-ḥr m mdw nṯr
wnfw-ib ʿqw m rḫ
ḥtpw ḥr spw n 3ḫt
sw3t(y).sn ḥr ḥt tn
ir.n(.i) r-ḫnt 3ḫw
... ...
ḏd.k3.tn ḥtp di nswt
Imn Tm Ḥr-3ḫty Ptḥ Skr Wsir Inpw
itrty šmʿ t3-mḥw
n k3 n mḥ-ib n nṯr nfr
sš nswt imi-r šnwty ... Ḫʿ-m-ḥ3t m3ʿ-ḫrw
... ...

He speaks to the people who will be,
and those on earth, great and small,
all the scribes skilled in script,
perceptive in the written word,
joyful in acquiring knowledge,
who delight in things of value,
who shall pass by this abode,
which I made among the spirits,
... ...
You shall say, A royal offering
to Amun, Atum, Harakhty, Ptah, Sokar, Osiris, Anubis,
and the temples, south and north,
for the ka of the trusty of the good god,
the royal scribe and chief of granaries ... Khaemhet, justified.
... ...

Self-praise (Urk. IV, 1846.6-16):
ḥḏ-ḥr pẖr-ib ir-3ḫt
iw.f dd.f snṯr ḥr st3t n nṯr nb
rḫ.n.f rnw.sn
sm3ᶜ.n.f wdnw nty ḥr.s m ḫt nb nfrt wᶜbt
iw.f drp.f n 3ḫw
stt.f mw n ntyw im
r3.f mḥ m iy.wy iy.wy m t ḥnqt n ḥr nb
iw ḥnq.n.f m3ᶜt n nswt
s3wš.n.f Ḥr nb ᶜḥ
swt nis.t(w) rn.f m-ḫnt m mnḫ
ᶜq3-ib mty-ḥ3ty

One generous, considerate, beneficent,
he used to place incense on the censer of each god,
knowing their names,
and made an offering on it of all good things.
He used to offer to the spirits,
he poured water to those who are yonder,
calling out "come, come", with bread and beer for all.
He has offered Maat to the king,
and adored Horus, lord of the palace;
his name was called within as one worthy,
upright and straightforward.

The Judgment (Urk. IV, 1846.17-1847.5):

h3.n sš nswt imi-r3 šnwty Ḫꜥ-m-ḥ3t pn r ẖrt-nṯr
swt m m3ꜥ-ḫrw tp t3
n ḫpr sḫr.f (*sic, for* srḫ.f)
n wnt ṯsst im.f ḫr wꜥtw n stp-s3 ꜥ.w.s.
spr.n.f r wsḫt n m3ꜥty
gm.n.t<w.f> m sšmw.f nb r-ꜥ mḫ3t
m-b3ḥ nṯrw imiw.s
iw ip.n sw Ḏḥwty m m3ꜥ-ḫrw
m ḏ3ḏ3t n nṯr nb nṯrt nb
iḫ nḏ.tn ḥr.f s3ḫ.tn sw
m-ḏb3 nfrw.f

The royal scribe and granary chief Khaemhet descended to the graveyard
as one justified on earth;
he had no accuser,
he was without reproach from the sole-one of the palace.
When he reached the Hall-of-the-Two-Truths
<he was> examined in all his conduct at the balance
before the gods who are in it.
Then Thoth accounted him justified,
in the court of all gods and goddesses;
now welcome him and transfigure him
in requital of his goodness!

There is here the complete union of ethical and magical thinking, more complete than in text 20. For here the judgment is not envisaged as a trial which the deceased is about to undergo, but as a trial already passed. The sḏmnf forms cannot be interpreted as present-tense 'performatives', for the final sentence in which the deceased asks the spirits to welcome him, proves that the judgment is seen as having been passed - in the manner envisaged in BD 125. Here then is the ethical core fully merged with the magical procedure.

The comparison of the Negative Confessions (better, Declarations of Innocence) of BD 125 with the autobiographic self-praises has revealed a large measure of congruence. The fact that the BD Declarations are formulated as denials (except for the positive sequence in the final speech to the gods) is the particular contribution of the BD scribes. The concept of a justification by means of a weighing of deeds, which was at least as old as the Instruction for Merikare and the Coffin Texts, had now been given its prevailing form: a weighing of the heart against the figure, or feather, of Maat. In this procedure, a weighing of all kinds of deeds (such as is indicated by the Merikare passage) would have been very complicated. The simple and logical solution was to weigh the heart's blanket denial of wrongdoing against the featherweight Maat figure, whereby the two scales would come out even.

Given this innovation on the part of the BD makers, our comparison does not require for its validation that we should match each BD negative declaration with an autobiographic negative declaration. Rather, our assemblage of them has shown, first of all, that negative formulations occurred in autobiographies at all times, and, secondly, that they were much more numerous in the 18th dynasty than in the earlier periods. That means, the BD scribes drew on a fund of autobiographic ethical declarations, comprising both positive and negative formulations.

Also documented here is the increase in autobiographic references to the judgment of the dead as part of the vastly expanded vision of the afterlife; and the perilous side of that vision tended to impart to usually confident self-praise a note of anxious self-justification.

The Egyptian was well aware of the distinction between a prayer and a magical spell; but he did not view the ethical-religious approach as incompatible with magical manipulation. Not being inimical, the two approaches could join forces; and their combination in the literary context was something that practiced scribes could evidently do with ease. By and large, the different literary genres were held to their distinctive tasks: autobiographies were designed to narrate and to declare, and - since the end of the Middle Kingdom - to approach the gods in prayer. But a magical element had been present from the beginning in the shape of the offering formula. Now, the intense preoccupation with the afterlife, and with safe arrival in the beyond, led to formulating a ritual which combined the declaration of ethical behavior with the binding power of the spell.

The Negative Confessions of BD 125 are not arranged according to a well planned scheme. There is, moreover, a large overlap between the two sets of confessions, the first addressed to Osiris the second to forty-two minor deities or demons. Summed up, they constitute two groups: wrongs against people and wrongs against gods. Taken together, they are denials of the following misdeeds: Killing. Stealing. Greed. Robbing the poor and the weak. Taking milk from infants. Causing terror, pain, and tears. Maligning a servant to his master. Adultery. Lying. Spying. Cheating with weights and measures. Misusing water and fire. Being hot-tempered, violent, aggressive, arrogant. Shouting and screaming. Offending a god or a king. Reviling a god. Stealing temple property and temple offerings.

If one compares these negative confessions with the self-praises of the autobiographies, and with the teachings of the wisdom literature, one finds a broad agreement in the naming of the major sins and vices: killing, stealing, greed, lying, cheating, violence, adultery, maligning, shouting, reviling a god - all these occur as denials in the Autobiographies and as prohibitions in the Instructions.

One major aspect of wrongdoing which is prominent in Instructions and Autobiographies but inconspicuous in the BD list, is corruption: taking bribes and rendering unfair judgments. The frequent refrain in autobiographies of officials, "I have not been partial", is missing from the negative confessions, except for allusions to "being deaf to the truth" and "winking" in text B, nos. 24 & 25 of BD 125.

On the other hand, it is interesting to find in the BD negative confessions a tenet of practical ethics which Amenhotep son of Hapu (text 19) had cited in describing his good labor relations: "I did not impose extra work", *n rdi.i irt ḥ3w*. This appears in text A as: "I did not in the morning increase the work quota I had set", *n ir.i tp-hrw nb b3kw m-ḥrw irt.n.i* (BD ed. Naville, pl. CXXXIII, cols. 8-9).

Lastly it is noteworthy that some of the most basic tenets of Egyptian ethics, which did not lend themselves to negative phrasing, are reproduced in the closing speech of BD 125 in their (slightly altered) traditional formulations, as found countless times in the autobiographical inscriptions:

I have done what people say and what gods are pleased with,
I have given bread to the hungry, water to the thirsty,
clothes to the naked, passage to the boatless.
(BD ed. Naville, pl. CXXXVII, cols. 10-11)

In sum, BD chapter 125 contains most of the major and some of the minor tenets of Egyptian ethics, as well as some prohibitions of a ritual nature. All these tenets were available to the compilers of the BD from experiences and practices which, in the course of a millennium, had been worked out in literary forms: autobiographies, instructions, and manuals of ritual. In their now ready-made form, the Negative Confessions found easy acceptance in the program of tomb equipment since there was no intrinsic conflict between prayers and spells.

As for the proposal that the declarations of priestly duties and prohibitions inscribed on Ptolemaic temple entrances constituted the actual "Sitz im Leben" of the BD Negative Confessions (so Grieshammer, Jenseitsgericht, p. 58, and in ZDMG Supplement II, 1974, pp. 19-25) it is quite implausible for two reasons: 1. The mere surmise that such priestly declarations already existed in earlier periods will not suffice as evidence. 2. These priestly declarations are by their nature much narrower in scope than the broad-based ethics of Everyman which, taught since the Old Kingdom, were put into ritual garb by the scribes of the BD. Hence I fully concur with the objections parallel to mine formulated by J.G. Griffiths (in his The Divine Verdict, Leiden 1991, 218ff.) where he called it "a matter of some surprise ... that the suggestion has been made that the priest's prelude to vocation and duty is the basic *Sitz im Leben* of the entire concept of the judgment of the dead as presented in the BD" (p. 218). The reader is referred to Griffiths' extensive refutation.

* * *

Where does this leave the stela of Baki? As I noted in the beginning, its iconography is entirely unlike that of stelae from the reign of Amenhotep III; for they are crowded with enthroned gods and adoring humans, and family members of the stela owner, whereas Baki sits all alone under the pair of magic eyes and is even separated from his offering table by the columns of the offering formula. I know only one other New Kingdom stela with a similar design, the stela of Kares (CG 43003, Lacau, Stèles, I/1, pp. 7-9, pl. IV). It has the winged sundisk in the lunette, a long text covering most of the surface, and at the bottom the figure of Kares sitting alone before an offering table. His wig, face, and posture resemble Baki's. The fact that the stela of Kares was found at Drah Abul-Nagah inhibits speculation about an Abydene workshop for the two. Nor does the iconographic resemblance extend to the inscription. For that of Kares tells a fact-filled story of his stewardship for, and devotion to, the queen mother Ahhotep in the reign of Amenhotep I (Urk. IV, 45-49). Baki's text is baffling because it is entirely devoid of facts. To get some grip on it one needs to observe its organisation and its style.

22) Baki's 15-line text employs a device which became common in the 18th dynasty: a division into major portions by repetition of the person's name, title, and the word *ḏd.f*. Thus the text consists of three main sections, plus a conclusion in the shape of an address to the living.

I. The Declaration of Innocence:

(1) ḥtp-di-nswt n k3 n imi-r3 šnwty B3ki m3ᶜ-ḫrw ḏd.f
ink mty m3ᶜ šw m ḫww
di nṯr m ib.f šs3 m b3w.f
iy.n.i r niwt (t)n imit nḥḥ
iw ir.n.i bw-nfr tp t3
n iwḥ.i nn wn.i
n nḏ rn.i ḥr sp nb
ḫsy isft (3) mi-qd
ḥᶜᶜ.i m ḏd m3ᶜt
rḫ.kwi 3ḫ.s n ir sy
tp t3 ḏr-ᶜ r mny
mwnf pw mnḫ n ḏd sy
hrw pf n spr.f r ḏ3ḏ3t
wḏᶜt s3rw wpt qdww
sswnt isfty dnt b3.f
wnn.i nn wn.i n wnt srḫ.i
(5) nn isft.i m-b3ḥ.sn pr.i m m3ᶜ-ḫrw
ḥs.kwi m-m im3ḫyw sb n k3w.sn

A royal offering to the ka of the granary chief Baki, justified,
he says:
I am one truly straight, free of wrongdoing,
who has the god in his heart and is aware of his might.
I have come to this town in eternity,

having done the good on earth.
I did not rob, I was blameless,
my name was not uttered for any mistake,
nor (3) any vileness and crime.
To speak the truth was my delight,
for I knew it profits its doer
on earth from birth to landing.
It is an effective guard for its speaker,
on the day he arrives at the court,
that judges the distressed, discerns qualities,
punishes the criminal, destroys his Ba.
I am without blame, there is not my accuser![1]
Without wrong before them, may I come out just,
and praised among the honored who joined their ka's!

II. The Faithful Servant:

imi-r3 pr imi-r3 šnwty B3ki m3ʿ-ḫrw ḏd.f
ink mḥ-ib ʿ3 n nb t3wy
špsy n ir sw ḥsy n bity
in bit.i iqrt sḫnt st.i
tn wi (7) m-m ḥḥ n rmṯ
m3ʿt.i rwd n Ḥr m-ḫnt ḥr-s3
šnw.i k3.f m pẖr ḫr.f m ḥʿt
r dw3 nfr.f m ẖrt-hrw
m sw3š w3ḏty.f r tr nb

The steward and granary chief Baki, justified, says:
I was a great trusty of the Lord-of-the-two-lands,
one valued by his maker,[2] one praised by the king;
it was my good character that furthered my rank,[3]
and singled me out among millions of men.
My rightness was strong for Horus in front and in back,[4]
I surrounded his ka with a jubilant circle,
so as to praise his goodness day by day,
and adore his twin serpents at all times.

III. The Virtuous Man:

imi-r3 šnwty B3ki m3ʿ-ḫrw ḏd.f
ink sʿḥ hr ḥr m3ʿt

sni r hpw wsẖt m3ᶜty
ẖmt.n.i (9) spr.i r ẖrt-nṯr
nn nḏyt ntt rn.i ḥr.s
n ir.i ḏwt r rmṯ
ṯsst nt nṯrw.sn
ᶜḥᶜw.i m ᶜnḫ n m3ᶜw
r pḥ.i im3ḫ im nfr
iw.i m ḥswt nt ḫr nswt
mrwt.i ḫr šnyw.f
pr-nswt tm m imity.f
nn ḏwt ir.n.i m ib.sn
rmṯ (11) n s3-pr mitt iry
ḥᶜᶜ.sn m bit.i iqrt
rn.i nḏ m stp-s3
m nb qd ir bw m3ᶜ
nfr.i m ib n it.i mwt.i
mrwt.i m-ẖnw ẖwt.sn
n sp t3ḥ sn mi ir.n.i ḫr.sn tp t3
tr.i ᶜ3.i wšd.n.i nḏs.i
nn ḥwr.i mnḫ r.i
nḏwt (13) r3.i m ḏd bw nfr
nn ṯs ᶜḥ3 ḏdt.n.i

The granary chief Baki, justified, says:
I am a noble pleased with right,
who conformed to the laws of the Hall of Truths;
for I planned (9) to reach the necropolis
without a baseness attached to my name.
I did no evil to people -
their gods condemn it;
my lifetime was lived with right wind,
to attain good reveredness yonder;
I had the king's favor,
and the love of his attendants;
the whole palace and its occupant
deemed me to have done no wrong.
The people (11) in back[4] likewise,
they rejoiced in my good nature;
my name was pronounced in the palace
as a man of character who does right.

My father and mother knew my goodness,
love of my dwelled in their bodies;
no ... equaled my acting for them on earth,[5]
I honored when grown whom I had hailed when little.
I had no spite for one better than I,
my counsel (13) was to say the good,
no hostile word was said by me.

IV. The Address to the Living:
sḏmw nn mitt ḏdt.n.i
rmṯ nbt wnnyw
hrw ḥr m3ʿt m ẖrt-hrw
mẖrw nn irt s3wt
nṯr nb 3bḏw ʿnḫ.f im.s rʿ nb
ir.ṯn st 3ḫ n.ṯn
sb.ṯn ʿḥʿw m nḏm-ib
r ḥtp <m> imntt nfrt
b3.tn (15) sḫm m ʿq prt
wstnw mi nbw nḥḥ
ḏdw ḫft p3wtyw

Listen to this as I said it,
all you people who exist:
Be content with Maat daily,
it is food that does not sate,
the lord god of Abydos lives on it daily!
If you do this, you will profit,
you will spend life's time in gladness,
till there's rest in the good west,
your Ba equipped to come and go,
you striding like eternal lords,
enduring like primeval ones!

Notes:

1. Most translators have rendered *wnn.i* as a past tense, e.g. Yoyotte, Jugement des morts, 67: "Ma vie durant je ne fus pas blâmé, il n'y eut pas d'accusation à mon encontre..." and he concluded that the sentences were "des phrases directement inspirées du chapitre 125". Such rendering encourages dating the stela to the reign of Amenhotep III rather than earlier. But compare the truly

past tense account of the judgment, spoken in the third person, of text 21! Baki's whole text does not suggest that he now claims to have already passed the judgment, rather that he expects full justification on account of his blameless conduct.

2.*ir sw*, "his maker", is the king, as for instance in Hammamat 114.7 (see my Autobiographies, p. 54, n. 12).

3.This is one of several New Kingdom variants of a Middle Kingdom phrase; Rediu-Khnum had said, "it was my heart that furthered my rank, it was my character that kept me in front", thus making a meaningful distinction between heart and character (Autobiographies, p. 45, n. 10). Having lost this point, the New Kingdom variants are banal.

4. I think that *m-ḫnt* and *ḥr-s3* are "front" and "back" rather than Spiegel's "drinnen und draussen", the front being the official parts of the palace, and the back the servant quarters, as also *s3-pr* in line 11. See also *ḫnt* and *s3-pr* in Merikare P 46.

5. The meaning of *t3ḥ* is obscure. Rather than the word for the Horus child of Wb. 5, 234.10, a sweet or medicinal plant or potion, such as *t3ḥt* of Wb. 5, 233.12-14, or *tḥwy* of Wb. 5, 323.1-3, may have been meant. In any case, the next sentence, "I honored, etc" rounds off the account of his excellent filial behaviour.

As for the date of the stela of Baki, neither its spare iconography nor its literary style support a dating to the reign of Amenhotep III. As already mentioned, its iconography resembles that of the stela of Kares, which belongs to the reign of Amenhotep I. Baki's style, too, is closer to the compact formulations of the early 18th dynasty than to the more involved and ornate phrasing discernible in the reign of Amenhotep III. What makes his text baffling is the complete absence of factual details. With nothing but the literary style to go by, it seems to me that his formulations have affinities with those of Ineni, also a granary chief, even though Ineni tells a fact-filled story of his long career, which lasted from the reign of Amenhotep I to that of Thutmosis III. See his autobiographical inscriptions in Urk. IV, 53ff., and the excerpts from them in our texts 11 and 12, in particular text 12 where the judgment is invoked (Urk. IV, 66-67). There, too, are two striking occurrences of *wnn.f* in the future/optatival sense, the existence of which is denied by Graefe in his Mittelägyptische Grammatik (2nd ed., pp. 81 & 145ff.), a denial not endorsed by Polotsky, whom I asked. For *wnn rn.i mn ḥr bi3wt(.i)* and *wnn ḫrw(.i) m3^{c} m wsḫt* can only mean, "may my name endure through my conduct" etc., or with Sethe, "Mein Name wird bleiben wegen meiner Vortreff-lichkeit ...". What matters here is that both Ineni and Baki are voicing their expectation of being vindicated in the judgment; they are not claiming to have already passed that judgment. That magic-oriented claim was made by Khaemhet (text 21) in the reign of Amenhotep III. It was, as far as I know, not made in the first half of the 18th dynasty. The reign of Thutmosis III is the time when BD 125 text copies first appear in Theban tombs (in TT 82). Thus, my proposed date for the stela of Baki is: reign of Thutmosis III, not later.

* * *

The common crime of cheating in the use of weights and measures does not feature in the denials of wrongdoing of the high officials whose inscriptions have been our principal sources. But it was a significant crime which is prominently mentioned in BD 125 and in the Wisdom of Amenemope. It is therefore interesting to encounter its denial in the biographic declarations of a minor official who spoke from the appropriate context: he was "keeper of the balance of the palace treasury". This is the autobiographical stela of Sekeb from Abydos, published only by Mariette as no. 1102 of his Catalogue des monuments d'Abydos, and translated by Barucq-Daumas, Hymnes et prières, as no. 14, p. 99. According to these scholars, the stela dates to the 18th dynasty; in its upper register the deceased adores Osiris and Isis, the lower register has the text in eight columns. Here is the transcription of Mariette's hieroglyphic text:

23) rdi(t) i3w n Wsir
in iry-mḫ3t n pr-ḥḏ m [^{c}ḥ] [S3-k3]-bw m3^{c}-ḫrw ḏd.f
inḏ-ḥr.k Ḫnt-imntt Wsir ḥr-ib t3-wr
iy.n.i n.k ib.i ẖr m3^{c}t
ḥ3ty.i nn grg im.f
nn ḥḏ(.i) p3wt nṯrw
nn w3ḥ.i ḥr mwt nt iwsw
nn snmḥ(.i) m tḫ n mḫ3t
iy.n.i m ḥtp r t3 ḏsr
iw ir.n.i mrr ib.k

n k3 n ḥsy n nb 3bḏw
<iry>-mḫ3t n pr-ḥḏ m ᶜḥ S3-k3-bw

Praise-giving to Osiris
by the keeper of the balance of the [palace]-treasury [Seke]b,
justified, he says:
I greet you Khentamenthes Osiris in Tawer!
I am come to you, my heart bearing Maat,
my heart is free of falsehood!
I have not pared the loaves of the gods,
I have not increased the weight of the hand-balance,
I have not altered the plummet of the stand-balance!
I am come in peace to the sacred land,
having done what your heart desired!
For the ka of one favored by the lord of Abydos,
<the keeper> of the balance of the palace-treasury, Sekeb.

Sekeb's three "I have not" declarations occur verbatim in the negative confession of BD 125 (BD ed. Naville, pl. CXXXIII, cols. 14 & 16-17). Such verbatim identity indicates that BD 125 was now in general use, and that a process of limited borrowing-in-reverse was taking place: BD declarations of innocence were cited in formulating self-justifications in autobiographies. This process could not have begun before the latter part of the 18th dynasty, and the stela of Sekeb is likely to belong there, unless it dates to the beginning of the 19th dynasty (without a photograph one canot tell).

It now remains for us to examine how the concept of the Last Judgment was dealt with in Ramesside and later times, in texts designed to teach, and to demonstrate, the performance of that uncodified code of ethics which was defined as doing Maat.

Sekeb's hymn to Osiris began with the declaration of coming before Osiris with a Maat-filled heart, continued with three declarations of innocence, and closed with his having come in peace to the sacred land. Taken together, the sequence suggests that the speaker envisages his standing before Osiris in the netherworldly hall of judgment, in the very situation depicted in the vignettes of BD 125. If so, the situation is implied rather than spelled out.

With some exceptions, Ramesside autobiographical inscriptions supply fewer factual biographical details than their 18th dynasty predecessors. Instead, the autobiographical statements are integrated with hymns to the gods in such a way that the self-presentations are linked to prayerful requests for a benign reception in the hereafter, and for the various benefits of the otherworldly existence. These requests are buttressed by strong affirmations of having done right *(m3ʿt)* and of being righteous *(m3ʿty, m3ʿ-ib)*. Now, Sekeb's self-introduction by means of the sentences "I come to you, my heart bearing Maat, etc." occurs frequently in Ramesside prayers, primarily (not exclusively) in prayers addressed to Osiris. For example, the vizier Paser adores Osiris and Maat in these words (TT 106, on pillar D in Broad Hall, KRI III, 5.7-8):

24) iy.n.i ḫr.k ib.i ẖr m3ʿt
nn isft m ẖt.i
nn ḏd.i grg m rḫ.i
n ir.i sp snnw

I am come before you, my heart bearing Maat,
without crime in my body;
I did not tell lies knowingly,
I did not practice deception.

Other examples of this sequence are KRI III, 143.8-9; III, 295.4-6; III, 312.11-12; IV, 115.15-16; VII, 215.12-13.

The prayers that contain this sequence do not spell out, but they suggest, that the speaker envisages his coming before the divine tribunal that will examine him and pass judgment on him. As for direct references to the judgment, here is one: Ptahmose, mayor of Memphis, inscribed the four faces of a tomb pillar with prayers to Re and Osiris (KRI III, 173ff.). On the fourth face he says:

25) i3w n.k bnr mrwt
Wsir nb ʿnḫ-t3wy
b3 nṯry imi ḥrt
tḫ pw wḏʿ m3ʿty
di.f rd rn.i m-ḫt nḥḥ ... (KRI III, 175.13f.)

Praise to you, lovable one,
Osiris, lord of Memphis,
divine Ba in heaven!
Plummet that discerns the righteous!
May he let my name flourish throughout eternity!

This is not only a clear reference to the judgment, but also one that projects the speaker's confidence in its outcome, because he is a righteous one!

Now we come to a major hymn to Osiris which is interesting on several counts including its invocation of the judgment.

26) Stela of Bak-aa with hymn to Osiris: HTBM 9, pls. XXI-XXIA, no. 164 = KRI II, 386-388. The same hymn is recorded on two other Ramesside stelae: Louvre C 218 of Minmose (Pierret, Recueil II, 134-138, and R. El-Sayed, Documents relatifs à Sais, pp. 1-28 & pls. 1-2) and BM 142 of Amenmose (KRI III, 218). Part of the hymn is also in the Ani copy of BD, ed. Budge, pl. XXXVI, p. 241. The upper part of BM 142 is missing. BM 164 and Louvre C 218 have the same iconographic scheme: under the two couchant jackals is the extended cartouche of Ramses II. Below, the deceased adores Osiris and other gods, and makes offering to his parents and other relatives. The lower half is filled by the text.

(1) rdit i3w n Wsir
sn t3 n Wnn-nfr
in ḥry-iḥw B3k-ʿ3 ḏd.f

i nb.i sbb nḥḥ
wnn.tyfy n ḏt
nswt nṯrw ḥq3 ḥq3w
ity Ḥrww

wnnyw mtn st ḫr.k
m nṯrw rmṯ
iry.k st.sn ḫnt ẖrt-nṯr
snmḥ.sn k3.k

(3) nty m iw n ḥḥ n ḥḥ
pḥwy mnit r.k
nty m ẖt ḥr.sn m ḥr.k
nn ḫpr isq m t3-mry

sn m-ʿ.k iww n.k tm
m wrw mi kttw
n.k im ʿnḫyw tp t3
spr n.k bw nb m bw wʿ

ntk nb.sn (5) n ky wp-ḥr.k
nn r-3w ṯww st
ir ḫd.tw ir ḫnt.tw
m-ẖnw km ʿḥʿw
iw ḥm.k dw3 dw3 m Rʿ
nty nb ḥr ḫt.k

B3k-ʿ3 m3ʿ-ḫrw ḏd.f
iy.n.i ḫr.k rḫ.kwi sḫrw.k
tr.kwi m irw.k m d3t
ḥms.k m3ʿt r ḫft (7) ḥr.k
ḥr wḏʿ ibw ḥr mḫ3t

twi m-b3ḥ.k ib.i ẖr m3ʿt
ḥ3ty.i nn grg im.f
dw3.i b3w.k m wsr.k
sḥtp.i psḏt ẖrt-nṯr
di.i n.k ḥknw
ir.i n.k hnw nn wrd

There follows an Appeal to the Living and a short self-praise, which is conventional except for the joyous tone of the last lines:

ir.n.i sp nb m nfrw
n sdḫ.i ḫr ḥr nb
ink ṯs w3s snḏm ih3w
wnf-ib šw m iṯ-int
hry ḥr nfrw nbw
ḥry-bit mdwt.f r st bw-m3ʿt *(sic)* (11-13)

Translation:

(1) Giving praise to Osiris,
kissing earth to Wenennofer,
by the stable-master Bak-aa, he says:

O my lord who bestrides eternity,
who will exist forever,
king of gods, rulers' ruler,
sovereign of Horus-kings!
Those-in-being stand before you,
gods and mankind;

when you assign them to the graveyard,
they implore your ka!

(3) Those to come in their millions,
in the end they land with you;
in the womb they face toward you,
there's no tarrying in Egypt.

They are with you, all come to you,
great and small alike;
yours are they who live on earth,
one and all will reach you.

You are their lord, (5) no one but you,
all of them belong to you;
be they faring north or south
in the course of life,
mornings, when you rise as Re,
all are in your wake.

Bak-aa, justified, he says:
I am come before you knowing your counsels,
respecting your countenance in Dat;
as enthroned with Maat (7) before you,
you judge hearts upon the scales!
I am before you, my heart bearing Maat,
this my heart is bare of lies;
I will praise your might and power,
will content the graveyard's gods,
I will give you acclamation,
I will laud you without fail!

Conclusion (11-13):

I handled all concerns with goodness,
and did not hide from anyone;
I am one who raised the fallen, consoled the sufferer,
one joyous, free of fidgeting,
who delighted in everything good,
a man of character who spoke what is right.

This hymn is a significant Ramesside contribution to the conception of Osiris as lord of death, and lord of all living beings destined to die, "gods and mankind", as the text has it. Having absorbed the death-fearing impulses expressed since the First Intermediate period ("O you who love life and hate death"), the hymn built up the proverbial "there is no tarrying in Egypt", which summed up the theme of transitoriness, a theme developed since the Middle Kingdom (Harpers' Songs, Lebensmüder). However, the hymn does not take up the doubt and disbelief concerning the reality of a hereafter, which had been so prominent in the Harpers' Songs of the "Antef Song" type, and in the Ramesside "Praise of Scribes" (P.Chester Beatty IV, verso 2,5-3,11). The hymn is fashioned in such a way that fear and grief have been replaced by a stoic acceptance of the inescapable reality of death. And that this acceptance is coupled with the hope of a blessed afterlife is brought out by the autobiographical ending, the coming-before Osiris speech of Bak-aa (the same speech is present in BM 142 but absent from Louvre C 218). By this ending the hymn obtains a note of confidence which balances its underlying melancholy. Louvre C 218 begins the hymn with an invocation of the god's mythology. The absence of a myth-telling introduction gives to the version of BM 164 its strongly focussed unity, to which Bak-aa's coming-before-the-god on the day of judgment adds not only the confidence of an afterlife but also its ethical foundation. Note, too, the excellence of Bak-aa's quatrain *iy.n.i ḫr.k rḫ.kwi sḫrw.k*, etc., with its marked rhythm and rhyme.

* * *

In the group of temple statues of the Theben clergy of Amun, which were reedited by Jansen-Winkeln (Ägyptische Biographien der 22. und 23. Dynastie) and which I excerpted for their Maat thinking (Maat study, chapter 6), there is only a single brief allusion to the judgment of the dead. It occurs on the cube statue of Harsiese, CG 42210 (= J.-W., Text A 5) for which Maat study, text 83, gives an excerpt of the inscription on the statue's right side. The inscription on the statue's back is its sequel and conclusion (J.-W., Text A 5, section e, 5, pp. 68 & 466). The text is a liturgical incantation urging the deceased's resurrection together with his earthly survival in his descendants: *ḥr nty ib.k ᶜq3wy n mḫ3t m3ᶜt*, "because your heart was exact for the balance of Maat".

* * *

With large numbers of biographical statues and stelae reposing unpublished in museums, it is not possible to determine adequately how the judgment of the dead was viewed in the course of the millennium which is lumped together as "Late Period". Altogether, that final millennium of pharaonic history is still so little known that generalisations about its thinking are liable to be premature and idiosyncratic. I conclude this sketch with four Late Period mentions of the judgment.

27) The Cairo statue of Iret-Hor-aa, dated to the reign of Psamtik II, was translated by Otto as no. 22 of his Biographische Inschriften (on the basis of the text publication by Piehl in ZÄS 25, 1887, pp. 120ff. I do not know if the statue has been dealt with since Otto's translation). The whole inscription, which is divided into five sections, is an address to Osiris in which the speaker outlines in traditional terms his right thinking and right acting throughout his life by following "the way of the god". Here is his initial declaration (section a, lines 3-8; I transcribe the way it is spelled):

(3) i Wsir nṯr ᶜ3 m nṯrw
ink ḥm.k ndr mtn.k
n ir.n(.i) msd.k
iw sḥtp.n(.i) n tm <m> (5) mr.f
ir.n(.i) iḫw n b(w) nb
iy.n.i ḫr.k n isft.i
n ḏw.i n mtr.i
iw (7) ir.n(.i) snḏm ib n rmṯ
hrt nṯrw ḥr.s
ḫw.kwi r.k nb.i
n smi r.i m-b(3)ḥ nb sᶜḥw

O Osiris, greatest of gods!
I am your servant who followed your way,
I did not do what you dislike,
I contented everyone <with> what he wished,
I did benefits to all!

I come before you without crime,
without a wrong, without an accuser,
for I did what pleases people,
and what gladdens the gods.
I am safe from you, my lord!
There is no report against me to the lord of the blessed!

The last two sections (d, e), are both introduced by *ḏd-mdw*, "recitation" or "spell"; and they form a matching pair, each beginning with the speaker's titulary and name, followed by some declarations of innocence that recur in BD 125. If the writer thereby drew a distinction between the self-presentations of sections a-c, and the recitations of sections d-e, both are nevertheless cut from the same cloth. For by declaring himself "safe" from the god, in section a, the speaker had adopted the tone of ritual urging whereby self-praise was turned into self-vindication.

28) Petosiris, however, observed a proper distance to the deity, and left the judging in the hands of the god. His strong speech on divine reckoning has been cited as text 98 of the Maat study. Both his oration and that of his father Sishu (Maat study, text 99) bear witness to a strictly ethical view of the judgment. Thus, autobiographical self-presentations in an ethical spirit, free of ritual manipulation, were still professed, and the partnership of Instructions and Autobiographies was intact.

29) On a more popular level, there is the visit which Setne Khaemwas, guided by his son Si-Osire, paid to the netherworld, where they observed the divine judgment in action (Second Tale of Setne Khaemwas). There, interestingly, a mere surplus of good deeds over bad ones sufficed to obtain vindication.

In sum, a sound moral view of the last judgment was alive and well in the final centuries of pharaonic culture:

30) The god lays the heart on the scales opposite the weight.
He knows the impious man and the man of god by his heart.
(PInsinger 5, 7-8)

* * *

While the sources here assembled confirm Spiegel's analysis of Egyptian views of the last judgment, a very different interpretation was presented by Morenz in his article Ägyptischer Totenglaube im Rahmen der Struktur ägyptischer Religion (Eranos Jahrbuch 34, 1966, reprinted in his Gesammelte Aufsätze, 1975) and developed at greater length in his Gott und Mensch im alten Ägypten (1964, 2nd ed. 1984). I quote from the second edition of Gott und Mensch:

> "So kam der Ägypter in ein ungeheures Dilemma, als ihm eine der Maat entsprechende Verhaltensweise von Gott nach dem Tode abgefordert wurde, d.h. als der Gedanke eines allgemein verbindlichen Totengerichtes nach sittlichen Masstäben Gestalt und Macht gewann. (p.162)
> Er bog das von der Macht ethischer Norm, also der Maat, geforderte Totengericht um und suchte es in Tat und Wahrheit nicht ethisch sondern rituell zu bestehen ... Aus diesen krummen Linien hat sich die nachmals klassische Form des Totengerichts gebildet, das in Wirklichkeit gar nicht mehr dies, sondern ein Ritus ist ... (p. 165)
> Wer sich für das Leben in dieser Welt angehalten weiss, Gott zu gehorchen und die Maat zu tun, wird sich trotz der generellen Vergewaltigung des Totengerichts durch den Ritus der Rolle bewusst sein, die die Ethik auch für den Eintritt ins Jenseits spielte. Dieses Bewusstsein war hellwach in den Zeiten, da die Idee des Totengerichts geboren und gepredigt wurde, also zunächst bei Ptahhotep ... dann sonnenklar bei Merikare ... Dieselbe Haltung erscheint am Ende einer langen Geschichte noch lebendig, die den Menschen gelehrt hatte, das Totengericht auf dem Wege des Ritus zu umgehen, Petosiris ... Sagen wir es doch ganz hart und realistisch: So selbstmörderisch sprang kein Ägypter mit seinem ewigen Leben um, dass er Sündenbekenntnisse dort abgelegt hätte, wo Gericht gehalten und für alle Ewigkeit abgerechnet wurde. Seine Sünde bekannte er in diesem Leben einem Gott, der nicht rechnete, sondern sich gnädig erwies. Der Fromme nahm die Maat als ethisches Prinzip ernst, er spürte ihr Walten im Zusammenhang von Sünde und Strafe. Aber gerade weil er sie ernst nahm, hütete er sich, ihr über das Leben hinaus auch noch das ewige anzuvertrauen." (p. 168)

Thus according to Morenz, the wholesale triumph of ritual over ethics with regard to the judgment could take place because even the truly pious person, one who was willing to confess sins in his lifetime, recoiled from the idea of a "Sündenbekenntnis" that would jeopardize his afterlife.

The theory is untenable, for it ignores the evidence. The sources here sampled of New Kingdom and post-New Kingdom autobiographies, which anticipated the judgment, were not taken into account. As for the early times in which the Egyptian had been "hellwach" to the moral demands of the judgment - that early wakefulness also fuelled the magical manipulations of the Coffin Texts. The contrast between Egyptian willingness to admit sins during life, and refusal to confess sins when envisaging the judgment, is an artificial one. In the literary works that are our sources for Egyptian ethical thought the concept of guilt, and its actual admission, appear in three contexts: in Instructions (e.g. Merikare, Amenemope, PInsinger); in the small group of votive stelae from Deir al-Medina where crimes are alluded to; and thirdly, in clear anticipation of the last judgment, on the 11th dynasty stela of Intef and in the Coffin Texts (see pp. 105f.). Thus contrary to Morenz's assertion, both situations - daily life and the anticipation of the judgment - engendered admissions of failings and guilt.[8]

However, the Deir al-Medina votive stelae represent not general confession of sins, but special cases in which persons smitten with blindness or some other affliction attributed their suffering to divine punishment for particular crimes. In almost all contexts, the discussion or admission of failings was low-keyed, forming an occasional murmured accompaniment to the strong affirmations of right-doing. Only the latest of the Instructions, that of PInsinger, by building up the contrast of the "wise man" and the "fool", made moral failings into a major theme.

The autobiographies being the principal sources for the affirmations of having fulfilled the ethical demands which the Instructions taught, it is primarily in them that we find the expectation of reward for right-doing. That expectation was threefold: a long and successful life; the survival of one's person in descen-

[8]It is interesting to compare Morenz's dismissal of the "crooked lines" of the magically performed judgment with Assmann's chapter on BD 125 in his new Ma'at, pp. 136ff. There BD 125 is the "Kodifizierung der Ma'at" by means of a magic which is "eine exakte Wissenschaft" (p. 136). "Der gereinigte und dadurch gerechtfertigte Initiand wird in die Gemeinschaft der Götter aufgenommen." (p. 148).

dants; vindication in the last judgment, followed by a transfigured eternal life.

But whatever apprehension of the judgment the Egyptian had, it was as nothing compared to his fear and hatred of death. By right doing and by ritual means as well, the judgment would be overcome. But death could not be evaded. With all his faith in the magical manipulation of his universe, the Egyptian, when not indulging in hopes and phantasies, was a pragmatist. Death was a massive reality. The hereafter? Except in imaginative tales, no one had ever come back from there to tell of it. These two things remained largely unresolved: the full-bodied fear of death, and the nagging doubt about the reality of a life in the beyond. To overcome these two required not self-assertion but rather a self-restraining sagacity and piety:

> The end of the man of god is to be buried on the mountain with his burial equipment. (PInsinger 18, 12)

III

THE MORAL VOCABULARY
An Annotated Index

The Index comprises the texts of Studies I and II and consists of three parts: A. Terms; B. Major Concepts; C. A ranking of Virtues and Vices. References are listed by the numbers of the texts, except in a few instances where a page number is given. The texts in Study II are preceded by the Roman numeral II. The Vocabulary is inevitably somewhat arbitrary in its inclusions and exclusions. The noun *m3ᶜt* has not been indexed, since it occurs in nearly all the texts; but the forms *m3ᶜ*, *wn m3ᶜ*, *bw-m3ᶜ*, *m3ᶜty,* and *m3ᶜ-ib* are included. Similarly, the word *ib*, "heart", has been omitted, but all compounds of *ib* are indexed.

The lists of Concepts (B) and Virtues and Vices (C) are also based only on the text citations of Studies I and II. They are meant to invite reflection on Egyptian moral terminology and on the moral selfview mirrored in it. They are not an outline of Egyptian morality as a whole.

A. Terms

3bt	crookedness	4
iwy, iwyt	wrong, harm	29,99
iwms	calumny	II/19
iwḥ	rob, theft	91,II/22
ib *compounds:*		
3wt-ib	joy	p.17,79
im3-ib	kind, gracious	33,96
ᶜ3 n ib.f	magnanimous	18
ᶜwn-ib	greedy	10

sp n ʿwn-ib	rapacity	59
ʿq3-ib	upright, straightforward	28, 38a, 39.3, 52, II/20, II/21
w3ḥ-ib	patient, steadfast, thoughtful, intent	28, 31, 77, 95, II/20
wn-ib	heedful	28
wnf-ib	joyful	II/21, II/24
wḥʿ-ib	skilled	46
wḏ3-ib	hale of heart	II/20
bq-ib	arrogant	II/11
pẖr-ib	considerate	II/21
m3ʿ-ib	rightminded, truthful	46, 55, 70, 83, 87, 88, 91, 96
mnḫ-ib	devoted, excellence	53, 92, II/11
mḥ-ib	trusty, trust	47, 76, II/21, II/22
nḏm-ib	gladness, joy	79, 81, 84, 94, 96, II/22
hr-ib	modest	46
ḥ3w-ib	sorrow	81
ḫrp-ib	forceful	28
ḫrt-ib	heart's desire i.e. pleasing	23
sḫm-ib	violent	75, II/12
im3	kind	15, 33, 90
ir-3ḫt	beneficent	II/21
isw	reward	82, 92, 94, 96
isft	wrong, wrongdoing crime, evil, falseness	p.17, 19, 20, 21, 37, 38a, 41, 43, 44, 46, 50, 52, 55, 60, 66, 71, 77, II/20, II/22, II/25, II/27
isfty	criminal	II/22
iqr, iqrt	worthy, trustworthy, good	52, 69, 74, 77, 84, 85, II/15, II/22
iqr *compounds:*		
iqr-bi3	good-natured	86
iqr-mdw	skilled in speech	86
iqr-sḫrw	resourceful	38a, 95
iqr-ṯsw	eloquent	28

iṯ-in	waver, fidget	74, II/24
ʿwn	rob, greed	59, 62
ʿrq	skill	28
ʿq3	straight, exact	29, 39.4, 62, 67, 98
w3t nfrt	good way	52
w3t nṯr	way of god	99
wʿ3	plot evil	28
wn, wni, wnt	shun, neglect, blame, fault	43, 46, 49, 60, 69, 74, 84, 87, 98, II/10, II/17, II/18, II/22
wḫdw	pained	28
wsr, wsrt	force, power, rich, strong, mighty	3, 8, 13, 26, 51, 53, 67, 81, II/26
b3w	might	97, 99, II/22, II/26
bi3, bi3t, bit, bi3wt	character, nature, conduct, qualities	22, 26, 62, 77, 79, 86, 90, II/12, II/22, II/26
bin	evil	14, 44
bwt, bwy	abhor, loathe	59, 60, 62, 66, 71, 76, 77, 82, 96, 99, II/20
bšt3 *in* mdt-bšt3	rebelliousness	59
bt3, bt3w	crime	58, II/20
prw	extra, profit	82, 87
pẖ3-ẖt	open-hearted	26
f3t	weight, gift	92, p.99
fq3	reward	84, 85
m3ʿ, wn m3ʿ	true, truly, just, rightful, rightly	3, 7, 8, p.17, 11, 20, 27, 31, 32, 47, 52, 59, 61, 62, 71, 92, 95
bw m3ʿ, ḫt m3ʿ	true thing, right, right thing	3, 4, 7, 97, II/22
s n m3ʿt, s m3ʿ	man of right	31, 95
st bw m3ʿt *(sic)*	what is right	II/26
ḏd m3ʿt	who speaks truth	28, 34, 87
m3ʿ-ib *see under* ib		
m3ʿw	rightness	19, 87
m3ʿty, m3ʿtyw	righteous, just	28, 38a, 44, 51, 58, 60, 70, p.77, 79, 87, 90, II/25

m3r	weak, poor, harm	8, 26, 39.3, 52, 53, 87
mit *in* iwty mity	not having two ways i.e. free of duplicity	83
mnḫ	worthy, effective, virtue, excellence	7, 28, 52, 53, 67, 84, II/17, II/20, II/21, II/22
mr-ḫt	greed	90
mhy	be slack, forget	53, 56
mkḥ3	fail, neglect	66, II/18, II/19
mty, mty m3ʿ	fitting, exact, truly straight	28, 29, 30, 31, 39.3, 59, 62, 69, 77, 88
mty ḥ3ty	straightforward	II/21
s n mty	man of rectitude	28, 29
mtn.k	your way (i.e. god's)	II/27
mtn nfr	good way	II/20
nfr, nfrt, nfrw	good, goodness, worth, beauty	4, 5, 7, 8, 9, 14, 15, 21, 29, 50, 57, 59, 60, 62, 65, 66, 67, 75, 80, 82, 90, 93, 96, 97, II/11, II/19, II/20, II/21, II/22, II/24, II/26
bw nfr	good, the good, goodness	2, 24, 44, 95, 99, II/11, II/22
tp nfr	the right manner, the best	8, 15
nfr-qiḥ	benign	96
nfr-qd	well-disposed	22
nmʿ	be partial	39.2
nḏyt, nḏwyt	baseness, calumny	10, II/8, II/22
rqi	rebel	II/16
hnw	attentive	28
hr	be pleased, content, contentment	47, 55, 59, 92, II/22, II/26
ḥnw	anger	28
ḥnt	greed	34
ḥr.wy	two faces = deceit	87
ḥḏi	neglect, damage	52, 55, 62, II/18, II/20
ḥḏ-ḥr	generous	26

ḫww	wrongdoing	II/22
ḫm-nṯr	godless	p.36
ḫm-ṯs	blameless	84
ẖsy	vileness	II/22
s3 *in:*		
wḏb s3 n / rdi s3 r	turn the back on	14, 38a, 87
sp	manner, concern, deed, occasion	9, 49, 53, 69, 74, 93, II/26
sp	blame, mistake	14, 49, 74, II/22
sp *compounds:*		
iwty sp.f	blameless	14
mʿr-spw	successful	95
nb sp	unfortunate man	92
sp n ʿwn-ib	rapacity	59
sp nfr	good deed	93
sp snnw(t)	deception	67, II/24
sp n sʿḏ3	mistake	63
sp n sk	failure	II/17
sp ḏw	harm	99
spw n ḏ3t	crimes	55
spd-ḥr	perceptive	II/21
sm3r	cause poverty	II/16
sh3	enmity	71
sḥwr	revile	II/14, II/18
sḫr, sḫrw	care, counsel, plans, condition	39.1, 43, 45, 53, 68, 98, II/26
sšwy	deprive	9
sšm, sšmw	guide, guidance, conduct, function	7, 24, 52, 75, 88, 92, II/21
sk	harm, fail	92, II/11
n sk	unendingly	81, 94
sgr	calm	39.3
sḏw, sḏwy	slander	82, II/19
šbw	gifts	51
špt	angry	1, 21
šnn, šnnt	affliction, hurtful	1, 57
šnt nṯr	profanation	23
šs3	skilled, aware	52, 68, 74, II/22
q3-ḫrw	loud-voiced	71, II/15

qi *in* ḥss m qi.f	dignified	95
qiḥ *see* nfr-qiḥ		
qb, qbḥ, qb-ẖt	cool, cool-bellied	22, 23, 69
qd, qdw, qdww	character, worth, repute, traits, qualities	7, 18, 19, 21, 22, 46, p.54, 52, II/19, II/22
nb qd	man of character	25, II/22
ḏw-qd	evil man	71
gr, gr m3ᶜ	silent, truly silent	75, 79
gm-gr	discreet	95
grg-ḥr	keen	28
grg, grgw	lie, lies, falsehood	7, 14, 34, 52, 59, 62, 67, 71, 72, 76, 82, 96, II/10, II/14, II/15, II/20, II/23, II/26
thi	stray, disregard, attack	52, 90, II/18
th-w3t	transgression	87
th-nmtwt	errancy	87
ṯs	blame, reproach	84, 93
d3r-srf	calm-tempered	23, 28
dns	weighty	95
ḏ3i-r3	covet	II/11, II/15
ḏ3t, ḏ3yt	wrong, crime	10, 33
spw n ḏ3t *see* sp *compounds*		
ḏw, ḏwt, bw-ḏw, bw-ḏwy	evil, crime, fault, harm, wickedness	2, 7, 8, 9, 14, 19, 21, 38a, 51, 74, 76, 99, II/22, II/27
ir bw-ḏw	evildoer	61, 88
ḏb3	repay	50

B. Aspects of Maat

Benevolence and Charity	1, 2, 3, 8, 9, 13, 14, 15, 20, 24, 26, 27, 28, 39.3, 52, 53, 59, 77, 87, 90, 99
Justice: Fairness and Impartiality to all	9, 24, 26, 27, 29, 30, 31, 34, 37, 39.2, 39.3, 40, 47, 53, 54, 61, 77, 88, 92, II/19
Justice: Conciliating contenders	8, 9, 24, 35, p.80
Shunning Evil and Evildoers	14, 38a, 61, 69, 71, 87, 88, 99
Loyalty and Obediance: "Acting/being on the water"	49, 56, 71, 81, 97, 98, 99
The Sum of Rightdoing: "What people love and gods praise"	14, 20, 35, 46, 49, 55, 59, 96, II/27
Knowing oneself	1, 18, 19, 20, 21, 22, 23, 28, 38a, 52, 69, 92, 95, II/22
Knowing and Doing the Will of the Gods	2, 3, 4, 7, 9, 35, 36, 45, 55, 59, 71, 77, 78, 79, 91, 94, 95, 96, 99, II/11, II/22
Raising up Maat *(si^c, si^{c}r m3^{c}t)*	11, 12, 13, 31, 32, p.35, 53, 65, 67
Offering Maat *(ḥnk m3^{c}t)*	67, 81, 82, 85, 88
The Way (good way, god's way)	52, 99, II/20, II/27
The Day of Judgment	35, 92, 98, 99, II/12, II/21, II/22, II/26, II/29, II/30
The Rewards of Rightness	14, 16, 33, 46, 49, 50, 51, 57, 58, 60, 61, 66, 82, 84, 85, 90, 93, 94, 96, 97, 98, II/19, II/22

C. A Ranking of Virtues and Vices

As far as is presently known, Egyptian moral thought was formulated in five types of literary sources. 1. Instructions in Wisdom, including the "Miscellanies" variety. 2. Autobiographies. 3. The Declarations of Innocence of BD 125. 4. Priestly prohibitions and declarations inscribed on Ptolemaic temple doors. 5. Imaginative Tales that conveyed moral lessons. There are then, for the time being, no indications that moral norms had been formulated as codes of ethics, that is to say, in a form stricter than that of the Instructions in Wisdom. Nor had the sages who composed Instructions appended lists of virtues and vices to their recommendations, prohibitions, and discussions. The closest approximation to such lists is found in the autobiographic self-praises with their extensive enumerations of rightness and denials of wrongdoing. Since the Middle Kingdom, such declarations often took the form of serried sequences of moral traits, as for instance that of Intef son of Sitamun (Study I, text 28), that one being a very sophisticated product, detailing the refined virtues of a royal steward. The New Kingdom further enlarged the scope of self-praises, especially by coining new abstract terms. Thus to some extent, the list form was there, but not as a deliberate ranking of virtues and vices. The ranked list that follows here is nevertheless legitimate in the sense that it is based on the prominence given to certain aspects of rightdoing and denials of wrongdoing, i.e. to certain virtues and vices, as they have emerged from the texts studied and from Indexes A & B.

Since the virtues appear mostly in adjectival form, they are so given here, whereas vices and crimes are more often expressed by nominal forms.

The Principal Virtues

Honest, true, upright	ʿq3, ʿq3-ib, m3ʿ-ib, m3ʿty, mty
Beneficent, kind, charitable	im3, im3-ib, wn-ib, ir-3ḫt, nfr, hnw, ḥḏ-ḥr
Just: fair and impartial	irt m3ʿt, tm rdi ḥr gs
Patient, steadfast, thoughtful	w3ḥ-ib
Selfcontrolled and calm	qb, qb-ẖt, d3r-srf, gr

Keen and competent	iqr, ʿrq, wḥʿ-ib, mnḫ, šs3, grg-ḥr
Loyal, devoted, trustworthy	iqr, mḥ-ib, mnḫ-ib, ir ḥr mw

Principal terms for being good: iqr, nfr, mnḫ, m3ʿty

The Principal Vices and Crimes

Lying, deceit, slander	grg, iwms, mdw, sḏw, nḏwyt, sp snnw
Greed and rapacity: robbing, stealing, cheating, coveting	ʿwn, ʿwn-ib, mr-ḫt, ḥnt, iṯi, ʿw3i, ḏ3i-r3
Aggression and violence	sh3, sḫm-ib
Anger, quarrel, shouting, cursing	ḥnw, q3-ḫrw, špt, šnṯ, šnt-nṯr, w3ʿ, sḥwr
Sloth, laziness, neglect	wni, mhi, ḥḏi

Principal terms for evil and crime: bin, bt3, grg, isft, ḏw, bw-ḏw, nḏyt, ḏ3t, ẖsy, ḫww

* * *

The abiding worth of this ancient ethic lies in its having placed the virtues of honesty and beneficence at the very center of its system. Modern philosophy reaffirms the primacy and universality of these two moral principles.

IV

THE "APPEAL TO THE LIVING" THROUGH THE AGES

This investigation was prompted by reading autobiographical inscriptions of the Late Period and encountering "Appeals to the living" which employ grammatical constructions different from those commonly found in the earlier periods and which have led the editors of the texts into believing that emendations were required. To cite now just one example: On the Saite statue of Nesnawiya, published by Ranke in ZÄS 44, 1907, 42ff., there occurs an "Appeal to the living" which begins thus:

i w^{c}bw nb srw nb sšw nb
^{c}q.sn r ir ẖt m ḥt-nṯr ...

Ranke's translation reads: "O all ihr Priester, Vornehmen und Schreiber, die ihr eintretet, um im Tempel von Edfu alltäglich zu opfern", etc. And he added the note: "*^{c}ḳsn* steht natürlich für *^{c}ḳtjwsn*".

The opinion that what looks like the sḏm.f form *(^{c}q.sn)* stands for the sḏmty.fy form *(^{c}qty.sn)* has prevailed until today, though two scholars, Clère and Caminos, have expressed some doubt or dissent (see below pp. 183f. & 188f.). The reigning view was stated quite recently by Jansen-Winkeln in his Ägyptische Biographien der 22. und 23. Dynastie (1985), p. 179, n. 29: "Die *sḏm.tj.fj*-Form wird in der Spätzeit häufig defektiv ohne *.tj* geschrieben." There follows a long list of alleged defective writings.

Since J.S.F.Garnot's dissertation on the "Appel aux vivants" in the Old Kingdom (Cairo 1938) the "Appeal" does not seem to have been studied, wherefore its Late Period forms have not been seen in the overall context. Hence the purpose of this study is to review the "Appeal" throughout its history. As Edel observed in his Untersuchungen zur Phraseologie der ägyptischen Inschriften des AR, pp. 2-3, the "Appeal to the living" should be distinguished from the "Address to visitors", even though the two are often intertwined. This study deals only with the "Appeal", but its results are also relevant to the "Address".

A few examples will recall the main forms of the "Appeal to the living", which began in the 5th and evolved during the 6th dynasty. The tomb of *Mry-rʿ-nfr,* called *Q3r,* had two matching Appeals (Urk. I, 252.2 & 255.9):

1) i ʿnḫw tpw t3
ʿqt(y).sn r is pn n ẖrt-nṯr
mrrw ḥs sn nṯr.sn
ḏdw t ḥnqt iḥw 3pdw ...

O living ones on earth
who will enter this tomb of the graveyard,
who wish their god to favor them:
Say, bread, beer, beef, fowl ...

2) i ʿnḫw tpw t3
sw3t(y).sn ḥr is pn
mrrw nswt ḏdt(y).sn
ḫ3 t ḫ3 ḥnqt ḫ3 iḥw ...

O living ones on earth
who will pass by this tomb,
the king's beloved are those who will say,
1000 bread, 1000 beer, 1000 beef ...

The two Appeals are clearly designed as a pair, and they show the basic tripartite scheme which was worked out during the 6th dynasty. Its three steps are: (a) The owner of the memorial hails the potential visitors; (b) he affirms that they possess the right motivation, or goodwill, for performing the pious act desired of them, which is to make an offering or to recite an offering prayer; (c) accordingly, he makes the request for an offering or a prayer.

For step (a) each Appeal uses one of the principal verbs denoting the approach to the tomb, *ʿq* and *sw3,* respectively. For step (b), the motivation, the Appeals refer to the visitators' desire to enjoy the favor of the god or of the king. As step (c) both Appeals request an offering prayer.

The one major difference between the two Appeals is that the first Appeal describes the motivation (b) by means of a participle clause which is syntactically independent of the request (c), while in the second Appeal the motivation and the request are construed as a single sentence (b) + (c). The point is worth noting because the manner in which motivation and request were linked became subject to many variations, and these variations are significant since they reflect the continuous evolution, or transformations, of the Appeal throughout the ages.

The linkage of motivation and request by means of the formulation *mrrw nswt ḏdt(y).sn* is common in Old Kingdom Appeals; and a significant expansion of the formulation was effected by means of the copula *pw* inserted between predicate and subject:

3) Appeal in the Deir el-Gebrawi tomb of *Ḏʿw* (Urk. I, 147):

i ʿnḫw tpw t3
b3kw mityw.i
mrrw nswt pw ḥssw nṯr.sn niwty ḏdt(y).sn
ḫ3 t ḥnqt ...

O living ones on earth,
servants like myself:
the king's beloved and favored of their town-god are they who will say
1000 bread, beer ...

4) And with further expansion in the Saqqara tomb of *Ḫwi* (Drioton, ASAE 43, 1943, 503):

mrrw nswt pw
mrrw Inpw tpy ḏw.f pw
ẖry-ḥb nb iwt(y).fy r ir n(.i) s3ḫw ...

Beloved of the king is,
beloved of Anubis on his mountain is
every lector-priest who will come to make my transfiguration ...

An unusual manner of linking the motivation with the performance is found on the Abydos stela of *Ppy-ni* (Urk. I, 112):

5) i ʿnḫw tpw t3
b3kw mity(w.i)

wnnt(y).sn <m> šms nṯr ḏdt(y).sn
ḫ3 t ḫ3 ḥnqt ...

O living ones on earth,
servants like myself:
Ones-who-will-be <in> the following of the god are they-
who-will-say
1000 bread, 1000 beer ...

Here the predicate of the sentence linking the motivation with the requested performance consists not of a participle *(mrrw)* but of the sḏmtyfy form *(wnnt(y).sn)*. The result is a very compact linkage between motivation and requested performance, whereas the construction with passive participle and *pw* (nos. 3 & 4) made it possible to expand, or double, the predicate. Additional examples of the construction with *pw* are Urk. I, 70 and Urk. I, 186; and see Edel, Altäg. Gr. §§ 957 & 968.

So far then, the "Appeal to the living" in the Old Kingdom may be said to have evolved from the briefest possible request (e.g. "O living ones ... pour water for me", Urk. I, 75) to a tripartite formula (address + motivation + request) in which the linkage between motivation and requested offering (or prayer) became the focal point. There were, however, Appeals in which the second step, the motivation, was absent. Instead, there appeared an alternative request, added on to the principal one:

6) Second Appeal in the Saqqara tomb of Khui (Drioton, ASAE 43, 1943, 503)

i ʿnḫw tpw t3 im3ḫw mrw nṯr
sw3t(y).sn ḥr is pn n ḫrt-nṯr
dd.ṯn n.i t ḥnqt m ntt m-ḫt.ṯn
ir nfr.n wnn m-ḫt.ṯn ḏd.k3.ṯn m r3.ṯn ...

O living ones on earth and honored ones beloved of god,
who will pass by this tomb of the necropolis,
you shall give me bread and beer of what you own.
If you own nothing, then say with your mouth ...

The main intent of this Appeal is to proffer an alternative method of giving and it does so emphatically by means of the substantival sḏm.f *dd.ṯn* stating the request, and the sḏm.k3.f *ḏd.k3.ṯn* proposing the alternative. This particular form of the Appeal occurs more than once, but it was distinctly a by-way and not the main road, for in the interest of stressing alternate methods of giving, it had omitted the all-important motivation for giving. Why could it not have done both? It could and did when an inventive scribe found the right balance in which the three main elements of the Appeal - address, motivation, request - were rounded off by a brief suggestion of alternate methods of giving, all done with that utmost sparseness and brevity of phrasing which governed all Old Kingdom pronouncements:

7) Tomb of Pepiankh the Middle at Meir (Urk. I, 223.17-224.3):

i rmṯ nb šmw m ḫd iw m ḫnt
ʿnḫ n.ṯn nswt ʿnḫ n.ṯn nṯr nty-ṯn ḫr.f
dd.ṯn n.i t ḥnqt m ntt m-ʿ.ṯn
f33.[ṯn] m ʿ.ṯn wdn.ṯn m r3.ṯn

O all people who go north, who come south:
As the king lives for you, as the god you are with lives for you,
you shall give me bread and beer of what is in your hand,
you shall proffer it by hand and offer it by mouth!

This Appeal is both a summing up of the old and a beginning of the new:

i. The "living ones" have been turned into "travellers north and south".
ii. The motivation for their readiness to give an offering - their being favored by king and god - has been turned into an oath formula.
iii. The request for making an offering with what is in hand is stressed by means of the substantival sḏm.f *dd.ṯn*.
iv. The alternative methods of either giving by hand or reciting by mouth are stressed by more substantival sḏm.f forms. In Orientalia 38, 1969, 472 Polotsky pointed out that these sentences were excellent examples of the substantival ("emphatic") sḏm.f stressing the contrasted prepositional phrases.

* * *

The Appeals of the First Intermediate Period range from very brief to very elaborate. Their principal innovation was to describe the "living ones on earth" as people "who love life and hate death".

8) A brief Appeal which lacks the element of motivation is that of the stela of Snni (Fischer, Dendera, 195ff. & 209ff.):

i ᶜnḫw i tpw t3
mrrw ᶜnḫ msḏḏw ḫpt
ḏd.ṯn ḫ3 mw ḫ3 t ḥnqt ...

O living ones, o earth-borne ones,
who love life, who hate death:
Say, 1000 water, 1000 bread, beer ...

The repetition of i creates two symmetrical phrases, and these are matched by the parallel "love-life, hate-death" epithets. This doubling of i recurs elsewhere, e.g. in our no. 10.

9) An Appeal that repeats the "alternate method of giving" of the second Appeal of Khui (no. 6) is the Naga ed-Deir Appeal of *K3k3* (Dunham, Naga ed-Dêr, no. 83):

i ᶜnḫw tpw t3
mrrw ᶜnḫ msḏḏw ḫpt
sw3t(y).sn ḥr is pn
iw.ṯn r dit n.i t ḥnqt m-ᶜ.ṯn
ir nfr.n wnn m-ᶜ.ṯn iw.ṯn r ḏd m r3.ṯn ...

O living ones on earth
who love life, who hate death,
who shall pass by this tomb:
You shall give me the bread and beer in your hand.
If there is none in your hand you shall say with your mouth ...

The principal change from the forms of no. 6 is the use of the iw.f r sḏm construction in place of the substantival sḏm.f and sḏm.k3.f forms.

10) The long Appeal in the tomb of the nomarch It-ibi of Siut (Griffith, Siut, pl. 11, top line; Brunner, Siut, pp. 42 & 17) develops the concept of piety as the motivation for the respectful acts which

future visitors should perform, all the enumerated acts being cast in the sḏmty.fy form:

i ʿnḫw tpw t3
msw ntyw r mst
ḫdwt(y).sn ḫntt(y).sn
iwt(y).sn m šms n Wpw3wt nb s3wt
irt(y).sn sw3w ḥr wʿrt tn
ʿqt(y).sn r is pn
m33t(y).sn ntt im.f
ʿnḫ n.ṯn Wpw3wt nb s3wt
Inpw nb r3-qrrt
iw.ṯn r dw3 nṯr r pr-ḫrw ...

O living ones, o earth-borne ones,
the born and to be born,
who will fare north and south,
who will come in the following of Wepwawet, Siut's lord,
who will do a march-past on this ground,
will enter this tomb,
will see what is in it:
As Wepwawet, Siut's lord, lives for you,
and Anubis, lord of *r3-qrrt,*
you shall praise god and make offering ...

Note that the request for offering is made by means of the iw.f r sḏm form, as was the case in text no. 9.

* * *

In the reign of Nebhepetre Mentuhotep II the "Appeal to the living" acquired its definitive direction: it became an Appeal addressed primarily to the priesthood and personnel of a temple.

11) The stela of Meru (Turin 1447, from TT 240, PM I^2, 331; Lichtheim, Autobiographies, 63f. & pl. III) has a double Appeal, one in the lunette, the other in the main text.
In the lunette:

i ḥmw nṯr ḥmwt nṯr
ḥsw ḥswt ḫnw ḫnwt

ẖrd nb nw t3-wr 3bḏw
rn pw nfr sḫ3.ṯn m 3bd ...

O priests, priestesses,
songsters, songstresses, musicians male and female,
all servants of Thinite Abydos:
It is a good name that you recall at the monthly feast ...

In the main text:

i ꜥnḫw tpw t3
wnnt(y).sn m šms n Ḫntimntiw n Wpw3wt
mrrw ꜥnḫ msḏḏw ḫpt
wꜥbw nw nṯr ꜥ3
ḥmw nṯr nb n 3bḏw
m mrr.ṯn wnn im3ḫ.ṯn ḫr Wsir
prr.ṯn ḫrw stt.ṯn m t ḥnqt wnnt(y).f(y) m-ꜥ.ṯn
iw ḏd.ṯn ḫ3 m t ḫ3 m ḥnqt ...

O living ones on earth
who will be in the following of Khentamenthes and Wepwawet,
who love life and hate death,
priests of the great god,
all priests of Abydos:
As you wish to have honor before Osiris,
you shall make a voice-offering and shall libate with the bread and beer that may be in your hand,
while you say, 1000 of bread, 1000 of beer ...

Here, then, the "living ones on earth" have become the personnel of the Osiris-and-Wepwawet temple at Abydos, whose occupation predisposes them to the performance of pious rites. Thus the motivation to perform an offering to the dead, the name of which is piety, is now fully established at the center of the Appeal, and fully linked to the actual request for offering. In addition to this innovating address to the priesthood the text offers a new formulation in the phrase, "it is a good name that you recall ...".

The division of the Appeal into two parts probably had to do with the newness of the round-topped stela which required new solutions for organizing the surface. The Abydene stela of *Mḥ3t*

(Leiden V 2 = Boeser, Beschreibung, v. II, no. 7 & pl. vi), bearing the regnal date "year 9" of Sesostris I, has an Appeal which is strikingly similar to that of Meru, except that the slight awkwardness of the earlier two-part Appeal has been eliminated and the whole is streamlined and simplified:

12) iʿnḫw tpw t3
wnnt(y).sn m šms n Wsir Ḫntimntiw
n Wpw3wt Inpw nb t3 d̲sr
ḥmw nt̲r nb wʿbw nb ḥmwt nt̲r
ḥsw ḥswt ḫnw ḫnwt
rmt̲ nbt nw t3-wr 3bd̲w
rn pw nfr sḫ3w.t̲n m r3-pr pn d̲d.t̲n
ḫ3 m t ḥnqt iḥw 3pdw ...

O living ones on earth
who will be in the following of Osiris Khentamenthes,
of Wepwawet and Anubis, lord of the sacred land,
all priests, web-priests, priestesses,
songsters, songstresses, musicians male and female,
and all people of Thinite Abydos:
It is a good name that you recall in this temple when you say,
1000 of bread, beer, beef, fowl ...

In the streamlined form, the phrase "it is a good name that you recall in this temple" also occurs on the 12th dynasty Abydene stela Durham-Alnwick Castle 1932 (Simpson, Terrace, ANOC 31.1) and, slightly varied, on the 12th dynasty Abydene stela CG 20088. It is still used in the 18th dynasty, e.g. on the stela Cairo JE 59636, published by Lacau in Mélanges Mariette (IFAO, Bibliothèque d'Etude 32, 1961, 211ff.). The phrase is worth noting, the more so since it was not understood by the editors of the Leiden Museum handbook De egyptische Oudheid (1981), where the stela of *Mḥ3t* is no. 44.

The new orientation toward the temple priesthood brought major changes in situating the persons addressed. The priests and other temple personnel were not viewed as future visitors but as being present at all times. That resulted in an increased use of participles and sd̲m.f forms in describing their motivations and actions, and a corresponding decrease in the use of the sd̲mty.fy form. It also led to the gradual avoidance of the phrase "who love life, who hate death", the proclaimed hatred of death evidently not being a suitable priestly and pious attitude. On the Abydene stela of Dedu-Sobk, in year 10 of Sesostris I (CG 20026) the Appeal reads:

13) iꜥnḫw tpw t3
m ḥmw nṯr ḥmwt nṯr wꜥbw
ḥnw ḥnwt nw r3-pr pn n Wsir Ḫntimntiw
irrw ḫt im.f n sꜥḥw.sn
ḏd.ṯn ḫ3 t ḥnqt ...

O living ones on earth,
namely priests, priestesses, web-priests,
musicians male and female of this temple of Osiris
Khentamenthes,
who perform rites in it for their blessed ones:
May you say, 1000 bread, beer ...

Here, the activities of the temple personnel are described solely by the active participle *irrw*. In the next Appeal, the motivation of the "living ones" is expressed by sḏm.f forms:

14) Stela of Shensetji (Faulkner, JEA 38, 1952, 3-5):
iꜥnḫw tpw t3
mrrw ꜥnḫ msḏḏw ḫpt
šms.ṯn Wpw3wt r nmtt.f nbt
ḥtp ibw.ṯn m ꜥnḫ tp t3
iw.ṯn r rdit n.i prt ḫrw m 3bd ...

O living ones on earth
who love life, who hate death:
As you follow Wepwawet in his every stride
and your hearts are content with life on earth,
you shall give me a voice-offering on the monthly feast ...

Here the "love-life-hate-death" phrase is present; in the next text it has been ousted by deliberate rephrasing:

15) Stela of Intef (Leiden V 6 = Boeser, Beschreibung, v. II, no. 4 & pl. iii; reign of Amenemhet II):

i ʿnḫw tpw t3
mrrw ʿnḫ msw.sn
ḥss tn nṯr.tn niwty ḏd.ṯn
ḫ3 t ḫ3 ḥnqt ...

O living ones on earth,
who wish their children to live:
Your town-god will favor you if you say,
1000 bread, 1000 beer ...

A new motif that gained currency in the second half of the 12th dynasty was the suggestion that reciting the offering prayer would benefit the doer as much as, or more than, the recipient. Many examples of this new formula were assembled by Vernus in RdE 28, 1976, 139-145, hence a single example will suffice here:

16) Stela of *Nfrniy* (Florence 1540 = Bosticco, Stele egiziane , no. 24; Sethe, Les., no. 28f.; Simpson, Terrace, ANOC 44.2 & pl. 63):
i ʿnḫw tpw t3
sš nb ẖry-ḥb nb sr nb
sw3t(y).sn ḥr šps pn
mr.ṯn w3ḥ n.ṯn Wsir nb ʿnḫ ḥq3 ḏt
ḏd.ṯn ḫ3 m t ḥnqt ....
ḏr ntt 3ḫ n ir r irw n.f
ṯ3w n r3 3ḫ n sʿḥ
nn nw m wrdt ẖr.s

O living ones on earth,
every scribe, every lector-priest, every noble,
who shall pass by this stela:
As you desire the grace of Osiris, lord of life, ruler of duration,
you shall say, 1000 of bread, beer ....
For it helps the giver more than the recipient;
breath of the mouth helps the blessed
and is not something that wearies.

The argument is designed to strengthen the motivation of the potential giver. The motivation itself is defined as desiring the grace of Osiris. Defining the pious motivation of the visitors, and linking it to the request for performing a donation by hand or by mouth, was the central intent of the Middle Kingdom Appeals. It was carried out by a variety of formulations: (a) Formulations relating to the priestly functions of the potential visitors (nos. 11-13). (b) Formulations describing the visitors in general as servants of a god and desirous of the god's favor (nos. 14-15). Here also belong those formulations which continue the Old Kingdom type (nos. 2-5) in which desire for the god's favor was linked with the requested performance of offering or prayer in a single brief sentence construed by means of a participle and a sḏmty.fy form. The Middle Kingdom formulations employ either the active or the passive participle. With active participle:

17) Abydos stela of *Q3y* (CG 20567). The Appeal begins the three-line text:

> mrr ḥss sw H̱ntimntiw ḏdt(y).f(y)
> ḫ3 m ḫt nb n im3ḫ(w) Q3y m3ʿ-ḫrw
>
> One desirous of the favor of Khentamenthes is one who will say,
> 1000 of everything for the honored Qay, justified.

The same formula occurs in CG 20046 and CG 20523. With passive participle:

18) Abydos stela of *Ptḥ-wr* (CG 20061; Sethe, Les., 87c):

> mrr(w) nṯr.f niwty nswt imi h3w.f
> sw3t(y).f(y) ḥr ʿb3 pn ḏdt(y).f(y)
> ḫ3 t ḥnqt iḥw 3pdw ...
>
> Beloved of his town-god and the king of his time
> is one who will pass by this stela and will say,
> 1000 bread, beer, beef, fowl ...

The main contribution of the Middle Kingdom, however, was to shape the motivation and the request in the form of a protasis-apodosis construction. In brief form we have it in exx. 11, 14, and 16. Since the middle of the 12th dynasty it was extended to lengthy sequences:

19) Stela of *Rmny-ʿnḫ* (CG 20748; Simpson, Terrace, ANOC 34, pl. 52):

i ḥmw-nṯr mty n s3w ẖry-ḥbw ḥm-k3w nb
wnnw n ḥt-nṯr nt Ḫntimntiw
ʿnḫw tp t3 sw3t(y).sn ḥr mʿḥʿt tn
m mr.ṯn grg ḥt-nṯr tn nt Wsir Ḫntimntiw
Wpw3wt nṯr.ṯn bnr mrwt
ʿḥʿ ẖrdw.ṯn ḥr nswt.ṯn
ḏd.ṯn ḥtp di nswt ...

O priests, phyle chiefs, lector-priests, and all ka-priests,
who are in the temple of Khentamenthes,
and living ones on earth who will pass by this memorial:
As you wish this temple of Osiris Khentamenthes to flourish,
and of Wepwawet, your lovable god,
and that your children stand in your places,
you shall say, An offering-that-the-king-gives ...

Both the temple personnel who are *(wnnw)* in the temple and the future visitors who will pass by *(sw3ty.sn)* are said to be motivated by the wish to see the Osiris-Wepwawet temple flourish (*grg* in the intransitive sense) and also to see their children prosper. The wish to see the Osiris temple of Abydos flourish is a specifically Abydene formulation, which recurs a number of times (e.g. Basel III 5002; Geneva D 50, both in Geschenk des Nils, ed. H. Schlögl, Basel 1978; BM 805 = HT III, 40; CG 20119; CG 20141 (with *ḥtp* instead of *grg*); CG 20224 (*rd* instead of *grg*); CG 20683. The most common and general formulation is the sequence, "As you desire the gods to favor you, so shall you say, an offering-that-the-king-gives ...". The protasis, "as you desire", is expressed by sḏm.f forms which either do or do not show gemination *(mrr.ṯn* or *mr.ṯn)* and either are or are not preceded by the preposition *m*. As for the apodosis, either it is construed with an optatival sḏm.f, "you shall say", as in no, 19, or it is introduced by the preposition *mi* with following sḏm.f: *mi ḏd.ṯn*; for example:

20) Stela of Sebekhotep (Tübingen 458; Sethe, Les., 88f., no. g = Brunner, Hierogl. Chrestomathie, pl. 11):

i ʿnḫw tp(w) t3
ẖry-ḥb nb sš nb wʿb sr nb

sw3tt(y).sn *(sic)* ḥr šps pn
ir.n.i r šwt n b3.i
r sḫn n šwt.i
m mrr.ṯn ḥs ṯn nṯrw.ṯn niwtiw
mn.ṯn ḥr nswt.ṯn
swḏ.ṯn i3wt.ṯn n ẖrdw.ṯn
pḥ.ṯn m ḥtp
sḏdw.ṯn mšʿw.ṯn n ḥmwt.ṯn
mi ḏd.ṯn ḥtp di nswt ...

O living ones on earth,
every lector-priest, every scribe, every web-priest and
official,
who will pass by this stela,
which I made as shade for my Ba,
as resting-place for my shadow:
As you desire your town-gods to favor you,
and that you endure in your positions,
that you bequeath your offices to your children,
that you reach (home) in peace
and relate your campaigns to your women,
so also shall you say, An offering-that-the-king-gives ...

Sethe in his Erläuterungen (88,23) explained the appearance of *mi* thus: "Die Worte *mj ḏd-ṯn* "wie ihr sagt", die hier mit "so saget" zu übersetzen sind, stammen wohl aus einer anderen Fassung der Anrufung, die etwa so lautete: "euch mögen eure Götter loben usw. wie (d.h. entsprechend der Thatsache dass) ihr sagt ..." The same explanation had earlier been given by H. Sottas in his La préservation de la propriété funéraire (1913), pp. 70-71, where he spoke of the reversal of the conditional and principal clauses, "Il vous arrivera tel bonheur, si vous dites ..." *(mi ḏd.ṯn)*. Le mélange des deux tournures aboutit souvent à des impossibilités grammaticales ..."

It has taken me a long time to realize that Sethe's and Sottas' explanation of *mi* as an intrusion from a differently structured Appeal, one in which the protasis was not a condition but a straight promise ("the gods shall favor you ...") is wrong. Such an intrusion from a different version of the Appeal did not take place because no such different version existed in the Middle Kingdom.

The explanation for the allegedly faulty *mi* is much simpler. The two parts of the sentence from "As you wish ..." to "so shall you say ..." were treated as an equation the meaning of which was: "just as you desire the gods' favor etc., so also shall you say ..." The preposition *mi* served to clearly mark the beginning of the apodosis while tying the two long halves of the equation together; and *mi* was perfectly capable of performing this function since it included the meanings "likewise", "accordingly", "so also", and "inasmuch as" (cf. Gardiner, Gr. §§ 170 & 205).

Sottas had listed two stelae as examples of Appeals with the alleged reversed construction in which the conditional clause would be the second member: CG 20093 and CG 20775. But CG 20093 has the usual form with conditional protasis. The text is a good illustration of the way in which the preposition *mi* functioned:

21) Stela of *Snb* (CG 20093; Simpson, Terrace, ANOC 49.1 & pl. 67):

i ꜥnẖw tpw t3
sš nb wꜥbw ḥm-k3 nb
mtyw nw s3w ḏ3ḏ3t pr Wsir
sr nb sw3t(y).fy ḥr šps pn
mrr.ṯn w3ḥ.ṯn tp t3
swḏ.ṯn i3wt.ṯn prw.ṯn n ẖrdw.ṯn
ḥs ṯn nṯrw.ṯn niwtiw
mi šd.ṯn ꜥb3 pn
mi ḏd.ṯn ḥtp di nswt ...

O living ones on earth,
every scribe, web-priests, every ka-priest,
chiefs of the phyles, council of the house of Osiris,
every official who will pass by this monument:
As you wish to endure upon earth,
to bequeath your offices, your homes to your children,
and to be favored by your town-gods,
so also shall you read this stela,
so also shall you say, An offering-that-the-king-gives ...

Here, the *mi* clearly shows that its function was to bring out the equation of protasis and apodosis, and by using *mi* twice the apodosis was lengthened so as to match the long protasis.

Appeals that are faultily constructed do occur in the latter part of the Middle Kingdom, but these faults are mere carelessness on the part of scribes or sculptors. They consist of omissions or misplacements of words or phrases:

22) The stela of Wahka I from his tomb at Qaw el-Kebir (Turin 1547; Steckeweh & Steindorff, Die Fürstengräber von Qaw, pl. 17a) begins with a prayer for offerings addressed to Osiris and abruptly turns into an Appeal to the living:

... rdi.tw n.i prt-ḫrw t ḥnqt iḥw 3pdw
ḥr ḫ3wt nt Wnn-nfr nṯr ʿ3 nb 3bḏw
Inpw nb t3 ḏsr
m mr.ṯn ḥs ṯn nṯrw.ṯn niwty
sw3t(y).fy nb ḥr wḏ pn
mi ḏd.tn ḥtp di nswt Inpw nb t3 ḏsr
n k3 n ḥ3ty-ʿ ...

... May be given me a voice-offering (of) bread-beer-beef-fowl
from the altar of Wenennofer, great god, lord of Abydos,
and Anubis, lord of the necropolis.
As you desire the favor of your town-gods,
every one who will pass by this stela,
so shall you say, An offering-that-the-king-gives
for the ka of the count ...

The actual address to the visitors is missing, and the phrase "everyone who will pass by ..." occupies the wrong place.

23) A similar omission occurs on the stela BM 240 (HT II, 32):

iʿnḫw tpw t3
sšw ẖry-ḥbw wʿbw ḥm-k3w nbw
rmṯ nbt sw3t(y).sn ḥr šps pn
mi ḏd.ṯn ḥtp di nswt ...

O living ones on earth,
all scribes, lector-priests, web-priests, ka-priests,
all people who will pass by this memorial,
so shall you say, An offering-that-the-king-gives ...

Here the entire protasis ("As you desire...") has been omitted.

Since the bulk of Middle Kingdom stelae belonged to ordinary citizens and minor officials, poor quality of carving style and text was of course frequent. However, the mediocre quality of Wahka's stela, coming as it does from a sumptuous tomb, is somewhat surprising. Chances are that this provincial noble had a mixed crew of craftsmen who produced work at differing levels. Officials posted at the royal residence must have had a clear advantage. The stela of Sehetepibre, treasurer of Amenemhet III, may serve to sum up the well-turned and elaborate Appeal in this latter part of the 12th dynasty. And note that this Appeal does not employ the preposition *mi*. Evidently the two types, with and without *mi*, were equally current in the second half of the Middle Kingdom.

14) Stela of Sehetepibre (CG 20538). The Appeal on the recto reads:

i ḥ3ty-ᶜ nb imy-r3 ḥm-nṯr nb ḥm-nṯr ᶜ3 nb
ẖry-ḥb nb sḏ3wty nṯr nb wt Inpw nb
ḥm-nṯr ᶜš3 nb mty n s3w nb
ᶜnḫ nb n niwt.ṯn ḫprt(y).fy m ḥt-nṯr tn
sw3t(y).sn ḥr mᶜḥᶜt tn
šdt(y).sn wḏ pn
m mrr.tn Wsir Ḫntimntiw
wḥm.tn irt ḥbw.f
m mrr.tn Wpw3wt nṯr.tn bnr mrwt
nḏm ib.tn m nswt r nḥḥ
mrw.tn ᶜnḫ sḫmw.tn mt
snb n.tn ẖrdw.tn
ḏd.tn m tp.t-r3.tn ḥtp di nswt ...

O every count, chief priest, high priest,
every lector-priest, god's treasurer, Anubis-priest,
every common priest, every phyle chief,
every one of your townsmen who will be in this temple,
who will pass by this memorial,
who will read this stela:
As you love Osiris Khentamenthes
and repeat performing his feasts,
as you love Wepwawet, your lovable god,
and your hearts rejoice in the king forever,
and you love life and forget death,

and your children thrive for you,
you shall say as your saying, An offering-that-the-king-gives ...

As for CG 20775 listed by Sottas as second example of a Middle Kingdom Appeal in which the conditional clause forms the apodosis (see p. 169) it is a stela found at Wadi Halfa of which its editors remarked "Wohl der 18. Dynastie angehörig", and that is surely the correct date. Its Appeal is of the kind discussed under no. 25.

In the 18th dynasty the repertoire of monumental biographic texts was markedly expanded by prayers to the gods for offerings and for an afterlife now formulated in detail as a vital otherworldly existence. The Appeal to the living became an adjunct to these lengthy orations.

On his Karnak statue from the temple of Mut, Hatshepsut's minister Senenmut declares that his statue is in the temple by royal grant, continues with an autobiographical narration, turns to the visitors with an appeal for recital of the offering formula and for their prayer to the goddess on his behalf, and concludes with a second appeal to visitors.

25) The two-part Appeal (Urk. IV, 412 & 415) reads:

a) i ꜥnḫw tpw t3 wnwt ḥt-nṯr
m3t(y).sn twt.i snn.i
[⸢n mrwt mn⸣] sḫ3.i m ẖrt-nṯr
ḥs tn nṯrt.tn ꜥ3t mi ḏd.tn
ḥtp di nswt ...

O living ones on earth and temple staff,
who will see my statue, my likeness,
[⸢which maintains⸣] my memory in the necropolis:
Your great goddess will favor you inasmuch as you will say,
An offering-that-the-king-gives ...

b) ṯ3w n r3 3ḫ n sꜥḥ
nn nw m wrdt ẖr.s
ink sꜥḥ n sḏm n.f
ꜥq.kwi grt ḥr sšw nb n ḥmw-nṯr ...

Breath of the mouth helps the blessed
and is not something that wearies;
I am one blessed to whom one must listen,
for I have entered into all the writings of the priests ...

By this last statement Senenmut not only tells his visitors that he is powerful by virtue of his knowledge; he also informs his present readers that he had studied the ancient writings: the reception of Middle Kingdom texts was in full flow; and just as in the Middle Kingdom, conservating and innovating tendencies were inextricably meshed. As for the syntax of Senenmut's Appeal, it is of the type which Sottas and Sethe had surmised to be the Middle Kingdom model from which the use of the preposition *mi* had been taken over: a main clause consisting of the promise "the gods will favor you", followed by a conditional clause with *mi* in the sense of "inasmuch as". This type of Appeal is indeed common in the 18th dynasty, but I do not know any examples of it from the Middle Kingdom.

26) The Appeal of Intef, count of Thinis, in the reign of Thutmosis III, (Louvre C 26 = Urk. IV, 965f.) has a similar mixture of Middle Kingdom phrases and new formulations:

i ʿnḫw tpw t3 rmṯ nb
wʿb nb sš nb ẖry-ḥb nb
ʿqt(y).sn r is pn n ẖrt-nṯr
mrw *(sic)* ʿnḫ sḫm.tn mt
ḥsw ṯn nṯrw.ṯn niwtiw
nn dp.ṯn snḏt nt ky t3
qrstw.tn m isw.tn
swḏ.ṯn i3wt.ṯn n ẖrdw.ṯn
m šdtt(y).fy *(sic)* mdwt.ṯn *(sic)* ḥr wḏ pn m sš
m sḏmt(y).fy st
mi ḏd.ṯn ḥtp di nswt ...

O living ones on earth, all people,
every web-priest, every scribe, every lector-priest,
who will enter this tomb of the necropolis:
you who love life and forget death,
your town-gods will favor you,

you will not taste the fear of the other land,
you will be buried in your tombs,
you will bequeath your office to your children -
be he one who will read this speech on this stela as a scribe,
be he one who will hear it -
inasmuch as you will say, An offering-that-the-king-gives ...

The Appeals of Senenmut and of Intef both employ the sḏmty.fy form to describe the standard actions of the visitors: "entering" the tomb or temple, "seeing" the stela or statue, and "reading" or "hearing" its text. In the next Appeal, however, the actions of the visitors are cast in sḏm.f forms.

27) Stela of Menkheperresonb, called Menkheper, reign of Thutmosis III, (Urk. IV, 1197):

i ꜥnḫw tpw t3
[wnn]yw ꜥnḫw nḥḥ ḥnty ḏt
[wꜥbw ẖry-ḥbw nw Wsir Ḫntimntiw]
šs3w nb m mdw nṯr
ꜥq.sn r is.i sw3š.sn ḥr.f
šd.sn m wḏ.i sḫ3.n *(sic)* rn.i
ḥs tn [nṯr.tn]
swḏ.tn i3wt.tn n [ẖrdw.tn m-ḫt i3wt w3ḥ]
mn s3 ḥr nst it.f m ḥswt nṯr niwty nb
ꜥnḫ n.sn Rꜥ m ḥrt Wsir m r3-[st3w]
[mi] ḏd.tw *(sic)* ḥtp di nswt

O living ones on earth,
[people] living in future times,
[web-priests, lector-priests of Osiris Khenamenthes,]
all those skilled in divine words:
As they enter my tomb, worship in it,
read my stela, recall my name,
[your god] will favor you,
you will bequeath your office to [your children in old age],
a son will abide in his father's seat in the favor of every town-god,
Re will live for you in heaven and Osiris in Ro[stau]
inasmuch as you will say, An offering-that-the-king-gives ...

The Appeal of Menkheper is part of a long prayer for a blissful afterlife, a text which is partly preserved on six other stelae ranging in date from the reign of Thutmosis III to that of Ay (Urk. IV, 1515ff. "der grosse Stelentext"). The Appeal is fairly complete only on the stelae of Menkheper and Nakhtmin (reign of Ay, Louvre C 55 = Urk. IV, 1536f.). The later text has the better scribal copy and gives the correct *sẖ3.sn* for Menkheper's *sẖ3.n*; it also has *ḏd.tn* in place of Menkheper's peculiar , an odd spelling which we shall encounter again.

28) A fitting counterpart to the long orations of the great officials is the terse Appeal on the stela of the craftsman *Iwn3*, a builder of sacred barks (HT VIII, 33 = Urk. IV, 1632):

ir s nb šdty.fy nb mdw pn
ḥsy tn nn nṯrw mḏḥ.i n.sn wi3w
di.sn n.ṯn ʿnẖ nfr i3wt nfrt qrst nfrt

As for every man who will read this speech,
the gods for whom I made barks will favor you,
they will give you a good life, good old age, good burial.

29) The reign of Akhenaten stifled the Appeal. Its place was taken by pious exhortations, such as the speech of the god's father Ay in his Amarna tomb (Urk. IV, 1998):

i wʿ nb ʿnẖ tp t3 ḏ3mw nb ẖpr
ḏd.i n.tn w3t n ʿnẖ mtr.i n.tn ḥswt
k3 šd.tn ḥr rn.i ḥr irt.n.i
ink m3ʿ tp t3

irw i3w n itn ʿnẖ
rwḏ.tn m ʿnẖ
ḏdw n.f ssnb p3 ḥq3
k3b.f n.tn ḥswt

O every living one on earth and all generations to be!
I will tell you the way of life and bear witness to you of favor;
then may you read of my name and my deeds,
I was a true one on earth!

Adore the living Aten,
so as to prosper in life;
tell him, "Give health to the ruler",
that he may double favors to you!

Two well turned quatrains.

The Ramesside Age revived the Appeal and introduced more innovations.

30) The stela of Didia, chief draftsman of Amun, in the reign of Seti I, has this Appeal (Louvre C 50, KRI I, 328):

i ḥmw nṯr wꜥbw ẖry-ḥbw
sš nb nw pr Wsir
šdd.sn wḏ pn n nbw nḥḥ
iḫ ḏd.tw ḥtp di nswt
ṯtf.tw mw ḥr st3w n Wsir
mr sš qd n Imn Ddi3 nbt pr Iwy
k3 ḥs tn Wnn-nfr
swḏ.tw i3wt.tn n mstw m-ḫt i3wt w3ḥ
šsp.tw snw pr m-b3ḥ Imn Mwt Ḫnsw
di.f pḥ.tw imi-wrt

O priests, web-priests, lector-priests,
and every scribe of the house of Osiris:
It is to the eternal lords that you shall read this stela,
and you shall say, An offering-that-the-king-gives,
and shall pour water on the ground to the Osiris,
the chief draftsman of Amun Didia, and the housewife Iwy!
Then will Wenennofer favor you,
you will bequeath your office to your children when old age
has come,
you receive loaves that came before Amun, Mut and Khonsu -
may he let you reach the west!

Here, by means of the substantival sḏm.f *šdd.sn*, the deceased makes the remarkable request that the temple personnel should recite the stela text to the gods! Then come requests for the offering prayer and for libation, and the promise of rewards expressed by means of verb forms ending in *t* plus plural strokes: 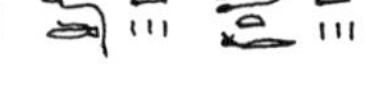

; even the noun *msw*, "children", has it: .
We have encountered the same in the appeal of Menkheper (no. 27) where the parallel text of Nakhtmin has *ḏd.tn*. Hence here also the peculiar ending replaces the second person plural ending *.tn*. And since even the noun *msw* shows this it is not possible to explain it as a writing of the indefinite pronoun *tw*. But why was it written at all? It can not be dismissed as a scribal error, since the scribe of Didia also wrote the normal endings *ḥs tn* and *i3wt.tn*, and because it occurs too often. In addition to the examples here given I have found two more, from the Third Intermediate and Late Period, respectively:
1. On the statue of Djedkhons-efankh, CG 42211, our no. 37: *iḫ ḏd.tw* ( ) *n.i ḫ3 m t* ... "may you say for me, 1000 of bread ...". In his new edition (Ägyptische Biographien) Jansen-Winkeln rendered, "Möge man für mich sprechen", and commented: "Oder, wenn man in emendiert, 'möget ihr'" (pp. 88 & 97). We have seen that can only have been a replacement for , not for ; and we are not entitled to dismiss and emend it.
2. Cairo statue 922 of *Pwbs* (Borchardt, Statuen und Statuetten, III, 155f.). This man was a high steward of a divine votaress *(mr-pr wr dw3t-nṯr)*. He makes an Appeal in which he requests: "May you say, drink till drunkenness, Count Pubes!" I propose that the writing for is the same phenomenon as the loss of *n* in the third-plural ending *sn*, where the no longer written *n* is also replaced by plural strokes. That loss of *n* is surveyed by B. Kroeber in his Die Neuägyptizismen vor der Amarnazeit (1970), 32-34.

Returning to our main theme - the grammatical and semantic changes of the Appeal with special attention to the use or non-use of the sḏmty.fy form - we have reached the time, the long reign of Ramses II, when the sḏmty.fy form is definitely receding, its function being assumed by participles and sḏm.f forms.

31) A statue of the vizier Paser, in the reign of Ramses II, has two Appeals, one on either side of the seat (CG 561, KRI III, 20)
Right side:

i ꜥnḫw ḥr t3
ẖry-ḥb nb sš nb wꜥb nb ḥm-k3 nb
sw3t(y).sn ḥr twt.i pn

ḏ3t.tn n.i ᶜwy.tn
dit n.i ḥtp m b3ḥ.i ...

O living ones on earth,
every lector-priest, scribe, web-priest, ka-priest,
who will pass by my statue,
stretch out your hands to me,
place an offering before me ...

Left side:

i ḥmw-nṯr itw-nṯr
iw.sn ḥr-s3 iry
ḥsy tn Imn-rᶜ Ḥt-ḥr nbt ḏsr
mi ḏd.tn ḥtp di nswt ...

O priests and divine fathers,
as they will come hereafter:
Amen-Re and Hathor, lady of holiness, will favor you,
inasmuch as you will say, An offering-that-the-king-gives ...

In these two complementary Appeals the sḏmty.fy form *sw3t(y).sn* and the sḏm.f *iw.sn* are balanced against each other. And from this time onwards the sḏmty.fy form becomes rare.

32) *Nfr-mnw*, mayor of Thebes in the reign of Ramses II, situated his Appeal in the context of the valley feast (TT 184, KRI III, 163):

i ḥmw nṯr itw nṯr wᶜbw ẖry-ḥbw
nty nb ḥr irt ḥnty.sn m-ẖnw pr-Imn
šmsw ḥr t3 r m33 Imn m ḥb.f nfr m int
stwt.sn m int špst ...

O priests, divine fathers, web-priests, lector-priests,
all who perform their task in the temple of Amun,
who serve on earth to view Amun in his beautiful valley feast,
as they walk in procession in the august valley ...

A timeless present reigns here: in the temple the priests are at their daily tasks *(ḥr irt ḥnty.sn)*, and at the valley feast they walk in procession *(stwt.sn)*. The same Appeal is inscribed in the tomb of a contemporary, the high steward *Nbswmnw* (KRI III, 185).

33) On the front of his statue in Munich the famous high priest Bakenkhonsu has this brief Appeal (KRI III, 297):

i ḥmw nṯr itw nṯr wꜥbw nw pr-Imn
imi ꜥnḫw n ẖntw.i st mw n ḏt.i

O priests, divine fathers, and web-priests of Amun's house:
give garlands to my statue, pour water to my body!

And on the dorsal pillar he addresses posterity thus:

i rmṯ nb ipw m ib.sn
wnnyw nty tp t3
iiyw ḥr-s3.i n ḥḥ n ḥḥ
m-ḫt i3wt kḥkḥ
nty ib.sn ꜥrq m m33 3ḫw
di.i rḫ.tn qi.i wn tp t3
m i3wt nb ir.n.i ḏr msy.i ...

O all people who ponder in their hearts,
beings who are on earth,
and who will come after me in millions,
after frail old age,
whose hearts are skilled in perceiving merit:
I will let you know my nature as it was on earth
in every office I held since my birth ...

Note the absence of sḏmty.fy forms. The priests are simply "of" the temple, and the people at large are defined by the participles *ipw* and *iiyw*.

34) The high priest Roma-Roy, on his Karnak statue CG 42186 in the reign of Amenmesses (KRI IV, 209), addresses the priesthood thus:

i ḥmw nṯr itw nṯr wꜥbw
ꜥ3yw nw pr Imn
ḏ3mw ꜥš3yw nty r ḫpr
imi [ꜥnḫw n ẖnty.i] ...

O priests, divine fathers, web-priests,
great ones of Amun's house,
and the many generations who will be:
give [garlands to my statue] ...

Note the construction *nty r ḫpr.*

35) On the 8th pylon at Karnak, the same Roma-Roy appeals to a long list of temple personnel (KRI IV, 288):

... nty iw.sn r ʿq r wʿbt pn nty m ẖnw [pr Imn] ...
... who will enter this workshop which is in [the house of Amun] ...

To sum up the evidence of the New Kingdom Appeals: In the early 18th dynasty the sḏmty.fy form is still in frequent use to describe the actions of future visitors. In the course of the 19th dynasty the sḏmty.fy form becomes infrequent, for it is increasingly replaced by participles, sḏm.f forms, and the future tense iw.f r sḏm. Altogether, the formulations of Ramesside Appeals are less traditional, more innovating, and infused with elements of the Late-Egyptian vernacular.

* * *

The largest body of source material for the Appeal to the living in the Third Intermediate Period derives from the statues of the priests of Amun found in the Karnak Cache. Selectively published by Legrain in the Catalogue général (Statues, III) they have now been republished in an improved edition with translations by K. Jansen-Winkeln: Ägyptische Biographien der 22. und 23. Dynastie (Wiesbaden 1985). Of the twenty-three fully published statue texts, numbered A 1 to A 23 in this new edition, eleven have an Appeal (nos. A 3, A 5, A 6, A 8, A 9, A 11, A 12, A 15, A 17, A 20, and A 23). Of these eleven, only one exhibits a sḏmty.fy form:

36) Statue of Hori (Cairo JE 37512 = Jansen-Winkeln, no. A 20, pp. 217 & 561):

i ḥm-nṯr nb sš nb ẖry-ḥb nb wʿb nb
m3t(y).f(y) ḥs pn m r3-pr pn
ḥs tn Imn ḥr ir.n.tn mi m3.tn wi ...

O every priest, scribe, lector-priest, web-priest,
who will see this statue in this temple:
Amun will favor you for what you do according as you see
me ...

Four of the other ten Appeals are cited here so as to illustrate their types.

37) Statue of Djedkhonsefankh (CG 42211 = Jansen-Winkeln, no. A 6, pp. 88 & 474):

i ḥmw-nṯr itw nṯr wʿbw ẖry-ḥbw
wnwt ḥt-nṯr mi qd.sn
ʿq pr <m> ḥt Imn m ipt-swt
iḫ ḏd.tw n.i ḫ3 m t ḫ3 m ḥnqt ...

O priests, divine fathers, web-priests, lector priests,
and the entire staff of the temple,
who come and go <in> the temple of Amun of Ipet-sut:
May you say to me, 1000 of bread, 1000 of beer ...

Here the participles *ʿq pr* express the regular activities of the priests. As for the optatival *iḫ ḏd.tw* () in place of the normal *iḫ ḏd.tn*, turn back to pp. 176f.

38) Statue of Amenemone (CG 42230 = Jansen-Winkeln, no. A 15, pp. 172 & 533):

[i rmṯw] iww
<u>iw.sn</u> ḥr wḏ sḫr m sbḫ šmʿ
snw.i msw gsw.i
ḥmw-nṯr ʿq ḥr nṯr
ink pw ḥsy n nṯr.f ...

[O people] who will come,
<u>when they come</u> to give instructions in the gate of Upper
Egypt,
my brothers, children, and my colleagues,
priests who enter in to the god:
I am one favored by his god ...

The opening of this Appeal was rendered by Jansen-Winkeln as: "[O (ihr)] zukünftigen [(Menschen)], die kommen werden, indem sie Anordnungen treffen im oberägyptischen Tor", etc.; and it was to this *iw.sn*, rendered "die kommen werden", that he attached his note 29, cited on our p. 155: "Die *sḏm.tj.fj*-Form wird in der Spätzeit häufig defektiv ohne *.tj* geschrieben", followed by a list of alleged defective writings.

At this point I express the hope that the reader who has followed the argument so far will be reluctant to accept the claim that forms that look like sḏm.f forms are in reality defectively written sḏmty.fy's, and would rather entertain the notion that forms that look like sḏm.f's are in fact sḏm.f's. For the moment let us continue our survey.

39) Statue of Horakhbit (CG 42231 = Jansen-Winkeln, no. A 17, pp. 194 & 543):

> i wnw nty r ḫpr
> iw.sn ḥr s3 rnpwt
> imi prw n šms Imn r ḏd m3ᶜt mrr.f
>
> O people who will be,
> when they come after years:
> Give an extra to the service of Amun by speaking the truth he loves!

The same *iw.sn* as in no. 38.

40) Statuette of Nesbanebdjed (Brooklyn 37.344E = Jansen-Winkeln, no. A 23, pp. 239 & 576):

> i wᶜbw nb sš nb ᶜq.sn r ḥt-nṯr
> ḥs tn nṯr ᶜ3 ḏd.tn ḥtp di nswt ...
>
> O all web-priests, all scribes, when they enter the temple:
> The great god will favor you when you say, An offering-that-the-king-gives ...

The sḏm.f *ᶜq.sn* functions just like the sḏm.f *iw.sn* in nos. 38 & 39.

Stylistically, the Libyan and Nubian period statues and stelae are often so similar as to be indistinguishable. The Cairo statue of

another Nesbanebdjed, also from the Karnak Cache, JE 38039, which Caminos published in the Korostovtsev Festschrift (Moscow 1975, pp. 52ff.) and dated "9th century B.C. or thereabouts", may be placed here to mark the transition to the Late Period proper:
41) The handsome cube statue of this Theban priest Nesbanebdjed has a single inscription starting on the front of the skirt and continuing on the dorsal pillar. After a lengthy titulary Nesbanebdjed addresses a warning to those who would remove and damage his statue and a blessing to those who would recite an offering prayer:

> ir rmṯ nb sšw nb nḏsw nb
> rḫw nb nt *(sic)* r3-pr pn
> šd.sn ẖnt(.i) m r3-pr pn
> ḥḏ.n.sn sšw.f
> ḫr.sn n ḏndn n Imn wr
> iw.sn r ʿḏd n nswt
> ir iw rmṯ nb nḏsw nb sšw nb
> wʿbw nb nt *(sic)* r3-pr pn
> m3.sn ẖnt(.i) pn ḏd.sn
> ḫ3 m t ḥnqt snṯr mrḥt ...
> iw.f r i3w n niwt.f
> im3ḫw n spt.f
> ẖr ḥsw nt *(sic)* Imn

> As for all people, all scribes, all commoners,
> and all learned men of this temple:
> If they remove (my) statue from this temple
> and damage its writings,
> they shall fall by the wrath of great Amun,
> and be subject to slaughter by the king.
> But as for all people, all commoners, all scribes,
> and all priests of this temple:
> If they view this (my) statue and say,
> 1000 of bread, beer, incense, ointment ...
> he will be an elder of his town,
> a revered one of his nome,
> and in the favor of Amun.

The text has some faults, such as *nt* for *nw* and *ir iw* instead of *ir swt*. But such faults do not justify emending all the sḏm.f's to sḏmty.fy's; nor did Caminos think so, for he wrote: "For the construction ir noun phrase sḏm.f in col. 9 cf. Schäfer, Klio 6, 288, 1.9." This is a reference to Schäfer's edition, "Die sogenannte stèle de l'excommunication", in Klio 6, 1906, 287-296 (= Urk. III, 108-113) where the sentence *ir ḥmw nṯr nb wʿbw nb ir.sn sp m r3-prw* has the same kind of sḏm.f construction, which Schäfer rendered, "Alle Propheten und alle Priester, die etwas Böses tun in den Tempeln ..." (similarly Sottas, Préservation, 135f.). Of course the more accurate rendering would be, "... if (or, when) they commit a crime ...", and this is the sḏm.f that we have been tracing in Appeals to the living since the Middle Kingdom.

Basically, the Appeals of the Third Intermediate Period continue the New Kingdom types. The visitors are characterized by means of participles and sḏm.f's; and the requests addressed to them are formulated with a protasis promising rewards, or going directly to the request, they add a promise in the end, such as becoming "an elder of his town and revered in his nome". This Middle Kingdom phrase (Urk. VII, 54; also Siut tomb IV, 78) was still alive in the New Kingdom and had a vogue in the Late Period.

In the 25th dynasty the archaizing and eclectic practices of the Late Period became extensive and varied. As far as the Appeal to the living is concerned, it continues to depend primarily on New Kingdom prototypes, which had of course incorporated Old and Middle Kingdom formulations. But there also seem to be direct borrowings from the Old Kingdom. The samples here assembled come from the statues of Montemhet and Harwa.

42) Statue of Montemhet CG 42236 (Leclant, Montouemhat, Doc. 1, pp. 2ff.; text B on dorsal pillar, pp. 6ff.):

a) wʿb nb mi n.i ʿ.k m qbḥw snṯr
ḫft m33 twt(.i)
m sni ḥr.i m wn
ḥr mw ḥnʿ ṯ3w tp-r3 3ḫ n.i sw r nḥḥ m ḫt
prw n.k m n-m-ḫt

Every priest, give me your hand with libation and incense,
when seeing my statue!
Do not pass by me hurriedly!
For water and the breath of speech help me more than a

million things,
and are profit for you in the future!

Here follows a warning not to steal the offerings, then comes an offering formula followed by a second Appeal:

b) i wnwt ḥt-nṯr nt Imn
ʿnḫ nb n niwt nb
s[w3].sn ḥr twt pn
ḥs ṯn Imn wr
mr tn nswt.tn
ḏd ḫ3 t ḥnqt ...

O staff of the temple of Amun,
and every citizen of every town,
when they pass by this statue:
Great Amun will favor you,
your king will love you,
when (you) say, 1000 bread, beer ...

43) Statue of Montemhet Berlin 17271 (Leclant, Montouemhat, Doc. 9, pp. 58ff.; text B, p. 60):

i ḥm-nṯr it-nṯr nb
ʿq.sn r wn ḥr m bw pn
ḥs ṯn Imn wr
sw3ḥ.f ṯn m msw.ṯn
mi nis.ṯn rn.i ...
ink sʿḥ n irt n.f
šps m3ʿ mr nb.f

O every priest and divine father,
as they enter to perform rites in this place:
Great Amun will favor you,
he will make you endure in your children,
inasmuch as you will call my name ...
I am one blessed for whom one should act,
one truly venerable, loved by his lord.

44) Statue of Montemhet CG 646 (Leclant, Montouemhat, Doc. 10, pp. 65ff.; text E, pp.73ff.):

iy n.i nb ḥr ḥtp di nswt
šsp.sn t ḥnqt qbḥw mrḥt
snṯr pr m-b3ḥ nṯr
mr(y) nswt pw
wnn.f ḥtp m ʿnḫ(t) ...

Whoever comes to me with an offering,
when they receive the bread, beer, water, ointment,
and incense that went up before the god,
he is one beloved of the king,
and he will rest in the land of life ...

Note the sḏm.f's *sw3.sn, ʿq.sn, šsp.sn,* in the position where, in the Old and Middle Kingdoms, sḏmty.fy's would have been. We have seen that in the New Kingdom the sḏm.ty.fy's were more and more replaced by sḏm.f's. Whoever emends the present sḏm.f's to sḏmty.fy's would have to emend the New Kingdom ones, too!

Observe also that no. 44 has the type of Appeal which was most widely used in the Old Kingdom, the type which combined the request for an offering and the promise of reward in a single brief sentence expressing the equation "one favored is one who will do", the predicate being a participle and the subject the sḏmty.fy form (nos. 2-4 & 17-18; no. 5 has two sḏmty.fy's). Now, in its revived form, both the subject and the predicate are participles, and the subject comes first.

Four of the eight statues of the high steward Harwa (published by Gunn and Engelbach in BIFAO 30 and 34) have an Appeal to the living. But only two Appeals, those on statues nos. II and VII, are adequately preserved.

45) Harwa statue II (Cairo JE 36711 = BIFAO 30, 1931, 796):

qʿh.f n(.i) ʿ.f m ḥtp di nswt
nis.f k3(.i) ḥr i(3)m-ib
iw.f r i3w n niwt.f im3ḫw n spt.f

If he bends the arm to me with an offering,
if he calls my name in kindness,
he will be an elder of his town and revered by his nome.

This is an interesting variant of the just discussed no. 44. Instead of the subject and the predicate being participles, the subject is construed as sḏm.f and the predicate is an iw.f r sḏm future tense. Gunn translated the passage, "He who will stretch forth his hand to me (?) in an 'Offering that the king gives', he who shall invoke my soul ..." and added the footnote: "Sḏmtj.fj forms written defectively." I propose to accept the forms as written.

46) Harwa's other Appeal, on statue VII (Berlin 8163 = BIFAO 34, 136) is conventional and could have stood verbatim on any New Kingom statue:

> i ḥmw-nṯr itw-nṯr wꜥbw ẖry-ḥbw
> ꜥq̠ nb r ḥt-nṯr nt Imn m ipt-swt
> r ir ḥssw r wdn ḫt
> r ir ḥnt nt imi 3bd.f
> ꜥnḫ n.tn nṯr šps wꜥb.tn n.f
> ḏd.f tn ẖr ḥswt.f
> mi ḏd.ṯn ḥtp di nswt ...
>
> O priests, divine fathers, web-priests, lector-priests,
> whoever enters the house of Amun in Ipet-sut
> to perform rites, to make offerings,
> to do the service of the monthly priest:
> The august god shall live for and you shall be pure to him,
> he shall make you endure in his favor,
> inasmuch as you will say, An offering-that-the-king-gives ...

Note the participle *ꜥq*, and the typically New Kingdom form of the promise-and-request sequence in which the request is introduced by the preposition *mi*.

This survey will conclude with four Appeals from the 26th dynasty. Post-Saite Appeals have been omitted, because grammatically they offer nothing new; their contents, however, are distinctly different from earlier Appeals and need to be examined in conjunction with the inscriptions of which they form part.

47) Statue of Djedptahefankh (Cairo JE 36949 H. de Meulenaere, BIFAO 63, 1965, 19-32 & pls. I-II, Appeal on p. 23). A block-statue from the Karnak Cache with cartouches of Psamtik I.

i ḥmw-nṯr itw-nṯr
ꜥq r bw ḏsr r ir ḫt m ipt-swt
mr.tn ꜥnḫ sḫm.tn mt
ḥs tn nb nṯrw
sw3ḥ.f tn m ḥt-nṯr.f
mi dw3.tn k3(.i) ḫft ḫt nṯr
ḏd.tn ḥtp di nswt ...

O priests, divine fathers,
who enter the holy place to perform rites in Ipet-sut:
You will love life and forget death,
and the lord of gods will favor you,
and will let you endure in his temple,
inasmuch as you will worship (my) ka according to the ritual,
and will say, An offering-that-the-king-gives ...

This Appeal, very similar to Harwa's second one (no. 46), is typical for the 25th-26th dynasties and is perfectly lucid, once one has realized that the priests' initial approach to the temple and the statue is rendered by the participle *ꜥq* and all other actions are expressed by means of sḏm.f forms, the whole being modeled on New Kingdom prototypes. The next example is much less clear, and not only because of its lacunae:

48) Statue of Ankhhor (Clère, RdE 24, 1972, 50-54). The text has two Appeals, both of them damaged; the second one reads:

--- ḥmw nb ꜥq r ḥt-nṯr
ꜥq.sn r ḥt-nṯr
nḏm ib.ṯn n nṯrw.ṯn --- ...
ink b3k m3ꜥ n r3-pr pn ...

all priests who enter the temple,
as they enter the temple:
May your heart rejoice in your gods --- ...
I am a true servant of this temple ...

The sequence *ꜥq ... ꜥq.sn* is odd, and so is the abrupt switch from the third-person *ꜥq.sn* to the second-person *nḏm ib.ṯn*. Clère rendered: "O tous prêtres qui entrez dans le temple, ou qui entrerez dans le temple, que votre coeur soit gracieux pour vos dieux", and he added the footnote, "Lire *ʿḳ(ty).śn*?". The question mark is well founded; for what sense could there have been in saying, "O priests who enter or who will enter"? Comparing with the similar Appeal of Nesnawiya, where Ranke emended *ʿq.sn* to *ʿqt(y).sn* (as was mentioned on p.155) will shed some light:

49) Statue of Nesnawiya (Berlin 17700); Ranke, ZÄS 44, 1907, 42-54):

i wʿbw nb srw nb sšw nb
ʿq.sn r ir ẖt m ḥt-nṯr bḥdt m ẖrt-hrw nt rʿ nb
ḏd.tn n.i ḥtp di nswt ...

O all web-priests, all officials, all scribes,
as they enter to perform rites in the temple of Edfu daily:
You shall say to me, An offering-that-the-king-gives ...

Here the sḏm.f third person *ʿq.sn* and the sḏm.f second person *ḏd.tn* make a perfectly normal sequence because *ʿq.sn* stands at the head of a whole sentence, instead of heading the truncated phrase *ʿq.sn r ḥt-nṯr* of no. 48. In other words, the sequence *ʿq ... ʿq.sn* is in order when *ʿq* denotes the general "entry" of the priests, i.e. their "having access" to the temple, while *ʿq.sn* denotes the specific occasions envisaged and elaborated in the Appeal.

Appeals in which some formulae appear to have been abridged are not rare. Consider the following:

50) Statue of Nakht-horheb (Tresson, Kêmi IV, 1931/33, 126ff.):

i ḥm-nṯr nb ʿq r ḥt-nṯr
wʿb nb m3.sn
mr ṯn nswt ḥs ṯn bit
w3ḥ.ṯn m ʿnḫ ẖr nṯrw.ṯn
mi ḏd.ṯn rn.i nfr rʿ nb

O every priest who enters the temple
and every web-priest when they view:
The south-king will love you, the north-king will favor you,
and you will abide in life with your gods,
inasmuch as you will pronounce my good name every day.

Here, after "when they view", one has a right to expect "this statue", as in nos. 25a and 41.

A summing up is in order. The gradual replacement of the sḏmty.fy form by participles and sḏm.f's is an observable fact, and one that nullifies the theory of defectively written sḏmty.fy's. That theory is anyhow inherently unlikely, since it taxes the scribes with the omission of the essential formative element of a particular verb form. The omission, or redundant writing, of feminine *t*-endings is not a comparable phenomenon.

A supplementary observation should also be made: the sḏmty.fy form had not died out in the Late Period. In our no. 36 we noted one occurrence in the 22nd dynasty. Eight further examples, gathered at random, will now be listed:

1. CG 42226 (Jansen-Winkeln, Biographien, A 11, pp. 141 & 511 & 180, no.1):
dmt(y).f(y) rn.i r 3ḫ n m-ḫt.
2. Tübingen 1734 (Catalogue 1981, p. 40, pl. 113 = Jansen-Winkeln, Biographien, p. 180, no. 3):
ḥm-nṯr nb ʿqt(y).f(y) r ḥt-nṯr tn ... dmt(y).f(y) rn.i.
3. Memphite stela of Apries (PM III^2, 840, Gunn, ASAE 27, 1927, 228):
ir sr ... nb th3t(y).f(y) mdt nt wḏt.
4. Louvre A 93 of Peftuaneith (Jelinkova-Reymond, ASAE 54, 1956/7,276):
wʿb nb irt(y).f(y) ḫt nṯr.
5. Cairo 672 (Borchardt, Statuen und Statuetten, III, 18ff.) on left arm:
ʿqt(y).f(y) r ḥt-nṯr.
6. Cairo 960 (Borchardt, Statuen und Statuetten, IV, 5):
ʿqt(y).f(y) prt(y).f(y) nb.
7. & 8. BM 1682 and 32183, unpublished, cited by Leclant & de Meulenaere, Kêmi 14, 1957, 37, n.6, both reading:
wʿb nb ʿqt(y).f(y).

The Late Period scribes used the sḏmty.fy form sparingly, correctly, and in fixed clichés. Such limited usage could be seen as corroborating evidence for the fact that defectively written sḏmty.fy's did not exist.

V

THE STELA OF PADISOBEK, A CHILDLESS MAN

(With Fig. 1 and Illus. 3-21)

The tall stela of Padisobek from Hawara, Cairo JE 44065, was published by G. Daressy in RT 36, 1914, 73-82. Its surface was even then weathered and damaged, and Daressy's copy has lacunae, uncertainties, and outright errors. The recto of the stela is inscribed with a version of the "Book of traversing eternity", the known copies of which are listed by J.-C. Goyon in Textes et Langages ... Hommage Champollion, III, 76. The verso is given over to the interesting autobiographical text which has claimed the attention of several scholars and is the subject of this presentation. In the absence of photographs and an accurate handcopy, the scholars who were attracted by the singular content of the verso limited their efforts to citing brief excerpts or giving partial translations as follows:

1. W.Spiegelberg, "Die Bitte eines kinderlosen Ägypters um Totengebete", Arch. f. Rel. Wiss. 18, 1915, 594-596, brief excerpts.
2. H.O. Lange, "Der Kinderlose", Mélanges Maspero I, 1935/38, 211-216, a partial translation with annotations.
3. A. de Buck, "Oudertrots, Kinderplicht en de Klacht van een Kinderloze", JEOL 11, 1949/50, 7-15, a partial translation, done with the aid of a photograph but lacking textual annotations.
4. E. Otto, Die biographischen Inschriften der ägyptischen Spätzeit, Inschr. 69, brief excerpts on his p. 62.

When two graduate students of egyptology at the University of California, Los Angeles, Mrs. Cynthia May Sheikholeslami and Mr. Jeffrey Cooper, were planning to spend the spring of 1980 in Egypt as members of the El-Hibeh expedition led by Robert J. Wenke, I asked them to take photographs of the stela's verso. This they did under hurried circumstances since the stela was locked away in a storeroom and an employee of the museum stood by while they worked. Even so, the photographs make a significant contribution in that they make it possible to obtain an overall control of Daressy's printed text and to recognize major and minor errors. Hence I publish a selection of the clearest photos. This is also the opportunity for thanking Cynthia May and Jeff Cooper for their substantial contribution.

The reading of several passages remains obscure, and I have not transliterated more than I can recognize. It is now possible to see where Lange, who had no photo, was misled by Daressy's text and made wrong conjectures. One can also reconstruct what de Buck, who had a good photo but did not comment on what he saw on it, was reading when he translated as he did. Altogether, a reader who takes the trouble can now get a grip on the text, even though a carefully done handcopy remains a desideratum. I have included Daressy's printed text along with the photographs. Thus, my transliteration and translation are based on Daressy's text as corrected by what I can see on the photos, and on close consideration of Lange's and de Buck's renderings and comments.

Though the text of twenty-one lines has a single topic, its treatment amounts to a division into three sections: 1. Padisobek appeals to the passersby to read his stela and heed his request to pronounce his name. 2. The long central portion narrates the misfortune of his life, his childlessness, and his resultant inability to provide for the customary funerary rites. To the description of this misery he adds impassioned affirmations of his faultless character and faithful performance of duties. 3. A strong plea to the visitors for recital of prayers on his behalf.

Fig.1: Daressy's Text (RT 36,1914, 78-79)

15
16
17
18
19
20
21
vers les 3/4
de la ligne

Transliteration

The First Appeal

(1) ḏd mdw in Wsir ḥm-nṯr Nt Pdi-sbk m3ʿ-ḫrw s3 n Wr[1] m3ʿ-ḫrw
ir.n nb(t)-pr iḥt n Sbk šd(y)t[2] Nfrw-sbk m3ʿ-ḫrw
i wʿb nb ḥm-nṯr nb ẖry-ḥb nb
[rmṯ nb] (2) [sšw] pr-ʿnḫ r ḏrw.sn
wtw[3] ḥmww ḥm-k3w[4]
ikdw[5] qris iriw sṯ3t mi-qd.sn
iw.sn r mnmntt[6] sw3.sn (3) šdyt
m tr n w3ḥ ḫt n sʿḥw.sn
m33.sn ʿḥʿy pn šd.sn sš-nṯrw.f
ndb.tn[7] smḥw ir.n.i m-ḥr.tn m ẖmsw[8]
(4) ḏd sḫ3.tn[9] siwy.tn rn.i iw (=r) nfr
ḥs tn[10] nṯr ʿ3 nb imntt ḥr.s
ḥr nty ink sʿḥ mnḫ[11] qd 3ḫ n 3ḫ [n.f]
(5) ir n iri.f twt n ir n.f
wʿb nḥ3 iw (=r) grg[12] nn ḏw ḫr.i

The Narration

ḏd.i di.i rḫ.tn m mdw ḫp n[13] iwms sš.n.i ... (6) tn ḥr.s[14] ir.n.i ʿḥʿw.i m ⌜3hm⌝ ... ḫpr im.sn ʿwnw m ḏt.f r ẖt.f nn ḥms.n.i m ḥmw m nḏm[15] (7) ...[16] nn n.i pẖr nst s3ḫ wi m sbẖt 3ḫt m iryw m k3t Inpw m hrw ... m qbḥw ... (8) ṯs m3qt ḥts.f wi m hrw sm3-t3 ḏd.f n.i s3ḫw m ... nb.f sʿq wi r wnt.i sḥtp.f wi m ʿʿw.i (9) sšm.f n.i ḫsw ḥḥ.f ist.i ḥr.i w3ḥ.f n.i ḫt mw mi ir.n s3 n it.f wnn.i m im3ḫw n sp3t.i nn n.i s3t (10) ikb.s n.i m hrw rnpwt ir.s n.i iwḫ[17] ḥ3y.s ḥr.i r nw n b3g sb is[18] ḫp(r) nn im.i r (=iw) nn wn ir n.i

ink (11) wʿb rḫ iry.f nn ḏw ḫr.f
twr ḏbʿty[19] m i.iry ḏrt.f nn ir.n.f ʿb
wʿb šm ḥr mw n nb.f
nn sbsb wp.f[20]
nn (12) wrd m šms.f
twr m pẖry.f r iw smn nb.f
nn wd iw (=r) s3w

ir wᶜb r tr[21] n ir ḫt nṯr
nn 3b ṯnw (13) i.iry.f[22]
wn.i nmḥw nn gm wn.f
ḏd tp[23] iwty g3s.f
wᶜb nḫt[24] nn ḏbᶜwt ḫr.f
... (14) ...[25] nn nmᶜ
ir mtwt k3[26] ... bwt.f pw grg

The Second Appeal

di.n.i nn m-ḥr.tn r rdit rḫ.tn inm(15).i ḥnᶜ ḫp(r).i iw (=r) srwd r3.tn n tm (=dm) k3.i m nḥw ir.n.i n tn[27] mtn ir[28] s nn bḫ.tw n.f tm (16) wn.f pw[29] nn pᶜpᶜ.tw.f rsy nn sḫ3.tw ir.n.f nn tm.tw (= dm.tw) k3.f mi nty nn wn [wn.i m][30] (17) imnw ft.tw.f ḥnᶜ w3bwy.f ḥr nn ḫpr im.i rdi.n.i nḥw m-ḥr.tn ḥr.s r rdit 3ḫ wnyw nty r ḫp(r) ḏt
(18) ḫpr n.i rsy nn nni ib.tn ḫft qm3.s
nn g3 iḥt.tn m wp.tw.s
nn wrd.n rs.tn m ḏdw
(19) nn mn [r3.]tn m wḥm.s
nn ḫt sswn m-ᶜ.tn ḫft ir.s
nn ... wḏ3.tn m ḏf3w ḥr.s
ḥr nty ṯ3w n [r3] (20) [3ḫ] n sᶜḥ ...
ᶜnḫ swt sᶜḥ n dm k3.f
ssn 3ḫ m nis ....

Translation

The First Appeal

(1) Speech of the Osiris, the priest of Neith, Padisobek, justified, son of Wer[1], justified, born of the housewife and musician of Sobek of Shedyt[2], Nefrusobek, justified.
O every priest, every prophet, every lector-priest,
[all people] (2) and all [scribes] of the house of life,
embalmers[3], servants, ka-priests[4],
all tomb builders[5] and funeral attendants,
when they come to Menment[6] while passing by (3) Shedyt,

at the time of offering to their deceased -
when they see this stela and read its inscription:
May you hear[7] the request that I make before you in humility[8],
(4) namely that you recall[9] and proclaim my name as a good one,
so that the great god, lord of the west, may favor you[10] for it!
For I am an excellent deceased,[11] a person who helps [his] helper,
(5) who acts for his companion, befriends him who acts for him,
one pure and hostile[12] to falsehood, there is no evil in me.

The Narration

I speak to let you know in words far from[13] untruth why I have written this (6) [account].[14] I have spent my lifetime in illness [and sickness] with pains thereof from morning till night; I could not enjoy [intercourse][15] (7) ...[16] I had no heir who would make me a glorified spirit at the portal of the horizon by rites and the work of Anubis on the day of ... with libations ... (8) ... would erect the ladder, would adorn me on the day of burial, would recite to me glorifications in ... of his lord, would enter me into my tomb, would lay me to rest in my sleep, (9) would perform the rites for me, visit my tomb for me, lay down for me offerings and water, as does a son for his father. Though being a revered one of his nome, I had no daughter (10) who could mourn me on the day of plant offerings, could weep[17] and wail over me at the time of weariness, which is death.[18] This happened to me because there was no one to act for me.

I was (11) a priest who knew his duties, who had no fault,
clean-fingered[19] in the work of his hand, who did no wrong,
one pure who walked on the water of his lord,
without neglecting his work,[20]
without (12) wearying in his service,
one clean in his time of duty
at the coming of the image of his lord,
not prone to dirtiness,
cleansed at the time[21] of making offerings,
and ceaseless in all (13) that he did.[22]
I was a citizen in whom no fault was found,
who made a statement[23] without partiality,

a valiant[24] priest without reproach.
One who ...[25] (14) without partiality,
who did Maat ...[26], who abhorred falsehood.

The Second Appeal

I have placed these things before you in order to let you know my character (15) and my being, and to strengthen your mouth to pronounce my name by the plea that I made to you.[27] For behold[28], a man to whom no child was born is one who does not (16) exist![29] He has really not been born! His deeds will not be remembered; his name will not be pronounced, like one who has not existed! [I am][30] (17) a tree that was torn out with its roots, because of what happened to me! Therefore have I put the plea before you that the living and those who shall be in the future shall serve (me)!
(18) If truly done for me, your heart will not tire by doing it,
your throat will not choke on uttering it,
your tongue will not weary by saying it,
(19) your [mouth] will not suffer by repeating it!
These are not goods that you lose when you do it!
Your storehouse will not [be emptied] of food thereby!
For breath of [the mouth] (20) [helps] the deceased;
... the deceased is revived when his name is pronounced;
the spirit breathes when one calls ....

Notes

1. Other readings of the name are possible.
2. Shedyt = Crocodilopolis = Medinet al-Fayyum.
3. Spelled *wdw.*
4. *ḥs-k3w* is written.
5. Spelled *iktw.*
6. Rather than Daressy's *n,* the photograph shows the hill-country sign.
7. Spelled *ntb.tn.*
8. Literally, "bowed down".
9. Spelled *sẖ3.dn.*

10. Spelled *ḥs dn*.
11. Here Daressy's text is very faulty and misled Lange. Read *ink sʿḥ mnẖ qd 3ẖ n 3ẖ* (not *s3*), and there is room for the suffix *f*.
12. After *wʿb* (with redundant *t*) I am guessing *nḥ3*, Wb. II, 290, with one of its negative meanings: "wild, schrecklich, gefährlich o.ä."
13. I follow Lange in thinking that *ẖp* here is *ẖpp*, Wb. III, 259, in the sense of "remote".
14. A no longer legible feminine word for the inscription.
15. Here are three words for illness, pains, and laments: the probable *3hm*, a second illegible one ending with the evil-bird sign and pluralstrokes, and the word *ʿwnw* of Wb. I, 172; and at the end of line 6 there are two words for sexual intercourse: *ḥm* (Wb. III, 80.6), and *nḏm* with no longer extant determinative (Wb. II, 381.15ff.). As Lange pointed out, the meaning must be that an illness had made him impotent. This interpretation of the passage, which seems to me well-nigh certain, was denied by de Buck, who however offered no alternative, but merely claimed that the man had worked ceaselessly for the common good (his note 37: "Op deze passage berust Lange's gissing, er is blijkbaar slechts sprake van P.'s rustelose werkzaamheid voor het algemeen welzijn.").
16. I cannot make anything of the damaged words at the beginning of line 7.
17. What is written looks like a mixture of *iẖw, iwḥ*, and *nḥi*.
18. Lange interpreted the words *sb is* as "als Ersatz dafür dass" and connected them with what follows; but misled by Daressy's faulty *ib nb* at the end of line 10, he obtained an entirely wrong sense. The word at the end of line 10 is *ink*, and with it begins a new sentence. This was recognized by de Buck who, however, omitted the words *sb is*. I attach them to the preceding *b3g*, "weariness/death" and see in *sb* a second metaphor which explains the first: "weariness, namely, departure". The heaping of parallels and synonyms is very pronounced in the whole text.
19. *twr ḏbʿty; twr* is spelled *diwr*.
20. What I read as *nn sbsb wp.f* was omitted by Lange and de Buck.
21. *tr* is spelled *dr*.
22. What Daressy read as the spittle sign D 26 at the end of line 12 I read as *ṯnw*, "all, every".
23. *tp* for *tp-r3*, as the determinative makes clear.
24. The branch under *wʿb*, "priest", I read as *nẖt*.

25. Of *bdti ḥww* I understand only that it is a beneficent action; *ḥww* might derive from *ḥwy,* Wb III, 45 "ach, ach doch", hence "pleaders" (?).
26. That *mtwt k3,* "semen of the bull", is a metaphoric term for Maat (it is guessed in Wb. II, 169.4) has now been worked out by Dieter Kurth in Studien zu Sprache und Religion Ägyptens, Fs. Westendorf, I, 273-281, on the basis of Ptolemaic temple texts. Kurth has not cited our stela; and I fail to understand the words that follow after *mtwt k3: n bs r šfn.* It is nevertheless gratifying to find that our priest was a declared follower of Maat and hater of falsehood.
27. *n tw* is written instead of *n tn.* This is the  that I discussed in the study of the Appeal to the Living, on pp. 176f.
28. What is spelled *mnti* I take to be *mtn,* "behold".
29. Daressy's *dm* at the end of line 15 is actually *tm,* the negative verb. Lange was misled by Daressy's *dm.*
30. The lacuna at the end of line 16 was restored to *wn.f m* by Daressy, and Lange accepted it. De Buck, however, restored the first-person suffix *wn.i m.* If so taken, the clause *ḥr nn ḫpr im.i* forms the end of this sentence rather than the beginning of the next. I have adopted de Buck's reconstruction.

Commentary

What is striking in this text is the extreme anguish, the intensity of the complaint, and its build-up to a climax: the man's childlessness has deprived him of all the services and comforts that normally pertained to death and burial, wherefore his very survival in the hereafter is jeopardized. Indeed his very existence is questionable. The tree torn up by its roots cannot sprout again, leaves no trace, and thus is as if it had never been. The image of the tree torn up by its roots is known from the stela of king Piye (line 133), where Tefnakht in his letter of surrender pleads for the life of his second son *(imi wḥ3 mnw r wʿbwy.f).*

The stress laid on the need to pronounce the name is also unusually emphatic. For the consequence of childlessness is a twofold nothingness: the earthly existence will leave no trace in the remembrance of descendants and the community, and the transfigured otherworldly existence may fail to materialize - unless the visitors will tarry at his stela and pronounce his name in prayerful recital.

Such unmitigated fear of death as a state of nothingness may have been common, but its expression in blank despair within the tradition of autobiographical inscriptions is most unusual. Quite lacking here are the consolations of wisdom and piety. There is not the resigned acceptance of the "coming to the realm of Osiris" found in the hymn to Osiris of the stela of Bak-aa (text II/26) nor a sage's calm acceptance of death as expressed in PInsinger (p.144). Yet Padisobek was a faithful priest and a good citizen who performed the tasks of Maat; and note how the doing of Maat is defined by its most essential features: truthfulness and fairness in dealing with other people.

It would be rash to invoke the often cited "anxiety" of the Hellenistic age; for that age also produced the serenity and trust of Somtutefnakht and Petosiris (texts 97-99). Thus, traditional phrasing notwithstanding, this seems to be the piercing cri de coeur of an individual who was lonely and afraid - a loneliness quite other than that of the Lebensmüder, who had yearned for the bliss of the heavenly beyond.

It will take a great many more text publications and incisive studies before Egyptian thinking in its many facets during that last millennium, from the time of the Saite state to the conversion to Christianity, is recreated in syntheses that shed light and invite assent.

LIST OF ILLUSTRATIONS

A SHORT BIBLIOGRAPHY OF MAAT STUDIES

Anthes R., Die Maat des Echnaton von Amarna (Journal of the American Oriental Society, Supplement 14) Baltimore 1952.

Assmann J., "State and Religion in the New Kingdom", in: Religion and Philosophy in Ancient Egypt, Yale Egyptological Studies 3, 1989, 55-88.

- Maât, l'Egypte pharaonique et l'idée de justice sociale. Paris 1989.
- Ma'at; Gerechtigkeit und Unsterblichkeit im alten Ägypten. München 1990.
- "Weisheit, Schrift und Literatur", in: Aleida Assmann ed., Weisheit (Archäologie der literarischen Kommunikation, III), München 1991, 475-500.

Bleeker C.J., De Beteekenis van de Egyptische Godin Maat. Leiden 1929.

Bonnet H., "Maat", in: Reallexikon der ägyptischen Religionsgeschichte. Berlin 1952, 430-434.

Brunner H., "Der freie Wille Gottes", in: Les sagesses du proche orient ancien, Strasbourg 1963, 103-117.

de Buck A., "Het religieus Karakter der oudste egyptische Wijsheid", Nieuw Theologisch Tijdschrift 21, 1932, 322-349.

Fairman H.W., "A Scene of the Offering of Truth in the Temple of Edfu", in: MDIK 16, Fs. Junker II, 86-92.

Helck W., "Maat", in: Lexikon der Ägyptologie, III, 1110-1118.

Hornung E., "Maat - Gerechtigkeit für alle?", in: Eranos Jahrbuch, vol. 56, 1987, 385-427.

Kurth D., "'Same des Stieres' und 'Same', zwei Bezeichnungen der Maat", in: Studien zur Sprache und Religion Ägyptens, Fs. Westendorf I, 273-281.

Morenz S., Ägyptische Religion, Kapitel 6. Stuttgart 1960.

Otto E., "Ethik", in: Lexikon der Ägyptologie, II, 34-39.

Schmid H.H., Gerechtigkeit als Weltordnung. Tübingen 1968.

Shirun-Grumach I., "Remarks on the Goddess Maat", in: Pharaonic Egypt, the Bible and Christianity, ed. S. Israelit-Groll, Jerusalem 1985, 173-201.
Tobin V.A., Theological Principles of Egyptian Religion. (American University Studies, series 7, vol. 59) New York 1989.
Westendorf W., "Ursprung und Wesen der Maat", in: Festgabe für Dr. Walter Will, Köln 1966, 201-225.

ABBREVIATIONS AND BIBLIOGRAPHY

ASAE	Annales du Service des Antiquités de l'Egypte.
BD	Book of the Dead.
BIFAO	Bulletin de l'Institut Français d'Archéologie Orientale.
CT	Coffin Texts.
HTBM	Hieroglyphic Texts from Egyptian Stelae etc. (in the) British Museum.
JEA	Journal of Egyptian Archaeology.
JEOL	Jaarbericht van het Vooraziatisch-Egyptisch Genootschap "Ex Oriente Lux".
JNES	Journal of Near Eastern Studies.
KRI	K.A. Kitchen, Ramesside Inscriptions, Historical and Biographical. Oxford 1975-1990.
MDIK	Mitteilungen des Deutschen Archäologischen Instituts, Abteilung Kairo.
PM	B. Porter & R.L.B. Moss, Topographical Bibliography of Ancient Egyptian Hieroglyphic Texts, Reliefs and Paintings. Oxford 1927-52; 2d ed. 1960-
RT	Recueil de travaux relatifs à la philologie et à l'archéologie égyptiennes et assyriennes.
SPOA	Les Sagesses du Proche-Orient Ancien, Colloque de Strasbourg, 1963.
TPPI	Textes de la première période intermédiaire, ed. J.J. Clère & J. Vandier. (Bibliotheca Aegyptiaca 10) Bruxelles 1948.
TT	Theban Tombs
Urk. I, IV, VII	Urkunden des ägyptischen Altertums: Abteilung I: Urkunden des Alten Reiches. Abteilung IV: Urkunden der 18. Dynastie. Abteilung VII: Urkunden des Mittleren Reiches, Heft I.
Wb.	Wörterbuch der ägyptischen Sprache, ed. A. Erman & H.Grapow. Leipzig 1926-1963.
YES	Yale Egyptological Studies

ZÄS Zeitschrift für ägyptische Sprache und Altertumskunde
ZDMG Zeitschrift der deutschen morgenländischen Gesellschaft

Aegyptische Inschriften aus den königlichen Museen zu Berlin. 2 v. Leipzig 1913-1924.

Baer K., Rank and Title in the Old Kingdom. Chicago 1960.

Barns J.W.B., Five Ramesseum Papyri. Oxford 1956.

Barucq A. & Daumas F., Hymnes et prières de l'Egypte ancienne. (Littératures anciennes du proche-orient) Paris 1980.

Brack A. & A., Das Grab des Haremheb, Theben Nr. 78 (DAI Kairo, Archäolog. Veröff., 35) Mainz 1980.

Brunner H., Altägyptische Weisheit, Lehren für das Leben. Zürich & München 1988.

Davies N. de G. & Gardiner A.H., The Tomb of Antefoker. (Egypt Explor. Soc. Theban tomb series, memoir 2) London 1920.

Drioton E., "Contribution à l'étude du chapitre 125 du livre des morts: les confessions négatives", in: Recueil Champollion, Paris 1922,545-564.

Dunham D., Naga-ed-Dêr Stelae of the First Intermediate Period. London 1937.

Dyroff K. & Poertner B., Ägyptische Grabsteine und Denksteine aus süddeutschen Sammlungen, vol. II. Strassburg 1904.

Edel E., Hieroglyphische Inschriften des Alten Reiches (Abhdl. d. Rheinisch-Westfälischen Akad. d. Wiss., 67) Opladen 1981.

- Inschriften des Alten Reiches II: Die Biographie des K3j-gmnj (Mitteil. d. Instituts f. Orientforschung I, 1953) 210-226.

- Die Inschriften der Grabfronten der Siut-Gräber in Mittelägypten aus der Herakleopolitenzeit (Abhdl. d. Rheinisch-Westfälischen Akad. d. Wiss., 71) Opladen 1984.

- Untersuchungen zur Phraseologie der ägyptischen Inschriften des Alten Reiches (MDIK 13/1) Berlin 1944.

Fischer H.G., Dendera in the Third Millennium B.C. Locust Valley 1968.

- The Orientation of Hieroglyphs, I. New York 1977.

Grieshammer R., Das Jenseitsgericht in den Sargtexten. (Ägyptolog. Abhandlungen 20) Wiesbaden 1970.

Garnot J.S.F., L'appel aux vivants dans les textes funéraires égyptiens ... (IFAO Recherches d'arch., de philol. et d'hist. 9) Cairo 1938.

Griffiths J.G., The Divine Verdict; a Study of Divine Judgment in the Ancient Religions. Leiden 1991.
Hayes W.C., The Scepter of Egypt. 2 v. Cambridge, Mass. 1953-59.
Jansen-Winkeln K., Ägyptische Biographien der 22. und 23. Dynastie. 2 v. (Ägypten und Altes Testament 8) Wiesbaden 1985.
Kruchten J.-M., Les annales des prêtres de Karnak. (Orientalia Lovaniensia Analecta 32) Leuven 1989.
Lacau P., Stèles du nouvel empire, I/1. (Catalogue Général) Cairo 1909.
Lefebvre G., Le tombeau de Petosiris. 3 v. Cairo 1923-24.
Legrain G., Statues et statuettes de rois et de particuliers. 3 v. (Catalogue Général) Cairo 1906-14.
Lichtheim M., Ancient Egyptian Autobiographies chiefly of the Middle Kingdom. (Orbis Biblicus et Orientalis 84) Freiburg-Göttingen 1988.
- Late Egyptian Wisdom Literature in the International Context, a Study of Demotic Instructions. (Orbis Biblicus et Orientalis 52) Freiburg-Göttingen 1983.
Limme L., Stèles égyptiennes. (Musées Royaux d'Art et d'Histoire, Guides du département égyptien, 4) Bruxelles 1979.
Mariette A., Catalogue général des monuments d'Abydos. Paris 1880. Reprint, Wiesbaden 1982.
Morenz S., "Ägyptischer Totenglaube im Rahmen der Struktur ägyptischer Religion", in: Eranos Jahrbuch v. 34, 1966, pp. 399-446. Repr. in his Religion und Geschichte des alten Ägypten, Weimar 1975, pp. 173-213.
- Gott und Mensch im alten Ägypten. Leipzig 1962, 2d ed. 1984.
Petrie W.M.F., Dendereh 1898 and Dendereh Extra Plates. 2 v. London 1900.
- Tombs of the Courtiers and Oxyrhynkhos. London 1925.
Pierret P., Recueil d'inscriptions inédites du Musée égyptien du Louvre. 2 v. in 1. Paris 1874-78.
Posener G., "Les douanes de la méditerranée dans l'Egypte saïte", in: Revue de philologie 21, 1947, 121ff.
Recueil d'études égyptologiques dédiées à la mémoire de Jean François Champollion. Paris 1922.

Roeder G., Der Ausklang der ägyptischen Religion mit Reformation, Zauberei und Jenseitsglauben (Die ägyptische Religion in Text und Bild, 4) Zürich-Stuttgart 1961.
Saleh M., Das Totenbuch in den thebanischen Beamtengräbern des Neuen Reiches. (DAI Kairo, Archäolog. Veröff. 46) Mainz 1984.
El-Sayed R., Documents relatifs à Sais et ses divinités. (IFAO Cairo, Bibl. d'étude 69) Cairo 1975.
Schenkel W., Memphis - Herakleopolis - Theben; die epigraphischen Zeugnisse der 7.-11. Dynastie Ägyptens. (Ägyptolog. Abhandlungen 12) Wiesbaden 1965.
Seeber Chr., Untersuchungen zur Darstellung des Totengerichtes im Alten Ägypten. (Münchner ägyptologische Studien 35) München-Berlin 1976.
Sethe K., Aegyptische Lesestücke zum Gebrauch im akademischen Unterricht. Leipzig 1924, repr. 1959.
Simpson W.K., The Terrace of the Great God at Abydos. (Pennsylvania-Yale Expedition to Egypt, Publications, 5). New Haven & Philadelphia 1974.
Spiegel J., Die Idee vom Totengericht in der ägyptischen Religion. (Leipziger ägyptologische Studien 2) Glückstadt 1935.
Studies presented to F.Ll. Griffith. London 1932.
Varille A., Inscriptions concernant l'architecte Amenhotep fils de Hapou. (IFAO Cairo, Bibl. d'étude 44) Cairo 1968.
- "La stèle du mystique Béky (no. 156 du Musée de Turin)" in: BIFAO 54, 1954, 129-135 & plate.
Vercoutter J., Textes biographiques du Serapéum de Memphis. Paris 1962.
Yoyotte J., Le jugement des morts dans l'Egypte ancienne. (Sources Orientales IV, pp. 17-80) Paris 1961.

ADDENDA ET CORRIGENDA TO MY ANCIENT EGYPTIAN AUTOBIOGRAPHIES CHIEFLY OF THE MIDDLE KINGDOM

The reader of that earlier volume is invited to note the following corrections.

1. On p. 61, Text 23: the number "Turin 1517" should read "Turin 1513". So also in the Index, pp. 157 & 162.

2. The word *ʿb3*, "stela", was consistently misspelled as *ʿbʿ*, on pp. 101, 103, 105, 109, 123 & 171.

3. In the bottom line of p. 140, in note 24, read: "The boat journey to", the words "journey to" having dropped out during the printing.

4. On Plate V, illustration no. 6 is described as "Temple of Ramses II and Coptic village Deir Sitt Damyana". What this photograph shows is not the temple of Ramses II found on the Porter-Moss plan on my plate X, near the temple of Sethos I, but rather the structure of Ramses II known as "the Portal" which is not indicated at all on the PM plan. It is located to the south-west of the Osiris temple enclosure and thus lies within the "North Cemetery of Mariette", the area currently studied by the Pennsylvania-Yale expedition.

5. On Plate VI, the directions indicated for illustrations 7 & 8 are reversed. Illus. 7 should read "looking South" and Illus. 8 should read "looking East".

6. In the Bibliography, p. 156, the entry "Vandier, Manuel d'archéologie égyptienne" should be adjusted to read: "6 v. Paris 1952-1978".

7. In discussing the word *inw*, on p. 141, I quoted Clère's study of the "autobiography of a Saite general" as being in "BIFAO 84, 1984" instead of "BIFAO 83, 1983". That inscription of a general named Psamtik was restudied by H. de Meulenaere in Chronique d'Egypte 61, 1986, where de Meulenaere gave a partly differing translation and concluded that the general belonged to the 30th dynasty rather than the 26th, and that the town for which he did construction work was Elkab.

PLATES

Plate 1

Stela of Horemwia

Plate 2

Stela of Baki

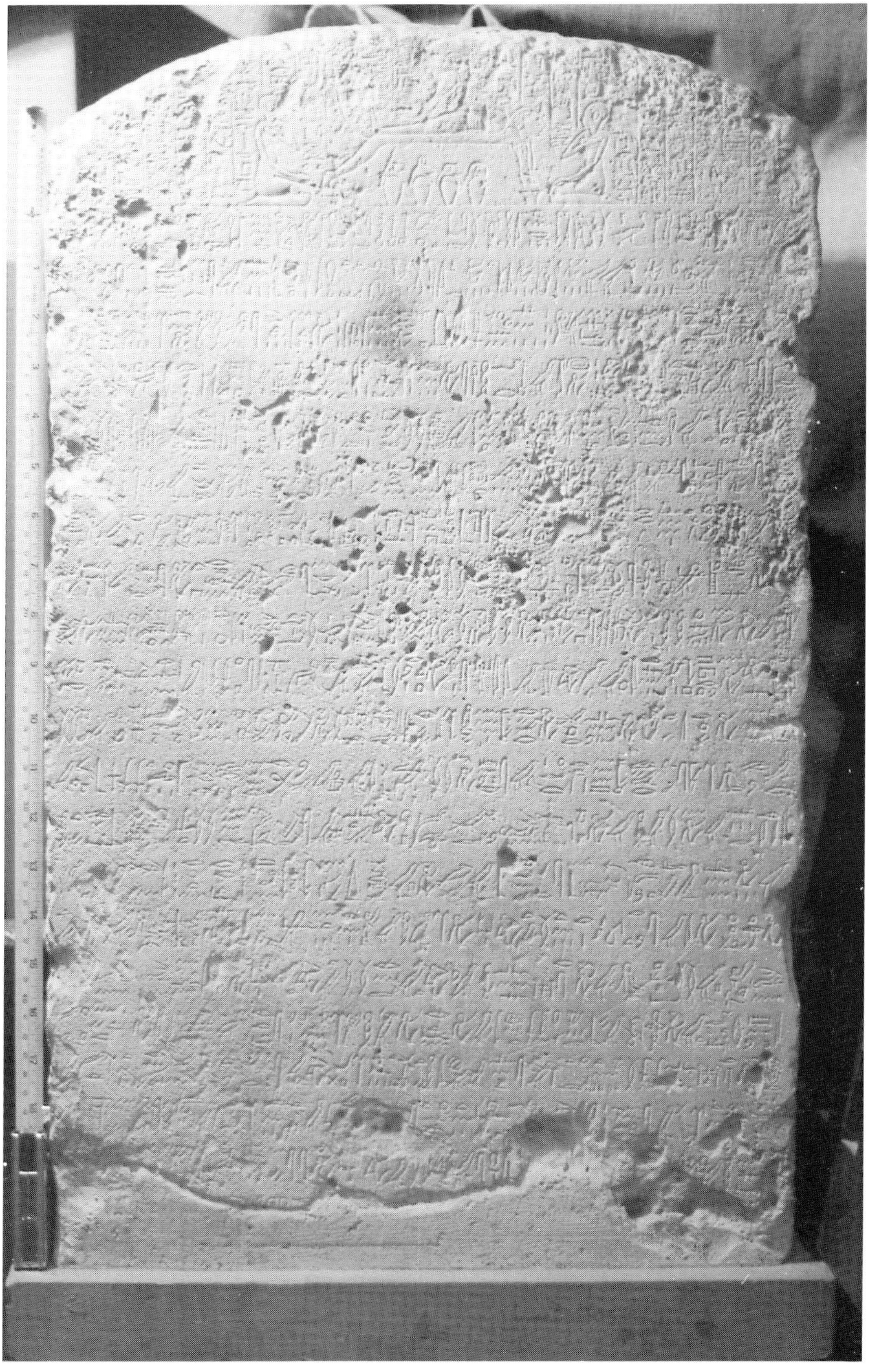

Verso of Stela of Padisobek

Plate 4

2
3
4
5
6
7

right

2
3
4
5
6
7

middle

2
3
4
5
6
7

left

Padisobek Lines 2–7

Plate 5

6
7
8
9
10
11

right

6
7
8
9
10
11

middle

6
7
8
9
10
11

left

Padisobek Lines 6–11

Plate 6

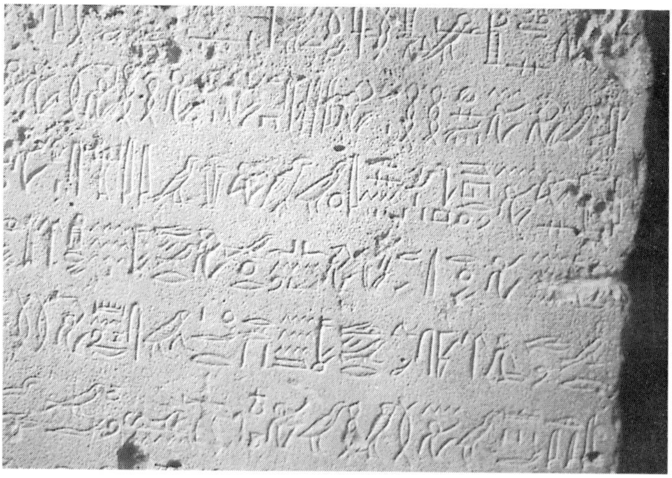

8 9 10 11 12 13

right

8 9 10 11 12 13

middle

8 9 10 11 12 13

left

Padisobek Lines 8–13

Plate 7

11
12
13
14
15
16

right

11
12
13
14
15
16

middle

12
13
14
15
16
17

left

Padisobek Lines 11/12–16/17

Plate 8

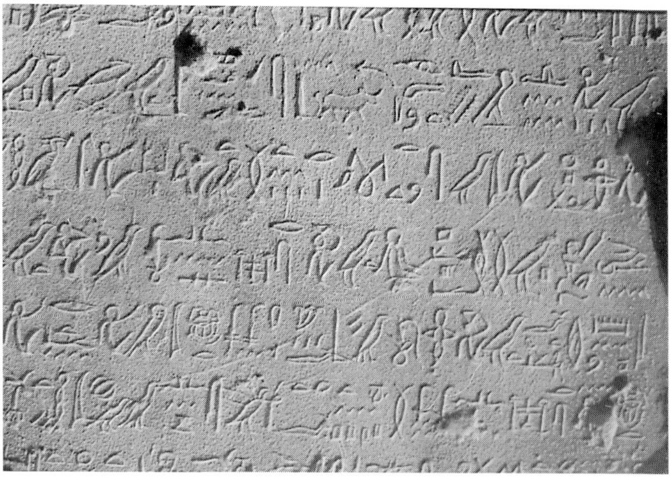

13 14 15 16 17 18 19

right

14 15 16 17 18 19

middle

14 15 16 17 18 19

left

Padisobek Lines 13/14–19

Plate 9

15 16 17 18 19 20

right

15 16 17 18 19 20 21

middle

15 16 17 18 19 20 21

left

Padisobek Lines 15–21

ORBIS BIBLICUS ET ORIENTALIS

Bd. 1 OTTO RICKENBACHER: *Weisheitsperikopen bei Ben Sira.* X–214–15* Seiten. 1973. Vergriffen.

Bd. 2 FRANZ SCHNIDER: *Jesus der Prophet.* 298 Seiten. 1973. Vergriffen.

Bd. 3 PAUL ZINGG: *Das Wachsen der Kirche.* Beiträge zur Frage der lukanischen Redaktion und Theologie. 345 Seiten. 1974. Vergriffen.

Bd. 4 KARL JAROŠ: *Die Stellung des Elohisten zur kanaanäischen Religion.* 294 Seiten, 12 Abbildungen. 1982. 2. verbesserte und überarbeitete Auflage.

Bd. 5 OTHMAR KEEL: *Wirkmächtige Siegeszeichen im Alten Testament.* Ikonographische Studien zu Jos 8, 18–26; Ex 17, 8–13; 2 Kön 13, 14–19 und 1 Kön 22, 11. 232 Seiten, 78 Abbildungen. 1974. Vergriffen.

Bd. 6 VITUS HUONDER: *Israel Sohn Gottes.* Zur Deutung eines alttestamentlichen Themas in der jüdischen Exegese des Mittelalters. 231 Seiten. 1975.

Bd. 7 RAINER SCHMITT: *Exodus und Passa. Ihr Zusammenhang im Alten Testament.* 124 Seiten. 1982. 2. neubearbeitete Auflage.

Bd. 8 ADRIAN SCHENKER: *Hexaplarische Psalmenbruchstücke.* Die hexaplarischen Psalmenfragmente der Handschriften Vaticanus graecus 752 und Canonicianus graecus 62. Einleitung, Ausgabe, Erläuterung. XXVIII–446 Seiten. 1975.

Bd. 9 BEAT ZUBER: *Vier Studien zu den Ursprüngen Israels.* Die Sinaifrage und Probleme der Volks- und Traditionsbildung. 152 Seiten. 1976. Vergriffen.

Bd. 10 EDUARDO ARENS: *The* ΗΛΘΟΝ-*Sayings in the Synoptic Tradition.* A Historico-critical Investigation. 370 Seiten. 1976.

Bd. 11 KARL JAROŠ: *Sichem.* Eine archäologische und religionsgeschichtliche Studie, mit besonderer Berücksichtigung von Jos 24. 280 Seiten, 193 Abbildungen. 1976.

Bd. 11a KARL JAROŠ/BRIGITTE DECKERT: *Studien zur Sichem-Area.* 81 Seiten, 23 Abbildungen. 1977.

Bd. 12 WALTER BÜHLMANN: *Vom rechten Reden und Schweigen.* Studien zu Proverbien 10–31. 371 Seiten. 1976. Vergriffen.

Bd. 13 IVO MEYER: *Jeremia und die falschen Propheten.* 155 Seiten. 1977. Vergriffen.

Bd. 14 OTHMAR KEEL: *Vögel als Boten.* Studien zu Ps 68, 12–14, Gen 8, 6–12, Koh 10, 20 und dem Aussenden von Botenvögeln in Ägypten. – Mit einem Beitrag von Urs Winter zu Ps 56, 1 und zur Ikonographie der Göttin mit der Taube. 164 Seiten, 44 Abbildungen. 1977. Vergriffen.

Bd. 15 MARIE-LOUISE GUBLER: *Die frühesten Deutungen des Todes Jesu.* Eine motivgeschichtliche Darstellung aufgrund der neueren exegetischen Forschung. XVI–424 Seiten. 1977. Vergriffen.

Bd. 16 JEAN ZUMSTEIN: *La condition du croyant dans l'Evangile selon Matthieu.* 467 pages. 1977. Epuisé.

Bd. 17 FRANZ SCHNIDER: *Die verlorenen Söhne.* Strukturanalytische und historisch-kritische Untersuchungen zu Lk 15. 105 Seiten. 1977.

Bd. 18 HEINRICH VALENTIN: *Aaron.* Eine Studie zur vor-priesterschriftlichen Aaron-Überlieferung. VIII–441 Seiten. 1978.

Bd. 19 MASSÉO CALOZ: *Etude sur la LXX origénienne du Psautier.* Les relations entre les leçons des Psaumes du Manuscrit Coislin 44, les Fragments des Hexaples et le texte du Psautier Gallican. 480 pages. 1978.

Bd. 20 RAPHAEL GIVEON: *The Impact of Egypt on Canaan.* Iconographical and Related Studies. 156 Seiten, 73 Abbildungen. 1978.

Bd. 21 DOMINIQUE BARTHÉLEMY: *Etudes d'histoire du texte de l'Ancien Testament.* XXV–419 pages. 1978. Epuisé.

Bd. 22/1 CESLAS SPICQ: *Notes de Lexicographie néo-testamentaire.* Tome I: p. 1–524. 1978. Epuisé.

Bd. 22/2 CESLAS SPICQ: *Notes de Lexicographie néo-testamentaire.* Tome II: p. 525–980. 1978. Epuisé.

Bd. 22/3 CESLAS SPICQ: *Notes de Lexicographie néo-testamentaire.* Supplément. 698 pages. 1982.

Bd. 23 BRIAN M. NOLAN: *The Royal Son of God.* The Christology of Matthew 1–2 in the Setting of the Gospel. 282 Seiten. 1979. Out of print.

Bd. 24 KLAUS KIESOW: *Exodustexte im Jesajabuch.* Literarkritische und motivgeschichtliche Analysen. 221 Seiten. 1979. Vergriffen.

Bd. 25/1 MICHAEL LATTKE: *Die Oden Salomos in ihrer Bedeutung für Neues Testament und Gnosis.* Band I. Ausführliche Handschriftenbeschreibung. Edition mit deutscher Parallel-Übersetzung. Hermeneutischer Anhang zur gnostischen Interpretation der Oden Salomos in der Pistis Sophia. XI–237 Seiten. 1979.

Bd. 25/1a MICHAEL LATTKE: *Die Oden Salomos in ihrer Bedeutung für Neues Testament und Gnosis.* Band Ia. Der syrische Text der Edition in Estrangela Faksimile des griechischen Papyrus Bodmer XI. 68 Seiten. 1980.

Bd. 25/2 MICHAEL LATTKE: *Die Oden Salomos in ihrer Bedeutung für Neues Testament und Gnosis.* Band II. Vollständige Wortkonkordanz zur handschriftlichen, griechischen, koptischen, lateinischen und syrischen Überlieferung der Oden Salomos. Mit einem Faksimile des Kodex N. XVI–201 Seiten. 1979.

Bd. 25/3 MICHAEL LATTKE: *Die Oden Salomos in ihrer Bedeutung für Neues Testament und Gnosis.* Band III. XXXIV–478 Seiten. 1986.

Bd. 26 MAX KÜCHLER: *Frühjüdische Weisheitstraditionen.* Zum Fortgang weisheitlichen Denkens im Bereich des frühjüdischen Jahweglaubens. 703 Seiten. 1979. Vergriffen.

Bd. 27 JOSEF M. OESCH: *Petucha und Setuma.* Untersuchungen zu einer überlieferten Gliederung im hebräischen Text des Alten Testaments. XX–392–37* Seiten. 1979.

Bd. 28 ERIK HORNUNG/OTHMAR KEEL (Herausgeber): *Studien zu altägyptischen Lebenslehren.* 394 Seiten. 1979.

Bd. 29 HERMANN ALEXANDER SCHLÖGL: *Der Gott Tatenen.* Nach Texten und Bildern des Neuen Reiches. 216 Seiten, 14 Abbildungen. 1980.

Bd. 30 JOHANN JAKOB STAMM: *Beiträge zur Hebräischen und Altorientalischen Namenkunde.* XVI–264 Seiten. 1980.

Bd. 31 HELMUT UTZSCHNEIDER: *Hosea - Prophet vor dem Ende.* Zum Verhältnis von Geschichte und Institution in der alttestamentlichen Prophetie. 260 Seiten. 1980.

Bd. 32 PETER WEIMAR: *Die Berufung des Mose.* Literaturwissenschaftliche Analyse von Exodus 2, 23–5, 5. 402 Seiten. 1980.

Bd. 33 OTHMAR KEEL: *Das Böcklein in der Milch seiner Mutter und Verwandtes.* Im Lichte eines altorientalischen Bildmotivs. 163 Seiten, 141 Abbildungen. 1980.

Bd. 34 PIERRE AUFFRET: *Hymnes d'Egypte et d'Israël.* Etudes de structures littéraires. 316 pages, 1 illustration. 1981.

Bd. 35 ARIE VAN DER KOOIJ: *Die alten Textzeugen des Jesajabuches.* Ein Beitrag zur Textgeschichte des Alten Testaments. 388 Seiten. 1981.

Bd. 36 CARMEL McCARTHY: *The Tiqqune Sopherim and Other Theological Corrections in the Masoretic Text of the Old Testament.* 280 Seiten. 1981.

Bd. 37 BARBARA L. BEGELSBACHER-FISCHER: *Untersuchungen zur Götterwelt des Alten Reiches im Spiegel der Privatgräber der IV. und V. Dynastie.* 336 Seiten. 1981.

Bd. 38 MÉLANGES DOMINIQUE BARTHÉLEMY. *Etudes bibliques offertes à l'occasion de son 60e anniversaire.* Edités par Pierre Casetti, Othmar Keel et Adrian Schenker. 724 pages, 31 illustrations. 1981.

Bd. 39 ANDRÉ LEMAIRE: *Les écoles et la formation de la Bible dans l'ancien Israël.* 142 pages, 14 illustrations. 1981.

Bd. 40 JOSEPH HENNINGER: *Arabica Sacra.* Aufsätze zur Religionsgeschichte Arabiens und seiner Randgebiete. Contributions à l'histoire religieuse de l'Arabie et de ses régions limitrophes. 347 Seiten. 1981.

Bd. 41 DANIEL VON ALLMEN: *La famille de Dieu.* La symbolique familiale dans le paulinisme. LXVII–330 pages, 27 planches. 1981.

Bd. 42 ADRIAN SCHENKER: *Der Mächtige im Schmelzofen des Mitleids.* Eine Interpretation von 2 Sam 24. 92 Seiten. 1982.

Bd. 43 PAUL DESELAERS: *Das Buch Tobit.* Studien zu seiner Entstehung, Komposition und Theologie. 532 Seiten + Übersetzung 16 Seiten. 1982.

Bd. 44 PIERRE CASETTI: *Gibt es ein Leben vor dem Tod?* Eine Auslegung von Psalm 49. 315 Seiten. 1982.

Bd. 45 FRANK-LOTHAR HOSSFELD: *Der Dekalog.* Seine späten Fassungen, die originale Komposition und seine Vorstufen. 308 Seiten. 1982. Vergriffen.

Bd. 46 ERIK HORNUNG: *Der ägyptische Mythos von der Himmelskuh.* Eine Ätiologie des Unvollkommenen. Unter Mitarbeit von Andreas Brodbeck, Hermann Schlögl und Elisabeth Staehelin und mit einem Beitrag von Gerhard Fecht. XII–129 Seiten, 10 Abbildungen. 1991. 2. ergänzte Auflage.

Bd. 47 PIERRE CHERIX: *Le Concept de Notre Grande Puissance (CG VI, 4).* Texte, remarques philologiques, traduction et notes. XIV–95 pages. 1982.

Bd. 48 JAN ASSMANN/WALTER BURKERT/FRITZ STOLZ: *Funktionen und Leistungen des Mythos.* Drei altorientalische Beispiele. 118 Seiten, 17 Abbildungen. 1982. Vergriffen.

Bd. 49 PIERRE AUFFRET: *La sagesse a bâti sa maison.* Etudes de structures littéraires dans l'Ancien Testament et spécialement dans les psaumes. 580 pages. 1982.

Bd. 50/1 DOMINIQUE BARTHÉLEMY: *Critique textuelle de l'Ancien Testament.* 1. Josué, Juges, Ruth, Samuel, Rois, Chroniques, Esdras, Néhémie, Esther. Rapport final du Comité pour l'analyse textuelle de l'Ancien Testament hébreu institué par l'Alliance Biblique Universelle, établi en coopération avec Alexander R. Hulst †, Norbert Lohfink, William D. McHardy, H. Peter Rüger, coéditeur, James A. Sanders, coéditeur. 812 pages. 1982.

Bd. 50/2 DOMINIQUE BARTHÉLEMY: *Critique textuelle de l'Ancien Testament.* 2. Isaïe, Jérémie, Lamentations. Rapport final du Comité pour l'analyse textuelle de l'Ancien Testament hébreu institué par l'Alliance Biblique Universelle, établi en coopération avec Alexander R. Hulst †, Norbert Lohfink, William D. McHardy, H. Peter Rüger, coéditeur, James A. Sanders, coéditeur. 1112 pages. 1986.

Bd. 50/3 DOMINIQUE BARTHÉLEMY: *Critique textuelle de l'Ancien Testament.* Tome 3. Ézéchiel, Daniel et les 12 Prophètes. Rapport final du Comité pour l'analyse textuelle de l'Ancien Testament hébreu institué par l'Alliance Biblique Universelle, établi en coopération avec Alexander R. Hulst†, Norbert Lohfink, William D. McHardy, H. Peter Rüger, coéditeur†, James A. Sanders, coéditeur. 1424 pages. 1992.

Bd. 51 JAN ASSMANN: *Re und Amun.* Die Krise des polytheistischen Weltbilds im Ägypten der 18.–20. Dynastie. XII–309 Seiten. 1983.

Bd. 52 MIRIAM LICHTHEIM: *Late Egyptian Wisdom Literature in the International Context.* A Study of Demotic Instructions. X–240 Seiten. 1983.

Bd. 53 URS WINTER: *Frau und Göttin.* Exegetische und ikonographische Studien zum weiblichen Gottesbild im Alten Israel und in dessen Umwelt. XVIII–928 Seiten, 520 Abbildungen. 1987. 2. Auflage. Mit einem Nachwort zur 2. Auflage.

Bd. 54 PAUL MAIBERGER: *Topographische und historische Untersuchungen zum Sinaiproblem.* Worauf beruht die Identifizierung des Ǧabal Mūsā mit dem Sinai? 189 Seiten, 13 Tafeln. 1984.

Bd. 55 PETER FREI/KLAUS KOCH: *Reichsidee und Reichsorganisation im Perserreich.* 119 Seiten, 17 Abbildungen. 1984. Vergriffen. Neuauflage in Vorbereitung

Bd. 56 HANS-PETER MÜLLER: *Vergleich und Metapher im Hohenlied.* 59 Seiten. 1984.

Bd. 57 STEPHEN PISANO: *Additions or Omissions in the Books of Samuel.* The Significant Pluses and Minuses in the Massoretic, LXX and Qumran Texts. XIV–295 Seiten. 1984.

Bd. 58 ODO CAMPONOVO: *Königtum, Königsherrschaft und Reich Gottes in den Frühjüdischen Schriften.* XVI–492 Seiten. 1984.

Bd. 59 JAMES KARL HOFFMEIER: *Sacred in the Vocabulary of Ancient Egypt.* The Term *D̲SR,* with Special Reference to Dynasties I–XX. XXIV–281 Seiten, 24 Figures. 1985.

Bd. 60 CHRISTIAN HERRMANN: *Formen für ägyptische Fayencen.* Katalog der Sammlung des Biblischen Instituts der Universität Freiburg Schweiz und einer Privatsammlung. XXVIII-199 Seiten. Mit zahlreichen Abbildungen im Text und 30 Tafeln. 1985.

Bd. 61 HELMUT ENGEL: *Die Susanna-Erzählung.* Einleitung, Übersetzung und Kommentar zum Septuaginta-Text und zur Theodition-Bearbeitung. 205 Seiten + Anhang 11 Seiten. 1985.

Bd. 62 ERNST KUTSCH: *Die chronologischen Daten des Ezechielbuches.* 82 Seiten. 1985.

Bd. 63 MANFRED HUTTER: *Altorientalische Vorstellungen von der Unterwelt.* Literar- und religionsgeschichtliche Überlegungen zu «Nergal und Ereškigal». VIII–187 Seiten. 1985.

Bd. 64 HELGA WEIPPERT/KLAUS SEYBOLD/MANFRED WEIPPERT: *Beiträge zur prophetischen Bildsprache in Israel und Assyrien.* IX–93 Seiten. 1985.

Bd. 65 ABDEL-AZIZ FAHMY SADEK: *Contribution à l'étude de l'Amdouat.* Les variantes tardives du Livre de l'Amdouat dans les papyrus du Musée du Caire. XVI–400 pages, 175 illustrations. 1985.

Bd. 66 HANS-PETER STÄHLI: *Solare Elemente im Jahweglauben des Alten Testamentes.* X–60 Seiten. 1985.

Bd. 67 OTHMAR KEEL / SILVIA SCHROER: *Studien zu den Stempelsiegeln aus Palästina/Israel.* Band I. 115 Seiten, 103 Abbildungen. 1985.

Bd. 68 WALTER BEYERLIN: *Weisheitliche Vergewisserung mit Bezug auf den Zionskult.* Studien zum 125. Psalm. 96 Seiten. 1985.

Bd. 69 RAPHAEL VENTURA: *Living in a City of the Dead.* A Selection of Topographical and Administrative Terms in the Documents of the Theban Necropolis. XII–232 Seiten. 1986.

Bd. 70 CLEMENS LOCHER: *Die Ehre einer Frau in Israel.* Exegetische und rechtsvergleichende Studien zu Dtn 22, 13–21. XVIII–464 Seiten. 1986.

Bd. 71 HANS-PETER MATHYS: *Liebe deinen Nächsten wie dich selbst.* Untersuchungen zum alttestamentlichen Gebot der Nächstenliebe (Lev 19,18). XII–204 Seiten. 1990. 2. verbesserte Auflage.

Bd. 72 FRIEDRICH ABITZ: *Ramses III. in den Gräbern seiner Söhne.* 156 Seiten, 31 Abbildungen. 1986.

Bd. 73 DOMINIQUE BARTHÉLEMY/DAVID W. GOODING/JOHAN LUST/EMANUEL TOV: *The Story of David and Goliath.* 160 Seiten. 1986.

Bd. 74 SILVIA SCHROER: *In Israel gab es Bilder.* Nachrichten von darstellender Kunst im Alten Testament. XVI–553 Seiten, 146 Abbildungen. 1987.

Bd. 75 ALAN R. SCHULMAN: *Ceremonial Execution and Public Rewards.* Some Historical Scenes on New Kingdom Private Stelae. 296 Seiten, 41 Abbildungen. 1987.

Bd. 76 JOŽE KRAŠOVEC: *La justice (Ṣdq) de Dieu dans la Bible hébraïque et l'interprétation juive et chrétienne.* 456 pages. 1988.

Bd. 77 HELMUT UTZSCHNEIDER: *Das Heiligtum und das Gesetz.* Studien zur Bedeutung der sinaitischen Heiligtumstexte (Ez 25–40; Lev 8–9). XIV–326 Seiten. 1988.

Bd. 78 BERNARD GOSSE: *Isaie 13,1-14,23.* Dans la tradition littéraire du livre d'Isaïe et dans la tradition des oracles contre les nations. 308 pages. 1988.

Bd. 79 INKE W. SCHUMACHER: *Der Gott Sopdu - Der Herr der Fremdländer.* XVI–364 Seiten, 6 Abbildungen. 1988.

Bd. 80 HELLMUT BRUNNER: *Das hörende Herz.* Kleine Schriften zur Religions- und Geistesgeschichte Ägyptens. Herausgegeben von Wolfgang Röllig. 449 Seiten, 55 Abbildungen. 1988.

Bd. 81 WALTER BEYERLIN: *Bleilot, Brecheisen oder was sonst?* Revision einer Amos-Vision. 68 Seiten. 1988.

Bd. 82 MANFRED HUTTER: *Behexung, Entsühnung und Heilung.* Das Ritual der Tunnawiya für ein Königspaar aus mittelhethitischer Zeit (KBo XXI 1 – KUB IX 34 – KBo XXI 6). 186 Seiten. 1988.

Bd. 83 RAPHAEL GIVEON: *Scarabs from Recent Excavations in Israel.* 114 Seiten. Mit zahlreichen Abbildungen im Text und 9 Tafeln. 1988.

Bd. 84 MIRIAM LICHTHEIM: *Ancient Egyptian Autobiographies chiefly of the Middle Kingdom.* A Study and an Anthology. 200 Seiten, 10 Seiten Abbildungen. 1988.

Bd. 85 ECKART OTTO: *Rechtsgeschichte der Redaktionen im Kodex Ešnunna und im «Bundesbuch».* Eine redaktionsgeschichtliche und rechtsvergleichende Studie zu altbabylonischen und altisraelitischen Rechtsüberlieferungen. 220 Seiten. 1989.

Bd. 86 ANDRZEJ NIWIŃSKI: *Studies on the Illustrated Theban Funerary Papyri of the 11th and 10th Centuries B.C.* 488 Seiten, 80 Seiten Tafeln. 1989.

Bd. 87 URSULA SEIDL: *Die babylonischen Kudurru-Reliefs.* Symbole mesopotamischer Gottheiten. 236 Seiten, 33 Tafeln und 2 Tabellen. 1989.

Bd. 88 OTHMAR KEEL/HILDI KEEL-LEU/SILVIA SCHROER: *Studien zu den Stempelsiegeln aus Palästina/Israel.* Band II. 364 Seiten, 652 Abbildungen. 1989.

Bd. 89 FRIEDRICH ABITZ: *Baugeschichte und Dekoration des Grabes Ramses' VI.* 202 Seiten, 39 Abbildungen. 1989.

Bd. 90 JOSEPH HENNINGER SVD: *Arabica varia.* Aufsätze zur Kulturgeschichte Arabiens und seiner Randgebiete. Contributions à l'histoire culturelle de l'Arabie et de ses régions limitrophes. 504 Seiten. 1989.

Bd. 91 GEORG FISCHER: *Jahwe unser Gott.* Sprache, Aufbau und Erzähltechnik in der Berufung des Mose (Ex. 3–4). 276 Seiten. 1989.

Bd. 92 MARK A. O'BRIEN: *The Deuteronomistic History Hypothesis:* A Reassessment. 340 Seiten. 1989.

Bd. 93 WALTER BEYERLIN: *Reflexe der Amosvisionen im Jeremiabuch.* 120 Seiten. 1989.

Bd. 94 ENZO CORTESE: *Josua 13-21.* Ein priesterschriftlicher Abschnitt im deuteronomistischen Geschichtswerk. 136 Seiten. 1990.

Bd. 95 ERIK HORNUNG (Herausgeber): *Zum Bild Ägyptens im Mittelalter und in der Renaissance. Comment se représente-t-on l'Egypte au Moyen Age et à la Renaissance.* 268 Seiten. 1990.

Bd. 96 ANDRÉ WIESE: *Zum Bild des Königs auf ägyptischen Siegelamuletten.* 264 Seiten. Mit zahlreichen Abbildungen im Text und 32 Tafeln. 1990.

Bd. 97 WOLFGANG ZWICKEL: *Räucherkult und Räuchergeräte.* Exegetische und archäologische Studien zum Räucheropfer im Alten Testament. 372 Seiten. Mit zahlreichen Abbildungen im Text. 1990.

Bd. 98 AARON SCHART: *Mose und Israel im Konflikt.* Eine redaktionsgeschichtliche Studie zu den Wüstenerzählungen. 296 Seiten. 1990.

Bd. 99 THOMAS RÖMER: *Israels Väter.* Untersuchungen zur Väterthematik im Deuteronomium und in der deuteronomistischen Tradition. 664 Seiten. 1990.

Bd. 100 OTHMAR KEEL/MENAKHEM SHUVAL/CHRISTOPH UEHLINGER: *Studien zu den Stempelsiegeln aus Palästina/Israel.* Band III. Die Frühe Eisenzeit. Ein Workshop. XIV–456 Seiten. Mit zahlreichen Abbildungen im Text und 22 Tafeln. 1990.

Bd. 101 CHRISTOPH UEHLINGER: *Weltreich und «eine Rede».* Eine neue Deutung der sogenannten Turmbauerzählung (Gen 11,1–9). XVI–654 Seiten. 1990.

Bd. 102 BENJAMIN SASS: *Studia Alphabetica.* On the Origin and Early History of the Northwest Semitic, South Semitic and Greek Alphabets. X–120 Seiten. 16 Seiten Abbildungen. 2 Tabellen. 1991.

Bd. 103 ADRIAN SCHENKER: *Text und Sinn im Alten Testament.* Textgeschichtliche und bibeltheologische Studien. VIII–312 Seiten. 1991.

Bd. 104 DANIEL BODI: *The Book of Ezekiel and the Poem of Erra.* IV–332 Seiten. 1991.

Bd. 105 YUICHI OSUMI: *Die Kompositionsgeschichte des Bundesbuches Exodus 20,22b–23,33.* XII–284 Seiten. 1991.

Bd. 106 RUDOLF WERNER: *Kleine Einführung ins Hieroglyphen-Luwische.* XII–112 Seiten. 1991.

Bd. 107 THOMAS STAUBLI: *Das Image der Nomaden im Alten Israel und in der Ikonographie seiner sesshaften Nachbarn.* XII–408 Seiten. 145 Abb. und 3 Falttafeln. 1991.

Bd. 108 MOSHÉ ANBAR: *Les tribus amurrites de Mari.* VIII–256 Seiten. 1991.

Bd. 109 GÉRARD J. NORTON/STEPHEN PISANO (eds.): *Tradition of the Text.* Studies offered to Dominique Barthélemy in Celebration of his 70th Birthday. 336 Seiten. 1991.

Bd. 110 HILDI KEEL-LEU: *Vorderasiatische Stempelsiegel.* Die Sammlung des Biblischen Instituts der Universität Freiburg Schweiz. 180 Seiten. 24 Tafeln. 1992.

Bd. 111 NORBERT LOHFINK: *Die Väter Israels im Deuteronomium.* Mit einer Stellungnahme von Thomas Römer. 152 Seiten. 1991.

Bd. 112 EDMUND HERMSEN: *Die zwei Wege des Jenseits.* Das altägyptische Zweiwegebuch und seine Topographie. XII–282 Seiten, 1 mehrfarbige und 19 Schwarz-weiss-Abbildungen. 1992.

Bd. 113 CHARLES MAYSTRE: *Les grands prêtres de Ptah de Memphis.* XIV–474 pages, 2 planches. 1992.

Bd. 114 THOMAS SCHNEIDER: *Asiatische Personennamen in ägyptischen Quellen des Neuen Reiches.* 408 Seiten. 1992.

Bd. 115 ECKHARD VON NORDHEIM: *Die Selbstbehauptung Israels in der Welt des Alten Orients.* Religionsgeschichtlicher Vergleich anhand von Gen 15/22/28, dem Aufenthalt Israels in Ägypten, 2 Sam 7, 1 Kön 19 und Psalm 104. 240 Seiten. 1992.

Bd. 116 DONALD M. MATTHEWS: *The Kassite Glyptic of Nippur.* 208 Seiten. 210 Abbildungen. 1992.

Bd. 117 FIONA V. RICHARDS: *Scarab Seals from a Middle to Late Bronze Age Tomb at Pella in Jordan.* XII–152 Seiten, 16 Tafeln. 1992.

Bd. 118 YOHANAN GOLDMAN: *Prophétie et royauté au retour de l'exil. Les origines littéraires de la forme massorétique du livre de Jérémie.* XIV–270 pages. 1992.

Bd. 119 THOMAS M. KRAPF: *Die Priesterschrift und die vorexilische Zeit. Yehezkel Kaufmanns vernachlässigter Beitrag zur Geschichte der biblischen Religion.* XX-364 Seiten. 1992.

Bd. 120 MIRIAM LICHTHEIM: *Maat in Egyptian Autobiographies and Related Studies.* 236 Seiten, 21 Tafeln. 1992.

UNIVERSITÄTSVERLAG FREIBURG SCHWEIZ

MIRIAM LICHTHEIM
IN DER REIHE ORBIS BIBLICUS ET ORIENTALIS

MIRIAM LICHTHEIM: *Late Egyptian Wisdom Literature in the International Context.* A Study of Demotic Instructions (OBO 52) 1983.

"On ne peut être qu'en admiration devant les traductions présentées, surtout quand on connaît les difficultés du texte démotique. D'autre part, la très grande culture de M. L. nous aide à mieux comprendre l'importance de la sagesse dans les différents contextes culturels de l'Égypte tardive."
R. Beaud, Revue Biblique

"Studies like these shed light on the larger critical question of the affinity other biblical books may have had with their respective environments. By eschewing 'parallelomania,' they encourage similar investigations of other ancient Near Eastern materials."
J. A. Gladson, Journal of Biblical Lierature

MIRIAM LICHTHEIM: *Ancient Egyptian Autobiographies chiefly of the Middle Kingdom.* A Study and an Anthology (OBO 84) 1988.

"Es ist Miriam Lichtheim gelungen, nicht allein ein bisher einmaliges corpus der autobiographischen Inschriften vorzulegen, sondern damit zugleich ein Stück ägyptischer Literatur-, Stil- und Religionsgeschichte zu schreiben, das in seiner Prägnanz und Dichte dem hohen Stil angemessen ist, der dieser Gattung seit der Zeit der 11. Dynastie eigen war."
O. Kaiser, Zeitschrift für die Alttestamentliche Wissenschaft

"Apart from the abundance of material contained herein, the book also offers much food for thought and insights that perhaps only a scholar of the calibre of Dr. Lichtheim, with her wealth of experience, could offer. For all this, the field of Egyptology is forever in her debt."
R. J. Leprohon, Journal of the Society for the Study of Egyptian Antiquities

English Summary

The first of the five studies explores «Maat», the Egyptian term for the moral order that governed men and gods in their respective spheres. The growth of the concept of Maat is traced from the Old Kingdom to the Late Period by a sequence of autobiographical and other texts in which individual Egyptians define and declare their understanding of, and adherence to, the code of right action termed «doing Maat». As the texts show, the essential features of right action were truthfulness and fairness. Adherence to Maat created the good order of society, while abandoning Maat plunged society into chaos. Man's knowledge of right, and his ability to do it, were defined as originating in his heart and in his nature: virtue was innate and inner-directed. In the texts of the New Kingdom the gods came to be addressed as partners of man's rightdoing by providing inspiration and guidance. At no time, however, were the gods given the role of formulating moral precepts. Man remained the maker of his ethos.

The second study demonstrates that the «Negative Confessions» of the Book of the Dead were based squarely on the moral declarations of autobiographical inscriptions, declarations which the scribes of the Book of the Dead rephrased in negative terms, in keeping with the BD's ritual-magical purpose.

The third study pinpoints in vocabulary form the principal terms for the virtues and vices used in the texts cited.

The fourth study shows that the grammatical constructions of the «Appeal to the Living» - the request by the deceased for the prayers of the living - underwent changes which scholars have failed to recognize, a failure resulting in unwarranted emendations and faulty translations.

Lastly there is a grave stela of Ptolemaic date with a text which, instead of the usual hopefulness, records a long cry of despair.